HEALING
My own story

THE LIFE AND TIMES OF AN
EXTRAORDINARY MAN

BY
BILL PARFREY

Published in the Republic of Ireland by

Bill Parfrey
62 Dosel Drive,
Grange Heights,
Douglas,
Cork 2,
Ireland

www.billparfrey.com
www.healingmyownstory.com

Cover Photo: ©Jean Forde

ISBN   0-9553553-0-3
            978-0-9553553-0-1

Printed by:
Lee Press Ltd.,
South Terrace,
Cork,
Ireland

Dedication

This book is dedicated to my mentor and good friend,

Professor George Canning

First printing   August 2006

Second printing   November 2006

Preface

Slán agus Beannacht[1]

If it is meant to be, it is not an accident. That is how I now sum up getting to know Bill Parfrey. As he wrote in his second e-mail to me:

"It was just pure chance that I made contact with you. I have a friend - Bill Murphy - also a Senator - and he makes a living doing various computer jobs for various companies and he has use of the Net. He came across a list of various Senators in the US and Canada and he gave me a few addresses to try out and yours was one of these! In my book, everything happens for a purpose and our coming together was no exception to the rule."

In his first e-mail to me, sent June 7, 1998 Bill wrote:

"A friend of mine told me that you are a Senator of JCI[2]. My name is Bill Parfrey and I live in Cork, Ireland. I was awarded a Senatorship in 1966 … . If you feel like getting in contact, send me an e-mail at your convenience. Every good wish. Bill Parfrey."

My reply to this stranger was cautious but apparently hit the right note. We quickly became 'cyber pals' and began to exchange many confidences by e-mail, supplemented by sporadic telephone conversations and correspondence and a few gifts. Bill had written for himself what he called "Bill Parfrey - My Story". When I received and read it in 1998 my reaction was that someday this fascinating life may be the basis for a book if only someone would devote the effort to get Bill to add to it, question Bill on what he reveals, get him to reveal more, do some independent research and then write it in a professional and marketable format.

A soft-spoken Irishman, of combined Anglican and Roman Catholic upbringing in Cork, Ireland, the Bill Parfrey of today is the result of a life-

1   An old Irish salutation meaning 'health and blessings (to you)

v

time of personal physical and spiritual struggle, of an often-emotional personal inquiry into the meaning of his life on "Spaceship Earth" while still encapsulated by his earthly skin or 'Diving Suit', of service to others who suffer from physical and mental and emotional pain, of a genuine love of humanity, of enjoying the Irish stereotype's fondness for 'friendship, fellowship, and the malt and the barley and the grape', and of dedication to his family's well-being despite the weight of the 'gift' of his psychic inheritance.

Bill has a way of combining a genuine humility with an innate stubbornness not to be readily dismissed or pigeon-holed into some descriptive framework based on conceptions held by others. He proceeds on his hero's journey very much his own man, and proud of it. For Bill, life on earth is a necessary station along the path of 'knowing and growing the spiritual being' we all are. He firmly believes that during our journey here on earth we must follow two precepts – First, to love others as much as we can, and this includes loving oneself as a prerequisite to being able to love others effectively; Second, to practice our God-given 'free will' in a manner that grows our spiritual being, as preparation for the next stage of existence that our spiritual selves must enter.

The other-worldliness or spiritual being of Bill has mixed with his love of this earth and humanity to produce a truly wonderful person, 'warts and all' as my mother used to say. He has the unique capacity to be firm in his beliefs, yet remains tolerant of those who do not share them or even denigrate them. He has remained humble and appreciative of the 'psychic gifts' he has developed and used to benefit others explaining, " It is God who does the healing, not me."

This book is worth reading because of the singular spirit of Bill Parfrey, which existed from before his birth as a son of Ireland and which has continued to develop. When he does pass through the final veil I am sure he will be welcomed on the other side as one who has completed his mission on 'spaceship earth' and is well-prepared to continue his spiritual growth in the hereafter. When that day comes, those who believe as Bill does can look forward to his continuing presence in their hearts and minds, and more.

Those who believe that we are 'spiritual beings in a physical body' will have little difficulty with this "hero's journey". All should find the life of Bill Parfrey a beacon of hope in a world where we need one. All should find his life will give them much to think upon and celebrate. All should enjoy the story for what it basically is, the captivating truth of one man who reveals his pre-birth, his life on 'spaceship earth', and looks into his future (we humans are time-oriented) - truth is stranger than fiction.

In closing, I must state that Bill has helped me in many ways, without being asked and without asking for anything in return. I thank him for that with all my being. Part of the medical doctor's creed is 'first, do no harm'.

Harry Weldon,
Ottawa,
Canada

FOREWORD

"Some are born great, some achieve greatness and some have greatness thrust upon them!"

All I can confirm is that I was born. I was not born great – I was lucky to have survived birth at all! I did not achieve greatness and any greatness that I am deemed to possess was thrust upon me by others.

I have no degrees. My university was the university of life, from where I learned all that I know. I must confess that help was coming to me from other sources – that inner voice that we all possess – but sometimes turn a deaf ear much to our detriment. I suppose that it is fair to say that I have had an extraordinary life with many varied experiences. It was suggested to me that I should record as many of these for posterity that I could remember.

Life goes by so quickly. When we are young time seems to drag but as we grow older time seems to speed up. Life is like a forty-five minute tape one plays and as the minutes go by, faster and faster goes the tape, as does life itself. Another staggering fact is the enormous list of changes that come about in a lifetime. Hard to imagine there was a time that the invention of the bow and arrow was looked upon as the weapon that would end all wars!

In my case it is hard to imagine the small room in a terraced house, lit by the incandescent gas lamps – the ultimate in modernity and here I am seventy-eight years later producing these few words on a computer. It is enough to blow one's mind. God be with the days of the quill pen.

We have all seen many changes in our lives both personally and collectively. Still we cannot get away from the fact that we cannot progress without change and so it will ever be. We all have our own personal Alpha and Omega – a beginning and an end. For me Alpha appeared on my horizon at 7.00 pm on the 23rd September, 1926 in the city of Cork in Ireland. Now I am rapidly approaching the very last letter of the Greek alphabet. Packed between these two letters are related some of the trials, vicissitudes, experiences good and bad, pathos and sadness, happiness and laughter, good health and bad and the many ups and downs of life.

Life is not easy but the test of a person is the fight that that person makes. I have come to the realisation that each of us has a destiny and whether we like it or not it is like a blueprint. To help us, we do have freewill and how we use this can ease or create more difficulties depending what decisions we make. If it happens to be the wrong one poor God gets all the blame!

My blueprint appears to embrace recording as much as I can of how life treated me and, more importantly, how I treated life.

This book is more like a long personal letter relating my story.

I have to thank my very good and valued friend Harry Weldon of Ottawa, Canada for the preface. I would like to thank those who very kindly wrote to me for the help I was privileged and guided to give them. These are reproduced in Part 5.

I have to single out my niece, Renate Kohlmann, for the trojan work she did behind the scenes. She is co-editor with my very good friend Bill Murphy. From a very busy schedule she found time to organise meetings on a regular basis at which the pros and cons of various parts of the book were discussed, often ad nausam. The format and layout of the entire work was designed and undertaken by Bill.

The striking frontispiece was photographed by my daughter, Jean Forde, who captured the author 'in vacant and in pensive mood'.

I must also pay tribute to my wife, Margaret, who for six months had to contend with files, photographs and copious sheets of paper scattered all over the house.

Finally to you, the reader. Thank you for taking the trouble to read this work of mine. I trust you will enjoy and perhaps learn something that can prove to be of value.

Contents:

Part Two

Part Three

Part Four

Part Five

Chapter 01

MY ARRIVAL AND THE FIRST FOUR YEARS

I came on board Spaceship Earth on the 23rd September, 1926 at 7.00 p.m. precisely. The street gaslight, which stood directly in front of the house – 16 Vincent View, College Road, Cork – filtered its light through the thin blinds of the windows into the room where my mother was giving birth to me. The glow from the streetlight was augmented by the glare and the hiss from two gas lamps which hung at each side of the fireplace. A warm fire blazed and crackled in the hearth.

Before my birth, my mother had numerous miscarriages. It was feared that I too was not going to make it. I learned that my birth was difficult, and that both my mother and I had pneumonia. This did not augur well for our survival.

16 Vincent View, College Rd.

As if an omen of some kind, I was privileged to have been born sporting a caul! This is the inner membrane enclosing a foetus, part of which is occasionally found on a child's head at birth and is thought to bring good luck! I was going to die and on the face of it, I was paying Mother Earth but a fleeting visit.

While my grandmother on my father's side, wrapped me up in the family magic shawl, our next-door neighbour who was Roman Catholic (our family being of the Protestant persuasion) baptised me on the spot. For as long as she lived she was invariably known as Granny Reilly! Growing up I felt so happy that I had no less than three grandmothers while all my friends had but two!

1

Whether it was the caul, the shawl or the baptism I cannot say. Perhaps it was the cumulative effect of them all, but I survived, as indeed did my dear mother who all of her life was a fighter.

Mercy Hospital, Cork.

My luck did not hold out in the health department and for the first four years of my life I was in and out of hospital with one complaint after another - Diphtheria, Scarlet Fever, Measles and so it went on. My father often told me that he was still paying off the chemist bills ten years after my birth!

In 1930 my sister Eileen was born. Things were not as bad as they had been at my birth in 1926, but my mother was, in the parlance of the time, 'run down' and had part-time help from a woman further down the street. As you can imagine, in the year 1930 there were not many vehicles on the roads, especially in the suburban area where we lived. Occasionally one would see the horse-drawn milk cart and that sort of thing, but traffic as we know it today just did not exist.

One day as I was walking along the path, I saw a strange woman pushing my sister's pram across the road. Not knowing that my mother had made arrangements to look after baby Eileen, I thought that the woman was stealing my sister! I ran across the road and as I did so, a bread-van suddenly made its appearance. I tripped and fell between the front wheels of the vehicle. The right side of my head was crushed, my leg, thigh and hip were all broken. I was rushed to hospital and believe it or not those were the days when you were asked if you could pay! My father told a lie and said he could. He was fortunate in having a very kind boss who gave him £100 - a huge sum in 1930.

The hospital was run by nuns most of whom I have to confess I found to be extremely harsh and unkind. All my curls were shorn off and, as I lay there with my left leg in a perpendicular position, I cried a great deal and lived for the short visits when my parents were allowed to see me. From where my cot was placed I could see out of a window that had a restricted view of the main road along which the trams trundled. I would keep looking out of that window for hours and when I saw a tram pass my heart leaped with the thought that my father was going to visit me. Alas, it was not always like that at all, but the ongoing hope that he would be on the next tram buoyed me up completely.

My mother had taught me some childish hymns and every so often I would start to sing them to myself. One I will always remember was entitled 'Jesus loves me this I know for the Bible tells me so'. Over and over I was reprimanded by my jailers - the nuns. In 1930 there appeared to be no love lost between those who were Roman Catholics [called 'Catholics' these days] and those who adhered to a different interpretation of the story of Jesus.

The day came when my leg was to be moved from its perpendicular to a prone position. The bandages that were glued to my limbs had to be removed. No spirits of any kind were used to remove the bandaging. Not a bit of it! It was simply torn off! I screamed in pain but all to no avail.

I will never forget the shock and the agony inflicted as long as I live.

I finally got out of the clutches of those holy nuns! Maybe they thought that I had to pay for the sin of being born of Anglican parents - I really do not know. They have all now passed to their reward and I wonder how they compared the way that I was treated with the words of Jesus when he said,

Patrick St., Cork in 1921. The Fr. Matthew statue is in the middle distance. It was here we met the Healer in 1931. He took us to his rooms and miraculously healed me so that I could walk again.

'Suffer the little children to come unto Me'.

I bear them no ill.

3

Chapter 02

MIRACLES DO HAPPEN

I came out of that awful hospital a cripple. My left leg was turned slightly outwards and a calliper stretched from the heel of my shoe to my hip. In order to walk, I brought forward my right leg and dragged my left.

One day in 1931, my father and I were standing in Cork city centre just opposite the statue of the Apostle of Temperance, waiting for a tram to take us to Donovan's Road by the university. My father would lift me up the hill and I would drag myself down the few hundred yards to our home (which was a terraced house).

Apostle of Temperance

Suddenly, out of the blue so to speak, a man approached my father.

'What's wrong with him?' he asked.

'He'll never walk again,' my father replied.

Back came the retort, 'I'll fix him!'

A conversation ensued after which I was brought to a building in MacCurtain Street. I found myself in a sparse room that contained a leather examination couch, covered with a green baize hairy material. It was illuminated by a dirty 60-watt fly-blown bulb which did not boast a shade.

I'd had so much of doctors and hospitals in my short life that I was screaming as I was laid on the couch. My trousers and the iron calliper were removed. As I lay on the couch I could feel the prickly part of the baize covering penetrate my skin. I was full of fear as that man came and placed his two hands on the right side of my body just above my hip.

4

Something happened! I could feel an electric shock course through the left side of my body. Suddenly, without any warning, my left leg turned itself around and shot out straight!

'Get off the table', I heard a gruff tone command. Trembling, I stood on the floor when I heard the next command,

'Walk!' I started to walk as I always did, dragging the left leg.

'Not that way!'

I hesitantly put my left leg forward and followed with my right! My father was astounded. He stood there holding the leg iron and asked in a dazed voice,

'What do I do with this?'

'Throw it away' came the reply!

'What do I owe you?' inquired my father.

'If you can afford a fiver [£5.00] that will be grand, but if you do not have it, forget it!'

It was a healer that made me walk in 1931.

Over 45 years elapsed before I heard about a boy who had been born with an extra bone in his foot. His parents were having him treated by a bone setter in north Cork. In the course of conversation I learned that the bone setter had the same name as the healer who had made me well in 1931! I was intrigued and ascertained the telephone number.

What followed was an amazing story. In deference to the man in question I am going to call him Mr. Leahy.

In the early part of the 18th century before Catholic Emancipation[2], Catholics were forced to worship at the local Mass Rock. The Mass Rock

2.   Catholic Emancipation — granting of freedom of worship.

was nearly always hidden and stood in a most inaccessible, secret location. To this day one may still visit such places of worship throughout the length and breadth of the country of Ireland.

Around about the year 1740 one of Mr. Leahy's antecedents was attending Mass at a secret location near a fast-flowing river. Half way through the ceremony a person on lookout warned that the 'Red Coats' had found the location and were coming to arrest the priest. People scattered for safety and the only way the priest could escape was to swim across the river. The priest was unable to swim and Mr. Leahy's ancestor came to the rescue. He was a powerful swimmer and he helped the priest to reach safety.

Overcoming the shock and dripping wet, the priest asked his rescuer how could he repay him. Now, as it happened an old man who was crippled with arthritis and whose hip was very painful hip had been one of the congregation.

'Say a prayer for the crippled man, Father.'

'I will do more than that', replied the priest as he instructed his rescuer to stretch out his arms, palms upward.

'By the power of Almighty God personified by His Most Bless-ed Son Jesus Christ I pass the gift of healing to you which will continue from this day forward from generation to generation through the male line.' And it has been so ever since. Mr. Leahy explained that at about the age of fourteen, the son begins to feel an awareness developing within himself. The inherited gift is making its presence felt. Under the tuition of the elder member of the family, the boy begins to develop further his gift.

I think of this wonderful story in awe, and of that bleak night in 1740, when that good man who rescued the priest was endowed with the Gift of Healing. This is the gift responsible for allowing me to walk at five years of age!

Chapter 03

EARLY SCHOOL EXPERIENCES

They say [and I often wonder who 'they' are] that schooldays are the best days of one's life. I deny this statement categorically for so far as I was concerned, most of it was hell on earth.

My earliest recollection of going to school was when at the age of three-and-a-half my father took me on his bicycle to Christchurch National School, in the heart of the city, not too far away from my father's place of work. Each morning I spent a couple of hours there with other infants. We played with building bricks, drew pictures on paper and made things out of play dough [called plasticine in my day]. This allowed my mother, who was pregnant and not feeling very well, to have me out of the way while she rested. My father collected me again on his way home for lunch. I can still recall the little hard seat with its short supporting sides, securely fastened to the crossbar of his bike, on which I made this daily pilgrimage. All good things come to an end and it was shortly after this that I had the accident chasing my sister's "captor" and found myself in hospital!

The months rolled by, as indeed did the years, and the day eventually arrived when I had to attend school regularly. I found myself in the Infants class of St. Fin Barre's National School, which was within walking distance of my home. My teacher was a most kind person and always willing to help me in every way. It was a two-teacher school and the principal was another lady somewhat elderly whose bark was worse than her bite. I was not in her section of the school and knew that the day would dawn when I would have to move to the higher classes. Before this came about the principal retired and her place was taken by a man who I feared on the spot. I was not the only one who felt like this.

The dreaded day dawned when I came under the full control of this sadistic and to me sinister headmaster. From day one it was painfully obvious that

7

he had his favourites and I certainly was not one of them. He always carried a thick bamboo cane and seemed to enjoy beating us with it, usually on the palms of the hands, which were numbed with the pain to the point one could not write properly. This meant more punishment.

I can recall a fellow pupil who was left-handed. This vile man insisted that my friend wrote with the pen or pencil in his right hand. It was nigh impossible for him to do so and the only way he could manage was to hold the pen in his right hand and using the forefinger of his left hand push the writing instrument along! That boy grew up to be a man with a constant twitch in his neck. He was unable to look anyone straight in the face as his head jerked to one side all of his life. He is dead now as I write this but sadly his affliction, together with a slight stutter, was one hundred percent due to this so-called teacher in the National School.

The school was co-educational and boasted a playground in which the boys and girls had forty minutes of free time daily. Boys congregated in one part, the girls in another. Those of us lucky enough to have sandwiches, ate our lunch and played various games, all of which were of a rough nature.

Although the school was under the auspices of the Anglican Church, the Government's Department of Education paid the salaries and decreed the teaching format. In 1922 the Irish Free State[1] came into being, with the obsession that everyone should learn to speak Irish. The Irish language was beaten into us in all the schools throughout the land.

When playtime ended the headmaster appeared with the school bell in his hand. He lined us all up along a concrete strip and ensured that we were in a straight line. Then, as if we were convicts or prisoners, he marched us back into the school – in step – to the sound of his calling out in Irish, 'a h-aon, a dó, a h-aon, a dó' [one two, one two] as we were herded back into class for more of the same.

[1] The **Irish Free State** (Irish: *Saorstát Éireann*) (1922–1937) was the name of the state comprising the 26 of Ireland's 32 counties that were separated from the United Kingdom of Great Britain and Ireland under the Irish Free State Agreement (or Anglo-Irish Treaty) signed by British and Irish Republic representatives in London on December 6, 1921.

While the pupils attending the school were all from the Protestant tradition of one kind or another, a number of Jews also attended. The large community of Jews in Cork around about this time numbered many hundreds. There was also the belief that all Protestants were rich! Such nonsense. There were five boys in my class who had neither socks nor shoes on their feet†and the clothes they wore were often threadbare. In my youth we had to make do with 'hand-me-downs' and I well remember my mother asking a poor widow woman, who was a seamstress, to turn some of my father's worn clothing into short pants, termed 'a pan-ses', for me to wear. There was an old song going round at the time with the opening line: 'Tis the poor that has to suffer, 'tis the poor that gets the blame'. I saw that borne out clearly during the hellish time I spent in that school. I remember one day when one of the lads - a big underfed boy - could not take any more and he lifted up a chair and threw it with full force at the principal. There was mayhem as others joined in for the battle royal. It was truly frightening and there were beatings right, left and centre.

No matter how I tried, I could not please the headmaster and had to continue with the taunts and gibes all along the line.

One day I was accused of being rude to this beast of a man. I was given the task of writing out the sentence, 'I must not be rude to Mr. X', one hundred times. It took a long time for me to do this and when I was finished I knew that my mother would be anxious to know why I had not put in an appearance at the usual time. I handed in my work and was about to pick up my school bag when the principal thundered,

'You have spelt my name incorrectly; go and write it out another hundred times and without a mistake'.

I could have cried and screamed in anger but there was nothing I could do. I had to start all over again.

I told my parents nothing about what was going on at school. They would not have believed me anyway. However, the day did come when they had to believe me. I always tried to avoid arriving home at the same time that my father was having his lunch, for I dreaded the inevitable question,

'How many socks did you get today?' ['Socks' was the word my father used to describe a cut across the hand with a cane.] It was winter and the school was heated by a massive coal burning stove. We dreaded the winter months, for our hated master would from time to time put his thick bamboo cane into the roaring fire. When it was red at the end he would hit a pupil severely across the palms of the hands.

For some reason I did not understand it was my turn to get flaked. I received four vicious cuts and the pain was excruciating. With swollen and bleeding palms I cried all the way home. That day I was shocked to find that my father was having a late lunch. He was in the middle of his meal when he noticed that I had been crying. I kept my hands in my pockets as he asked me the dreaded question. When I showed him my hands his face blanched. He dropped his knife and fork and without saying a word he stormed out of the house down to the school. What transpired there I really do not know. My father was a big man and I have always felt that he had given my tyrant teacher the hiding of his life.

I never returned to that school from that day onwards. The happiest days of your life, how are you?

Chapter 04

OUT OF THE FRYING PAN AND INTO THE FIRE

I was a changed person. The clouds had disappeared from the sky and left a golden sun that shone daily, figuratively speaking. I was free from that hellhole of a school and the devil that ran it.

Schools were closed for the summer and I was as free as a bird. The relief was startling and I revelled in cycling around the countryside. One of my favourite past times was swimming in the river Lee.

I learned that I was to commence my secondary education in September 1936 at the coeducational Cork Grammar & High School. Prior to my becoming a pupil, the Grammar School & High Schools were separate entities for boys and girls respectively. So far as I know, in the interests of economy the two schools were merged.

Attending my new school necessitated being rigged out with a uniform of grey trousers, a red vee-necked pullover embellished with a yellow band on the neck and wrists, a tie to match and the head gear was a red cap with the school ensignia. I was very proud of my new clothes. We were taught to respect the school uniform and the code stated that when out and about the full ensemble was to be worn.

Before the new term commenced my father took me to meet the headmaster - Rev. John Hobson. All sorts of rumours were rampant about this august principal and I felt that I was entering the holy of holies when we entered the drawing-room of his home. He had a rugged expression and his head sported a shock of grey hair. My impression was that he could be severe but fair and would stand no nonsense. This was well and truly borne out, especially for anyone who was instructed to 'Report to the Head!' I always seemed to be in trouble and whether I was directly responsible or not the cant was, invariably, 'Where was Parfrey at the time?'

The great day dawned in September when I entered the hallowed school building. Not that it was huge, but in comparison to my old school it contained a labyrinth of passageways, staircases, classrooms, toilets, the sum of which produced its own unique atmosphere once experienced never forgotten. There appeared to be teachers everywhere, all of whom were teaching this and that different subject. I had to get used to dropping the word 'class' and substituting it with 'form'. I found myself in form two and could not get over the relief I felt as I made new friends. I was introduced to new subjects such as French, Maths, History, Drawing, etc. It was all so different from my old school. The more senior pupils spent their lunch hour in the old Grammar School but junior students like me were confined to the building until such time as gravitating to a higher form, which I did at the end of term the following year.

My first visit to the headmaster, known throughout the school as 'the Boss', resulted from a simple action of mine. It was lunch break and I was eating a sandwich. The crust was a bit hard so I threw it out the open window of the classroom and thought nothing more about it. After the break we had our French class, with a very dour teacher, Miss Norton. She mounted the dais and addressed the class,

'Bon jour la classe.'

As if it were a signal of some sort, suddenly my crust of bread came flying through the window hitting Miss Norton on the face. There was stunned silence as a very angry Miss Norton demanded to know how it was that she should be in receipt of a crust of bread fired with deadly accuracy from the garden next door. I had to own up to the fact that the crust that did the damage had been thrown out the window by me.

'Report to the headmaster at once,' she said, her face still red with fury.

With fear and trepidation I knocked on the door of the headmaster's office, entered and was confronted by the Boss. Apparently when I threw the crust out of the window it hit a large cat slumbering in the sunshine that belonged to a spinster who occupied the house next door to the school. The woman made a complaint to the school to the effect that her cat had been attacked! Working on the principle of tit for tat she retrieved the missile and returned it with deadly accuracy from whence it came! I received a caution from the headmaster and had to visit the spinster to apologise for the incident. She turned out to be a pleasant old lady, not at all the ogre I expected to meet. This was the start of a very long line of incidents during my sojourn in the Grammar School which led to my being blamed for everything straight off the belt-head, to such an extent the cant 'where was Parfrey at the time' was born and it never died!

The first year rolled by and I got into the swing of things. Moving from what could be termed the sheltered accommodation of form two, form three was the proverbial horse of a different colour. Sticking with metaphors, the blinkers came off and I saw and became part of a whole new world. I made my first acquaintance with Latin, Greek, Geometry, Algebra, Trigonometry, Geography as well as a whole new field of History and English Literature, including Shakespeare. Irish as a subject seemed to be far down the list and I found that the appalling grinding I had received in the National School put me light years ahead of my fellow students.

Another subject was Art which I must confess I enjoyed. While I was not too bad on Celtic diagrams I was unable to draw the proverbial cat! The classroom in which form three students worked and had their being was very cramped and was dubbed by one of the teachers as 'The Cell'. The name stuck like glue. Individual rickety desks were jammed close together so one had to be like a contortionist to pass through the sparse few inches that separated one desk from the other.

Overall I did not think of myself a good student. My one ambition was to be a doctor but there was as much chance of going to the university as there was of taking a trip to Saturn. The end result was that I just did not work like the others. I energised myself for the subjects that I liked, and for those that I found difficult I just went with the flow. Maths was a difficult subject and when it came to studying Euclid I could readily understand why his wife thought the man she married was mad and burned many of his books!

Strangely enough, book one made sense, as did books three and six, but the second book of Euclid was on a league of its own. It was the Boss who taught us mathematics. He was a man with the patience of Job and God knows he needed it where I was concerned. Problem five, I think it was in the first book of Euclid, stated that: 'the square on the hypothesis was equal to the sum of the squares on the other two sides.' As far as I remember it took forty-six individual actions to prove that this was in fact true. It was known as 'Pons-ass-an-aurum': the Bridge of Asses! I hate to think back on the number of weeks that I was held in 'Detention' [DT for short] on Saturdays until I finally managed to prove that what Euclid stated was in fact the truth!

I dreaded the day we had 'cuts'. These were problems the Boss put up on the blackboard and asked the class in general if anyone could solve the problem set. I sat as far back in the class as possible - 'cuts' were way out-side my league.

Once in a while I would be picked upon by the Boss to come up to the front of the class, whether I liked it or not, to prove a problem. There I would stand in fear and trepidation, not having the slightest idea what I was to say or do. With the chalk held in a trembling hand I would blurt out,

'That line is equal to that line.' Back would come the retort,

'That line is NOT equal to that line.' Then I might say,

'That angle is equal to that angle.' There would be a further remark,

'That angle is NOT equal to that angle.' In frantic desperation I would take a chance and stutter,

'That angle is equal to the sum of the two other angles.'

The Boss would explode:

'That angle is not equal to the sum of those two angles. If the Archangel Gabriel came into this classroom and told me that the angle in question was equal to the sum of the other two I would say to him, prove it!'

'Comrade Parfrey', he would go on, 'You are suffering from 'Bullockdom'.

Turning to the class in general he would ask all and sundry if they knew what 'Bullockdom' was? They would invariably nod sagely for they knew what was coming. Taking a deep breath he would say,

'There are three degrees of 'Bullockdom' and they are, first not knowing what you are given, secondly not knowing your own construction, and thirdly and worst of all, setting out to prove something but you do not know what it is!'

One can appreciate why I kept my head down.

One day the Boss put a 'cut' on the blackboard and holding out the piece of chalk asked those of us in the class if anyone would like to come up and prove the problem. As usual, I was keeping my head down waiting for the star of the class to get up and take on the challenge. No one volunteered. I took a casual glance at the proposition and, for the first time in my life, saw the solution.

I raised my hand and the Boss asked me if I wanted to go to the toilet! I replied in the negative and said hesitantly,

'I think I can solve the problem, Sir.' There was a stunned silence and then, as if a miracle had come about, he said to me in hushed tones at the same time extending the chalk,

'My dear Comrade Parfrey, come up.' There was an eerie feeling as I stood up and endeavoured to manipulate the obstacles of the closely placed desks. I was just at the front line of desks when an awful thing happened. The fly of my trousers caught in a projecting piece of one of the battered desks and with a deft flick opened all the buttons so that my manhood was exposed.

15

Bear in mind that this was a co-ed class and there was no possible way I could go forward and take the extended piece of chalk. It was as if I was unable to accept an Olympic Gold medal that had been well and truly earned. To my chagrin I had to tell a lie and confess that I did not see the solution after all. As I made my way back along the obstacle course to my desk I was subjected to a tirade from the Boss,

'You ignorant bostoon; you misguided son of a Hottentot!'

That was the last time I stood up and claimed I knew anything!

Chapter 05

O ANNIE – ANNIE – ANNIE – ANNIE – O!

In my youth there were many characters, all of whom were poor. They eked out a living by doing odd jobs, playing tin whistles, repairing leaking saucepans and kettles, sharpening knives. Added to the list would be street musicians of all sorts - the barrel organ player, not forgetting the vocalists. In complete contrast, from time to time a trio of musicians would set up playing classical music! The group comprised of an elderly man and his two sisters. He was the trumpet player and hoisted the large harp played by one of his sisters. The second sister played the violin or cello. The pavement was their stage complete with music stands! A massive seashell was used for collecting the many coins after each performance. I learned years later that they visited all of the cities in the country on a regular basis. Their infrequent visits to our area were always a highlight. Looking back it was incongruous. Times were hard in the1930s and living from day to day was not easy. I often wondered what story lay behind each of those characters I met in my youth. I am sure that had they an ability to put pen to paper, their experiences would have become books of note in their own right.

We lived not far from one of Cork's many slum areas where people lived without proper sanitation. Raw sewage was thrown into the gullies passing the doors of the tiny houses to find its way to the nearest manhole connected to the sewage system. At least in my home we did have a flush toilet! Money was scarce and jobs few. Many a time a coat was 'turned' - taken apart and put together again - to all intents and purposes making a new coat but it looked and felt odd to wear. Taking all this into consideration one can but imagine how the homeless fared!

The one character who stands out in my mind is O Annie Annie Annie Annie O. Everyone called him Black Ned. No one knew what his real name was, except his father and mother. To me he was a loveable old man, about six feet in height, with a rotund weather beaten face that shone like a polished rose-hued apple beneath about three or four days growth of hair. His head sported a shock of closely cropped white hair. He was a man of the roads and carried all his belongings in a sack on his back shielded from the weather by a black tarpaulin cape. I often thought that he must have been a man who was down on his luck - who knows - and just took to the roads. His peculiar name came about from the little street performance he did on a regular basis to collect a few coins to keep body and soul together.

Black Ned and his little wooden doll. Photograph by kind permission of Amy and Chris Ramsden

He sat on a little collapsible stool. A narrow board projected out about two feet at the end of which was a little wooden doll. As he tapped the board with a coin the little doll started to danced to a tune he had made up. Over and over again he repeated his song of words, 'O Annie Annie Annie Annie O' up the scale and descended one note to a word back to middle C.

One day he called at our home and asked my mother for some hot water so that he could make a cup of tea. She was only too pleased to do so. She brought him some bread and butter and a small piece of cake. There in the postage stamp size of our front garden, using the front room window sill as his table, he enjoyed his meal. It was only after he had finished his repast that I found some symbols scratched into the brickwork of the front wall of the house. It was a symbol to tell other travellers that our home was 'a good house!' Whoever occupies my old home today is not aware of the cryptic sign but must often wonder why people call to the house so often for a handout or help. He was a lovable old man of whom I was very fond. He always had a good word. That was nearly seventy years ago; my memory of him is as fresh in my mind today as if it were yesterday.

I learned one great lesson in my life from knowing 'O Annie Annie Annie Annie O'. I think it was in the year 1936 and I had just celebrated my tenth birthday. I had a half-a-crown to spend. In old money that was two shillings and six pence - a fortune in those days. Worth nothing at all today. A half-a-crown could buy a full four-course lunch in a good restaurant! I planned to spend the money and have a wonderful time in the city. Plans embraced buying chocolate slices, which were my favourite cakes, and going to the cinema. With my mother's 'have a great day son,' ringing in my ears I set off for town. We did not live too far from the city centre and my foot was light at the thought of the great afternoon in front of me.

I must make mention of the fact that in addition to my silver half-crown I had a halfpenny. As I made my way in to town, I held on closely to the two coins. I reached a point where I had to decide to take a longer route or a shorter more direct route. What prompted me to take the circuitous route I do not know, but I did. Very few people used this route for it just passed a large college institute and a couple of factories. Fate decreed I take this path.

The road went by the south channel of the River Lee and as I turned to walk along the quayside who should be there but O Annie Annie Annie Annie O! I could not believe it. There he was sitting on his stool with the little doll dancing away and not a soul in sight. I knew in my heart of hearts I could not pass him by without giving him something. What should I do? Give him the silver half-a-crown or the virtually worthless brass coin? It was as if I was walking the proverbial plank. As I passed him by I found myself throwing the silver coin into his hat. All I was aware of was tremendous emotion within myself as the doll stopped dancing and the song ended. As I crossed Clarke's bridge [dating back to the year 1776] I looked back. There was O.A.A.A.A.O mouth agape. So far as he was concerned all his Christmases had come together.

At that time in Cork City the Salvation Army was very active in helping the poor and destitute. They ran a hostel where they supplied what was known as 'a two-penny doss', a night's shelter that provided rough sleeping accommodation. They also had what was known as 'penny dinners' where a meal was provided for only one penny. So far as O.A.A.A.O was concerned at the drop of a coin he had fifteen nights shelter or thirty meals.

I had a lump in my throat as I walked to the city centre hugging my brass coin. There was no visit to the cinema, no chocolate slices but it did not seem to matter. I looked at various toy shops and wended my way to a huckster's shop where they made lock-jaw toffee. It got the name because once you put a piece into your mouth you would not be able to open it for hours. The cost of a square was one half-penny. After six in the evening I returned home and my mother asked me if I had a good day. I replied in the affirmative. I never told her or anyone else about what happened that day. On the following Wednesday I received a short letter from an aunt of mine in Scotland. I seldom heard from her. The letter contained a belated birthday card together with a postal order for five shillings! This was twice what I had given away on Monday! I was staggered.

I had always wanted to have an air gun that fired lead 'bullets'. Now, with my five shillings I bought a Diana gun. My purchase however led to another lesson I had to learn. Namely, if one has a firearm of any sort, one is never content until something is killed with it.

I took a few shots at cans and glass bottles, etc. It was not a powerful weapon. One morning in the garden I looked up and saw a little sparrow chirping away on the rooftop of the house next door. I do not know what prompted me but I lifted my gun and aimed at the little bird. The chances of hitting him were remote, but I did. In his death throes he flew down and landed at my feet. I took him in my hands, crying and said how sorry I was. I was destitute. He died in my hands. It was a lesson I have never forgotten.

The other lesson I learned that I have proven to be true, is that whatever one gives without expecting it to come back, WILL always come back. If one gives and expects it TO come back it never will. The real secret is to give when it really hurts and while doing so TRUST. Another throw-away: money on MONDAY is ALWAYS lucky!

Chapter 06

SCHOOL INITIATIONS

It did not take long for me to discover the truth in the saying, "there is always calm before a storm". I had heard that "new boys" were initiated into the school and when it came to my turn, believe me I grew up fast! There was a scale of initiations, what one might term junior and senior.

My first encounter came about a couple of months after becoming a student. One day, I was surrounded by a gang of six and frog-marched to the toilets. I confess that I was a bit scared but it did not take me long to realise that it was far better not to show fear as this was looked upon as a sign of weakness and could result in a double dose.

I took some solace in the fact that there were at least three more of my school companions lined up ahead of me for the same treatment, whatever that was going to be. Not knowing was the worst part, I waited in trepidation as I heard squeals and a cry or two coupled with the flushing of the toilets. Those who went before me were directed out another exit so one had not the slightest idea what was in store.

It came to my turn. I was blind-folded and brought to the toilets. My head was forced into the bowl and then I felt a gentle stream of water running over my head, neck and face. I was full sure that I was being urinated upon and got the impression that this was so when my head was pushed further into the toilet bowl and a couple of gallons of water from the tank cascaded over me. I was determined not to cry out and bit my lip while undergoing the ordeal. The blind-fold was removed and I was given a towel by a group of grinning students with which to dry myself! One's imagination runs riot at times like this and what I thought was urine was merely slightly warmed water. I was slapped on the back and congratulated. I had passed the test and had to swear to keep that particular initiation ceremony a secret. I had become one of the boys!

The senior initiation ceremonies were far worse. These took place in the old Grammar School where the seniors spent their lunch break. There was a large concrete play area bounded on the left by a brick wall, which separated the upper part of the school from the lower portion. Conveniently placed steps led to the lower level and the difference between one level and the other was about a ten feet drop. I use the word "drop" advisedly as it was the key component for this torture; and torture it was. The victim was left hanging by his hair over the ten-foot drop! The more he screamed the more he was held by the hair. To my mind this was vicious in the extreme. I was fortunate to have escaped this initiation.

Then there was "the black hole of Calcutta". This was a store-room in one of the blocks of buildings that was utterly dark. If you suffered from claustrophobia it was just too bad. One had to run the gauntlet of students on either side hitting you with wet knotted towels - these hurt like hell. The misfortunate was locked up in this hole and water bombs were hurled through a small opening at the top of the door. These were large paper bags filled with cold water that rained down on the misfortunate who was being subjected to this type of initiation. Looking back, this was very cruel and I hate to think of the number of boys that were affected by this treatment for the rest of their lives. Of course, at the time, nobody gave a thought to the psychological damage that was being done.

I had many pals who attended the Christian Brothers' College, which was just down the road from my school. Very often friends and neighbours of mine would cycle together to our respective schools. Whatever seemed bad about my school, the reports of what was happening to my friends attending the Christian Brothers' College made our experiences seem like a picnic. The brothers were armed with a long double leather strap with a line of old copper pennies stitched in between both lengths. A flake from this awful weapon could really and truly inflict terrible pain.

Reports I received from various friends who had the misfortune to attend this college, told of beatings inflicted for even a minor infringement which were horrific. In one particular case a so-called Christian Brother pulled the ear out of the head of a student! On another occasion a frightened young boy was locked in a small room at the top of the building and was so scared that he jumped out of the window. I do not recall whether he died or was very badly injured. School in my day was tough and one had to be tough to endure what went on. There was little purpose in relating to one's parents what was going on for they just did not believe it. The same thing held sway for the girls attending most of the convent schools. Looking back I feel that these adults had major problems and vented their spleen on the misfortunates who had no redress.

God forgive them all.

Chapter 07

A POT-POURRI OF MEMORIES

The one great advantage of growing old, so far as I am concerned, is that my long term memory becomes stronger as the years roll by while, at the same time, I could forget what I had for breakfast on any given morning! Musing in front of a comfortable fire I could see in the flames, as if scrying a crystal ball, faces and situations from the past. A kaleidoscope of patterns and events, some funny, some frightening, some sad but all mixed together to produce a pot-pourri which went to make up my life.

I think of school friends long since dead who having joined the British forces, lost their lives during the war. Two brothers went down with their ships while yet another was shot down somewhere over France. All were in their late 'teens. The most gruesome memory I have to this day is in respect of a pupil who was liked by all his schoolmates. He went to live in South Africa where he was married. Shortly afterwards in a fit of rage he murdered his wife and paid the ultimate penalty; he was hanged by the neck until he was dead! Shivers still run down my spine when I think back as if it was yesterday.

On a lighter note, the Savoy cinema was opened in 1931 and could seat up to 2,000 people in the auditorium. There was a hard seat for the organist, Fred Bridgeman who came from England and he entertained countless numbers of Corkonians during those halcyon days. He had a son Philip who was also a pupil in the school and even then showed business potential in various ways.

Thompson's bread and cake factory was close to the school and when the wind was in the right direction carried wonderful smells of luscious cakes in the making that permeated the building and had us with our tongues hanging out! As most of us had very little pocket money Phil arranged a weekly draw whereby we paid in the princely sum of one penny per week.

The prize? Two Thompson's cakes daily for six days in one week, the school being open from Monday to Saturday inclusive. The gamble was well worthwhile and Phil did very well financially, especially as he purchased cakes which were slightly below the set quality control and were sold from the factory at half price!

Another of the services Phil rendered, at a price, was the selling of "lines". For being disorderly in class or some other misdemeanour a teacher would give as a punishment the writing out of 20, 50 or 100 lines such as, "I must not talk in class" and similar other old chestnuts. The writing of lines was a thorn in the side as it meant spending valuable time churning out repetitive stuff over and over again. Our ingenious entrepreneur had invented a type of frame that held four pencils so that with the writing of one line, as if by magic, four lines were written simultaneously. He had large stocks of the various lines that were normally dished out, which he sold to any student who wanted to save time and had money to boot. I often wonder if he became a millionaire!

Another pupil I recall to mind was Frank Heney. He was a strange guy and had a photographic memory. We had a really good teacher of English and I learned so much from him. English was my favourite subject and over the years I was privileged to have been taught six or seven Shakespearean plays and sonnets. We were invariably given the task of learning up to twenty lines of Shakespeare at a time. This took me a long time to do. In contrast, Frank could open the appropriate passage five minutes before the class commenced, read it once and still be word perfect. It was a wonderful gift to have and stood him in great stead. When he left school he joined the Irish army and became a medical orderly.

War clouds gathered in 1938 and despite Mr. Chamberlain's "Peace in our time" speech after his return from meeting Hitler in Munich, the following year war was declared on 3rd September, 1939. Having gained possession of the ports from the British in 1937 the government declared Eire would remain neutral. War brought unbelievable changes with food shortages and rationing became the order of the day. New pupils started to attend the school. They came from war-torn Britain and it was so incongruous to see pupils from Wales and elsewhere coming to grips with the Irish language, the learning of which was compulsory.

Our annual "Speech Day" was held in the Central Hall in Academy Street. This was the day when the parents of the students came to hear the school hierarchy give an account of its stewardship. It was also the day that the school prizes were presented to outstanding students. I never came into this category but I did win a minor prize on at least two occasions where drawing was concerned. After all the formalities were over a concert followed with various songs and recitations, and the evening was crowned by the school play. I will never forget the year that it was decided to produce the musical, "The Willow Pattern Plate."

Because it was thought I possessed the best voice, I was shanghaied and given the principal part of The Prince. I may have had a good voice but in no manner of means was I an actor. I will never forget that day. The dais at the end of the hall, while raised, was not a stage in the accepted understanding of the word. The curtain, in two halves, was suspended on a strong wire that ran across the stage from the right to left, and the actors and actresses entered and exited stage left. The small space on the left was crowded as all those taking part in the play awaited their cue to come on stage. Though I could remember most of the words of the songs I could not remember all my lines and from start to finish it was a disaster!

There I was, all dressed up in my finery with my wooden sword painted silver to give the audience the impression that it was a deadly instrument. I was continually being prompted and a couple of times looked in the direction of the prompter and was heard to ask,

"What did you say?"

This was much to the amusement of the audience who could not but help laughing. The whole thing began to fall apart and develop into a farce, and as I ad libbed the leading lady did her best to reciprocate. The show ended rather abruptly. I was singing an aria and will always remember the words:

"And I slash and I gash".

As the part called for the raising of my sword, with gusto I swung it up, down and sideways as I sang the words. It is possible to be in the wrong place at the wrong time in life and this was one of those times.

I was too far forward on the stage as I waved my sword about to such an extent that I dislodged the supporting wire, and the whole curtain came crashing down. Those waiting on the left to make their entrance were shown up in all their glory!

I took off, leaving the producer of the musical to make clucking noises to the audience. Looking back, I think that it was a success but the headmaster certainly did not. He came down after me and gritting his teeth told me in no uncertain terms that I was a ham actor. I was never again asked to take part in any future productions. I think the stage lost out but I gained!

I have already mentioned "DT", which was the abbreviation for "Detention." All pupils received marks from their form teachers based on ability to learn, behaviour and so forth and these were recorded faithfully. Three zeros in any given week saw a pupil having to stay in school on Saturday after 12.30 p.m. closing time for the full DT period which, from memory, was two hours and study whatever subject was thought appropriate by the teacher. Everyone endeavoured to avoid being awarded three zeros in the week. If one was unfortunate enough to pick up an extra zero, you were already booked for the following week. I knew of pupils who were never free on Saturdays! As you can guess I did quite a bit of "time" for no matter how hard I tried I was always in trouble, much of it not of my making. Trouble seemed to follow me around like the plague and continues to do so to the present day.

All I could do was offer it up!

Chapter 08

A TROUBLED UPBRINGING

Four years prior to my birth the Irish Free State came into being. From an early age I was always conscious and proud to be Irish. My parents on the other hand, while they too were Irish, had an affinity with England. My maternal grandmother came from that country, my grandfather had been in the British Army, and my father fought in the 1914-18 Great War.

As an aside, in latter years my father told me how foolish he had been to join up. He had been gassed and shot through his left leg and suffered shell shock for many years. At certain times of the year, especially around the time of Armistice Day - 11th November, he would become morose and would relive some of the appalling things he had seen and experienced. For all this he ended up with a pension of one shilling per week from the British government!

To me and my generation it was history and we could not get worked up like our parents when the King broadcast to the nation and the annual Armistice Day parade took place in Cork. Catholics, Protestants, Jews and dissenters came together on that day for a march to the cenotaph. A special Service was held in St. Fin Barre's Cathedral while at the same time a Memorial Mass was celebrated at St. Mary's Cathedral, know affectionately as "the north chapel". I remember that the Gardai were out in force on those days and there were many who resented the red poppy. Most of my fellow cho-risters did not agree with a number of the prayers used and we steadfastly refused to say them. This caused quite a bit of friction.

As recorded in another part of this book, not all the members of my family were of the same faith. The Parfreys were apt to change their religion at the drop of a hat and many of them, including me, detested all the divisions. For better or worse I was brought up in the Anglican tradition. I had many cousins and friends who were Roman Catholic and more who followed the teachings of the Church of Christ Scientist [Mary Baker Eddie]. One of my uncles had a great regard for Communism and often requested that when he died his body was to be cremated and his ashes sprinkled over the Red Square in Moscow! For the record, he didn't make it.

So far as my section of the family was concerned we had no difficulty in attending ceremonies in the churches of various relations who followed different faiths. Regrettably they found it difficult to reciprocate even when my grandmother's son – an uncle of mine – passed away. Wild horses could not get them to step through the portals of the church for the obsequies. It was a sad state of affairs. While we got on well with our neighbours there were, I am sorry to say, many who were quite bitter.

I dreaded Sunday mornings as I made my way to sing in the choir. I had to run the gauntlet of "Proddy woddy green-gut, never says his prayers; catch him by the left leg and throw him down the stairs. The stairs gave a crack and Proddy broke his back and all the little proddies went 'quack, quack, quack'". Often sods of grass and sometimes stones where thrown at me and others. On one occasion I was physically attacked and had the indignity of having sods of grass pushed up the leg of my pants! Hard to believe today that such things went on when I was a child. Some areas were worse than others. The word "Protestant" embraces all those who are not Roman Catholics, viz. Methodists, Presbyterians,

Bill Parfrey, choir boy!

Quakers, Plymouth Brethren, et al. The word "Catholic" means universal. All Protestants without exception accept this tenet so why is it that the Anglican Church is not known as The Catholic Anglican Church? The difference between it and the Roman Catholic Church [called the Catholic Church today] is separated by a doctrinal point only?

I often wonder what the Master Himself must think of it all!

The St. Fin Barre's Cathedral Choir

Chapter 09

SNIPPETS FROM THE WAR YEARS

The war brought huge changes. Cars were put off the roads except where doctors and priests were concerned. Petrol was rationed to four gallons per month and one could not do much travelling on that amount of juice. Bus services were curtailed and the last bus left the city centre at 9.30 p.m.

In 1940 cars and vans were converted so that they could run on coal gas and it was a strange sight to see vehicles sporting huge rubber balloons on the roofs to contain the gas. A fill would allow an eight horsepower vehicle to travel thirty miles. One windy day, I saw a small vehicle lifted two feet in the air! Their lives were short lived, for coal became a luxury item and what was imported went to the gasworks throughout the country. Only a limited period was available daily when one could cook a meal or light up a room.

In those days many homes were dependant on gas for illumination. Gas was supplied each day from 8.00 a.m. until 9.30 a.m. and then the supply was turned off. It came on again at 12.30 p.m. until 2.00 p.m. and there was no further supply until 6.00 p.m. which lasted until 9.30pm. After this one had to depend on a candle if one was lucky enough to have one!

Necessity being the mother of invention, all sorts of things came on the market. The sawdust stove, once it got going, could cook all before it. Then there was the hay-box, which was used to continue cooking a meal in a saucepan after the gas supply was shut off. Company representatives adapted their vehicles to run on charcoal, the burner being fitted to a stand that projected from the front bumper. It was a tough job to get things started in the morning. Once, I saw a long-distance bus pulling a charcoal-burning unit. I think it was on its way to Dublin!

There were three trains per week to Dublin and three per week to Cork. The official departure time was 8.00 a.m. and arrival scheduled for 6.00 p.m.

Seldom if ever did the train get within shouting distance of the official timetable. More often than not it took sixteen hours to make the journey of 150 miles. No catering facilities or heating was provided for the passengers. It took three engines to haul the train up the hill through the tunnel to Kilbarry. The drivers and firemen performed Herculean tasks endeavouring to get up steam, burning cement and coal dust mixed together. They had appalling problems with clinkers and many a time a train had to make an unscheduled stop to clean out the fire box. Even to re-light the fire!

Apart from wood everyone had to depend on turf from the bog to try and heat the home and keep warm. Unscrupulous merchants would soak the fuel in water so that a bigger profit was made as the consumer was paying for water along with the turf. Here and there one could see turf hanging on a clothes line to dry in the breeze. People had to resort to cooking in the fire-grate. Getting turf to burn was a skilled operation and could be a soul-destroying job.

The average family in my day could not afford to either purchase or cover the cost of keeping a car on the road so the humble bicycle reigned supreme. As the war dragged on it became nigh impossible to purchase an inner tube or a tyre. I remember when none were available we had to pack grass tight-ly into the tyre, which itself was in a bad condition, and make sure it stayed attached to the rim by binding it securely with tar tape! Of course this meant that one had to dispense with brakes for the front wheel! I saw people rid-ing bikes on the rims alone - a very dangerous and rough ride but there was nothing else one could do. There was a thriving black market if one only knew where it was. Most things, including food and cigarettes were on sale at exorbitant prices.

Food was rationed and at one stage where tea was concerned the allowance was a quarter of an ounce per week! The sugar ration was half-a-pound weekly and, from memory, the butter ration was four ounces per week. Every bit of available ground was used to grow vegetables and hundreds of allotments were to be seen all around the outer periphery of the city where people grew what was necessary. The terrace of houses where we lived had a fair size garden in which we grew potatoes and all sorts of fruit and vegetables, including tomatoes. We had a couple of apple trees, one pear and one plum tree. We grew raspberries, loganberries as well as blackcurrants. Some years there was a bumper crop and provided that sugar was available, we would make jam.

Jam manufacturers had to resort to sugar beet to replace sugar and often beetroot was brought into play. Bread was made with 100% wheat extract so the resultant product was black and virtually inedible. For quite a time one would find potato in a loaf of bread. This diet did a lot of damage to the innards of many people. People sieved the flour available and the amount of roughage left afterwards was just incredible. Occasionally one could buy a small white Vienna loaf costing one shilling, a prohibitive price in those days. These loaves were made from [so I was given to understand] flour smuggled over the border from the north of Ireland. At one period people found that their throats were bleeding after consuming these loaves. It transpired that the flour used was stored in a warehouse in an area that had been bombed by the German Luftwaffe. Minute shards of glass had penetrated the sacks and this accounted for the bleeding in the throat. That was the end of the Vienna loaves.

The Government issued gas masks primarily to those living in cities rather than the country at large. I stand to be corrected on this point. Total blackout was enforced and windows were not allowed to show the slightest bit of light. Wardens from the Air Raid Precautions checked houses constantly to enforce the regulations. Over-ground reinforced concrete air raid shelters appeared on the streets and there was the distinct possibility that the country would be invaded. Feelings ran high and in certain parts of Ireland there was quite a pro-German empathy and anti-British feeling.

I recall spending a family holiday in a remote part of county Kerry in a cottage overlooking Dingle Bay. Early one morning a German submarine commander called to the lady who owned the cottage and purchased supplies of fresh vegetables for the crew. The sub was well and truly gone by the time one of the few aeroplanes the state possessed - an old Avro Anson[1] – flew flat out at 130 mph up and down the bay in an abortive search. In 1943, in Cork, I saw a German aircraft chase an English Spitfire. These incidents were the closest I ever got to the action.

We had a radio and listened to the propaganda that was coming our way from each side. It was never clear what was the real truth. I can well recall the day my father bought the radio. It was in the year 1933. Prior to that we had a small crystal set with earphones and after hours of adjusting the set, we might be lucky to pick up 2LO, the Irish station that broadcast for a couple of hours each day. The new radio was a five valve set and afforded the listener to tune in to stations on the medium and long wave bands. To us kids it was sheer magic. At Christmas time when Dickens' "A Christmas Carol" was transmitted, there with the lights out and only the glowing embers of the fire for illumination, we sat enthralled as we listened to the ghosts of the past, present and future. No TV could match the images conjured up in our respective minds. To this very day, for me the radio reigns supreme and I hardly ever watch television programmes.

The history of what went on in the country during the war years is well documented in far more comprehensive and detailed books.

I write simply about my personal experiences and knowledge.

---

[1] The **Avro Anson** was a British twin-engine, multi-role aircraft that served with the Royal Air Force, Fleet Air Arm and numerous other air forces during World War II and afterwards. Named for British admiral George Anson, it was originally designed for maritime reconnaissance but was soon rendered obsolete.

Chapter 10

THE YEARS ROLL BY

The war years dragged on, as indeed did my schooling. I was always in trouble but I hasten to say that I was not troublesome. At least I thought so but perhaps others thought otherwise. I endeavoured to keep as low a profile as possible but that did not help me when I had to report to the headmaster for misbehaviour in class. To tell you the truth I cannot remember what it was for, but with fear and trepidation I approached the head's study and knocked on the door. A gruff command to enter and suddenly I came face to face with a grim-looking headmaster whose countenance spelt out clearly that he would brook no nonsense. He took down his cane telling me that I was to receive "two of the best".

My mind flashed back to the sadistic master who ruled the roost in the primary school. I held out my right hand. The cane rose in the air and came down with all the power the headmaster could muster. It seemed like an eternity as I waited for the cane to cut into my hand, thinking at the same time that my other hand would also have to bear an equal amount of pain. I closed my eyes as the cane descended and I felt the turbulence as it whizzed past my extended hand.

"Let that be a lesson to you," the headmaster said, his expression softening. I could not believe it. There was to be no corporal punishment. I learned a lesson that day which I never forgot. The headmaster was not a tyrant but scrupulously fair and his bark was much worse than his bite. I was a mediocre student and really had no incentive to study as opportunities to fulfil my ambition to become a doctor just did not exist. I did not even sit for my Leaving Certificate examination and left school when I was sixteen.

Times were hard and jobs virtually non-existent. I was lucky and procured a job as a clerk in a small stockbroker's office where I slaved away for the princely sum of fifteen shillings [about €1.00] per week. It was a one-man business and starting at 9.00 a.m. it was often after 7.00 p.m. before I was allowed to leave. I also had to work for half a day each Saturday. There was one other member of staff there - a 27 year old woman who showed me what to do. My employer was very mean and would supply me with a new ribbon for the portable typewriter upon which I was forced to work only when the ribbon was worn through. Even though young, I was no fool and saw many people making money by inside trading. It was like a club. I detested the job but stuck at it.

One day an advertisement appeared on the local daily paper seeking an assistant Estate Clerk to work with Cahir Estates Company in Co. Tipperary. Knowledge of rentals and accounts was essential. On the advice of my father, I made application for the position. My father gave me a crash course on gale days and tenancy agreements; he was well versed in this type of work. As you can imagine my C.V. was not very impressive but it did include my schooling. Imagine my surprise when in 1944, I received a letter from the company asking me to attend for interview on the 8th August. There was a hand-written postscript telling me to visit my old headmaster before the date of the interview. This I did. Seated in the headmaster's sitting room I showed him the letter.

"Well, well, well," he exclaimed, "my old friend George Robinson."

Fate decreed that the father of my former headmaster had been the head game-keeper on the estate! He spoke about Cahir and its environs with great affection and before I left he handed me a letter which he told me to give to Mr. Robinson at the interview. Many years later I came across the short letter in the office vault. It stated simply and I will never forget the words,

"Unless some bright star appears, give the job to Bill Parfrey."

By a strange coincidence [I know today that there is no such thing] I was in line for a job with a large printing company in Cork. In this day and age it is hard to believe, that in 1944, the vast majority of us had never travelled very far and the town of Cahir, even though it was but fifty miles from Cork, might as well have been in another country so far as I was concerned. The night before I was to travel on the 8.00 a.m. bus I was very sick and when I should have been looking my best I was as sick as the proverbial dog. As the bus left, I inquired of the bus conductor how I would know when we reached Cahir. The answer he gave me was,

"It is the first town you come to that has trams!"

I was so ignorant and naive that I actually believed him! I thought to myself it must be quite a big place. I found that it was anything but big and boasted a population of sixteen hundred people!

I found my way to the estate office where I met the secretary and overall administrator of the Cahir estate, which comprised the best part of 10,000 acres. The interview went well and while I had the ability to do the job I was just eighteen years of age. It was agreed that should I be successful in being appointed to the position I was to add a further three years to my age, so there and then I received the proverbial key of the door! Ten days later a letter arrived appointing me to the position at a salary of £10.00 per month! I was also informed that there would be a probationary period of six months. This was to be followed by a five-year period of learning estate management, each year bringing with it an incremental increase in pay.

By the same post came a letter from the printing house offering me a job. What was I to do? The pay was a little more than what I would earn in Cahir with the added bonus that I would have my own warm bed, food and home life. I asked my father for advice. He told me to leave home. It was a difficult thing to do but weighing up the pros and cons his advice was sound. On the 4th September, 1944 I left home for good. Suddenly I was not a boy any longer but grew up quickly in every sense of the word and became a man. I had to face the world on my own - a daunting undertaking.

Much to the satisfaction of my employers I was very quick to learn, and long before the five years had elapsed I was 'au fait' with the workings of the company. I had an ability to see ways of streamlining many aspects of the business which included farming, a commercial dairy, market gardens with glasshouses producing fruit and vegetables for the Dublin and local markets, sawmills, forestry, fisheries, 300 properties, the upkeep of Cahir castle and a waterworks. The company had the distinction of being the only privately owned waterworks in the country at that time and even supplied the Tipperary S.R. County Council! My talent for administration and the ability to produce innovative ideas in solving various problems came to the fore and I became second in command! The firm had a staff of eighty spread over a wide area. Even after the eighteen years of my employment there were still parts of the estate I never saw.

The decision to leave home was the makings of me but I still had to steel myself for what lay ahead.

Chapter 11

SETTLING DOWN IN A SMALL COUNTRY TOWN

After spending one's life in a city, going to live in a small town is tanta-mount to putting oneself under a microscope. It takes a bit of getting used to. In a city people pass in the street without thinking, whereas in a small town one is expected to bid the time of day to everyone you meet. Again, things taken for granted in a city stand out in relief in a small town. In a closely-knit community, concern would be expressed if one heard of a neighbour getting a bad dose of 'flu for example. If someone from the town died, every shop would close as the cortege went by. Night-life was virtual-ly non-existent save for the pub or the cinema. It took me a long time to adjust. Coming to terms with living in digs, facing pigs head and other such delicacies was just too much for me and many a dinner [termed lunch today] found its way into the river. I did not complain, believe me. Where I was staying was looked upon as being the best lodging house in the town!

For a number of months I was homesick and it took grit and determination on my part to stick it out while I thought of the comforts of home. I made it my business to return for a week-end once every month. As I did not have enough money to pay for a return fare, this necessitated taking the bus to Cork on Saturday afternoon together with my bike, which I needed for my return journey. On principle I would not ask my father to help me out.

The first 33 miles of the return journey was virtually up-hill all the way to Mitchelstown, which is seven hundred feet above sea level. From here to Cahir was a further seventeen miles but with just one or two inclines. Believe me as I sped down the last hill to the town I was saddle sore and muscle weary. My best time for the journey was four-and-and-a-half hours and my worst - 10 hours! I mounted the bike outside my home and set off on a nightmare journey with the wind against me. Conditions were so bad that when I was on the last stretch of seventeen miles I could but walk as the wind was so strong. I could not continue in this manner so, having received permission to be half-an-hour late on a Monday morning every four weeks and with financial help from my father, I travelled by bus to and from Cork. What a contrast it was to enjoy my mother's cooking as distinct from the fare I had to endure in the digs.

Standing on suspension bridge outside Cahir Park House, residence of Colonel Richard Butler Charteris, owner of Cahir Estate where I was employed from 1944 to 1962

I called the place "Bleak House". Elsewhere I relate the strange happenings that went on there. The man whose position I was taking over had lived there for a number of years. The landlady affectionately known as "Miss" to all and sundry and well over seventy years of age thought very highly of him. He died at an early age from cancer and "Miss", who was a little eccentric, told us that we were to leave the inner doors open at all times so that the ghost of Bob Brady could pass through! I had the weirdest feeling living in that house and especially at night. While I did not know the man when he was alive I heard many stories about him. He was an outdoor type and tramped the mountains and woods of the estate in search of game.

One day after returning to Bleak House weary and wet but well satisfied with what he had bagged he found that the cartridges for his double-barrelled shotgun were damp. "Miss" did all the cooking and baking using a large steel range. As usual she had retired to bed at 7.00 p.m. and as the oven was warm, Bob put the cartridges into the oven to dry them out. The following morning he left for the office forgetting about the cartridges! "Miss" stoked up the fire and left the house to go to the butcher around the corner.

40

While placing her order the sound of a muffled explosion could be heard and a neighbour ran to tell her that the range had blown up! It was the mercy of providence that she was not in the kitchen at the time for the force of the explosion blew the strong steel oven range door across the room, embedding itself deeply into the opposite wall. The oven was never used again and all meals from then on had to be pot-roasted, fried or boiled.

While on the subject of meals, for dessert we received stewed apple every day for up to six months. There was a variation on Sunday when a crushed biscuit was placed underneath. It turned me off stewed apple for life.

Eventually I settled in and adapted to my new life. I became used to the stillness and aware of the rushing of the river Suir over the salmon weir by the bridge; the walks through the 1,000 acre Cahir Park with the famous Swiss Cottage [since donated to the State] in which the park ranger lived. He was a brilliant fisherman and tied his own flies, many of which were sent worldwide. I was never a fisherman but during my time in Cahir Park I fished! I was the envy of many an angler for I had permission to fish the park stretch of the river which abounded with very big trout. One evening after numerous occasions of losing flies and cat gut [the forerunner of nylon cast], I got fed up and threw rod, line and net into the river. I never tried my hand at angling ever again. I mollified myself by saying that I gave up because I did not like to think of the fish having barbs stuck in their mouths!

The estate office displayed on the wall two perfectly reproduced models of salmon caught on the River Suir by the then owner of the estate, Colonel Richard Butler Charteris. The larger of the fish, forty and one half pounds, was caught in 1926 and the second, a 38 pound specimen, caught in 1938. I believe this record was broken by an English lady who was fishing in the northern part of the county. She had never previously taken a salmon rod in her hands in her life and landed a fish over 50 pounds in weight!

The office was situated at the rear of Cahir House Hotel just off The Square of Cahir. The company sold the premises to the Burke family in 1922 or thereabout for the princely sum of £700.00! The hotel built up an excellent reputation both countrywide and even further afield. The estate office looked out on to the garden of the hotel. The office comprised of a large reception area with a counter over which rents were received and wages paid out each Saturday. The inner sanctum comprised of two very large rooms with ornate designs on the walls and a large open fireplace. The smaller of the two rooms contained the estate strong room and also the office of the Secretary and administrator of the estate. At one time, the town of Cahir boasted a gas works. The area where I worked was in the past illuminated by a one time splendid chandelier which now sported five defunct gaslights - a relic from the past as the gas company had long since gone into oblivion.

As estate clerk it was made clear to me that the town of Cahir and its people came first while the estate itself played second fiddle. An example of this was the fact that the town was also illuminated by street gas lamps the maintenance and running costs of which were borne by the estate at an annual cost of £8.00 per annum each! I will make subsequent references to the munificence of the company at a later point in this narrative.

Three events stand out in my mind in relation to the office.

A small two-bar electric fire was expected to warm the huge office area in winter, which was an impossible task. The cold permeated the bones to a degree that I had to wear a heavy overcoat together with a scarf to keep some heat in my body. Gloves also had to be worn and taken off when I had to write something down. I approached my boss and told him of the situation. The result was magical. Huge amounts of timber, cut to size, were sent to the office from the woods and a large fire was kept burning in the grate specially adapted to burn wood. What a difference it made.

A middle-aged lady was employed to clean the office once a week and was paid on a monthly basis. She was very conscientious. The office sparkled and glowed after she had been there with polish, dusters and all the other cleaning paraphernalia. In one corner of the room, tucked behind an obsolete piece of office furniture stood a gun! To me it looked like something one would use to kill an elephant. For some reason best known to herself, the cleaning lady [the salt of the earth "can I do you now, Sir?" brigade] decided for reasons best known to herself to clean out the corner in question.

Gingerly she lifted out the heavy gun – she was a small woman – and as she turned the stock of the gun came in contact with the obsolete furniture. There was a huge bang that knocked the cleaner off her feet and the antique lamps were blown to smithereens. The wall was peppered with shot. No one realised that the gun had been there for years fully charged. The woman resigned on the spot and got married! Whether it was a shotgun wedding or not, I really do not know.

There was a large picture on one of the office walls depicting a herd of horses. They were brown in colour and stood under a tree. I always thought that it was a depressing picture. One day, a Colonel South-Bombard [not his real name] who was residing in Cahir House Hotel while a large local mansion which he had purchased was being renovated over a three month period, came down to breakfast and ordered a triple Remi Martin brandy. The manageress commented, "drinking brandy before your breakfast?" As he moved into the hotel garden he replied, "but my dear lady, this IS my breakfast!" He looked in the window of the estate office and saw the painting. He became very excited and being a connoisseur rushed into the office and immediately offered to purchase the painting. It was not for sale but as a result of his knowledge we learned that the painting was by a man called Furney and was valued at £2,000. That would have been around the year 1947.

About three months afterwards the artist killed himself!

Chapter 12

CAHIR – THE CROSSROADS OF THE SOUTH

I coined the phrase "Cahir - the crossroads of the South" after living in the town for two or three years. The main roads from Cork to Dublin and Limerick to Waterford ran through the town, resulting in there being no less than sixteen buses passing through the town each day. In addition Cahir was on the main railway line from the ferry port of Rosslare on the southeast coast of Ireland, passing through the city of Waterford and on to Limerick. There was a connection at Limerick junction for trains to Cork and Dublin. The slogan was apt and later was adopted by the Cahir Development Association, which I was instrumental in bringing into being.

Before I ever went to live in the town I had heard the expression, "When you are in Cahir you are in trouble!" From where it originated I have not got a clue, but I did find that one had to mind one's Ps and Qs and be careful what one said. Out of a population of 1,600 souls, no less than 100 came from Cork! These were people who came to work in the area, the two largest employers being the Cahir Estates Company and the flour mill of Going & Smith Ltd. There was a section of the local population who gave the impression that they resented newcomers. I regret to say that this group did not appear to want any changes, and operated on the principle that what was good enough for their fathers was good enough for them! To my way of thinking those who live and earn their living in any given place have an obligation to do all that is possible for that place in return.

Where religion was concerned, the town of Cahir seemed to cater for all sorts and conditions in addition to the Catholic faith which, as one might expect, had the largest number of adherents. There was quite a large Church of Ireland congregation as well as Presbyterians, Methodists, Quakers, Evangelists. The number of pupils attending the Church of Ireland primary school in 1944 was over 60. When my own family and I were later forced to leave the town in 1962 the average attendance was down to seven! The maxim "close the school and you close the church" was ultimately borne out. This did not mean that the doors of the church were closed for good, rather that the parish did not boast the services of a full time rector. The Irish government supported minorities and provided that the number of pupils averaged seven, the State was prepared to bear the cost of a full-time teacher. Contrast this with the Catholic primary school next door where the ratio of teachers to pupils was roughly one to 35! In effect this meant that Protestant children of all denominations were in effect receiving individual tuition and their education went forward by leaps and bounds as a result.

It did not take me long to come to realise that most of the top jobs were held by Protestants who were also the main employers. I was told that in times prior to my arrival, employees of Going & Smith Limited had to attend a prayer service on Sunday afternoons and it was as much as their job was worth if they failed to do so! There was a definite class distinction and I never came across a place which boasted so many upper class colonels, captains, commanders and brigadiers most of whom were looked upon as snobs. I abhor this kind of thing. I was not a good church goer but showed the flag every so often.

In addition to the Catholic church there was the Church of Ireland building and the Presbyterian edifice which did duty for all those who were not members of the Anglican tradition. There had been a very big British barracks on the outskirts of the town where many soldiers had been stationed going back to the Crimean war. I remember there were four wall plaques commemorating the four war horses that had survived the battle of Savastapol. Perhaps they are still there to this day.

Because so many of the soldiers stationed in Cahir were members of the Church of England, St. Paul's Church was filled to capacity every Sunday. The numbers were so great that a series of services had to be arranged each week. That was not the case in 1944, but there was a still a sizeable congregation nevertheless. The interior of the church comprised a long aisle with a nave and seating on either side. There were also galleries that could accommodate quite large numbers. In my time it was seldom that the galleries were open but they were from time to time.

One Sunday I decided to go to the church and say a few prayers. All the pews had doors and at one time pew rents were charged so that only the same families could sit in 'their' pew. While this tradition had died out, families still occupied the same seats weekly. I was unaware of all this and when I entered the church I sat in the first pew I saw. Imagine my surprise on Monday morning when I received a peremptory command to call and see a Mr. Stravley who was I think the secretary of Going & Smith Limited.

I had no idea why he wanted to see me but out of courtesy called to his office that morning. He was not in a good mood and told me in no uncertain manner how outraged he was that I had occupied his pew the previous day. I could not believe this and that finished me so far as church-going was concerned. I mentioned the matter to the rector of the parish, Canon Armstrong, later to become an Archdeacon. He listened to me and it was obvious that the poor man had a difficult job in running with the hares and chasing with the hounds. I thought to myself that perhaps the cant I heard long before I ever set my eyes on Cahir was the truth!

Whether to make amends or to fill a gap I, was invited to the rectory for dinner one evening. Although I accepted the invitation I was conscious of the fact that I was stepping out of my league. I was not 'au fait' where silver service was concerned or the correct etiquette. However, the thought of a good meal was bait enough.

On the day in question I dressed myself up in my best bib and tucker. My heart was beating a little faster than usual as I walked up the avenue to the large rectory. The VIPs who attended included the Bishop of Cashel, Emily, Waterford and Lismore, the Dean of Cashel and an Archbishop of the Church. One of the guests - another stopgap - was the Rev. John Pleare, a curate in the parish of Clonmel, the county town eleven miles distant from Cahir. Like me he was out of his depth and kept his head down.

Pre-dinner drinks were served in the drawing room and we did our best to keep out of sight and out of mind. After pleasantaries and small talk we trooped into the dining room.

It was very large and the centre-piece was a huge highly polished mahogany table with neat place settings. All I knew was that etiquette dictated to start with the outside spoon or fork and work inwards. Both the curate and I watched out of the corner of our eye to make sure we were doing the right thing. A very large shaded light illuminated the tableware and the silver and glassware glistened and sparkled.

Prayers were said by His Grace the Archbishop and the meal commenced. The first course was a type of fruit cocktail. This was followed by a soup and bread course and then came the 'piece de resistance'! It comprised of two snipe on a large plate with a selection of vegetables on the side.

I had not the slightest idea how to handle the small birds which on such a large plate looked as if they floated on a pond. As if in slow motion I ladled the vegetables on to the plate, all the while keeping an eagle eye out to see what the curate who was sitting opposite me might do. He was in the same boat as myself.

None of the dignitaries seemed in any hurry to commence the main course as their animated conversation flowed north, south, east and west of the large table passing right over the heads of the curate and me. Finally the curate had had enough. Taking up a fork he drove it into one of the twin birds.

To his consternation and mine he either missed his target or the skin was too tough. Either way, the fork slipped and as if a bullet from a gun, the snipe shot across the polished table and landed right in front of me. I was nearly hysterical as the curate got up from his place and walked all around the large table. Apologetically, he leaned over me, skewered the bird as if a trophy and proudly marched back to his seat. Whether it was politeness on the part of the dignitaries or not, the conversation on the Ming dynasty carried on as if nothing had happened! I think that the excellent wines had something to do with it! That night as I lit my oil lamp in my sparse bedroom in Bleak House one thing was clear to me - there are those that have it, and there are those that don't!

I belong and have always belonged to the latter group and it has done me not the slightest harm all my life.

Chapter 13

THE WATERWORKS AND THE MONTHLY FAIR

As I've said, the Cahir Estates Company had, to the best of my knowledge, the distinction of being the only private company in the country that supplied piped water to a town's inhabitants. Colonel Richard Butler Charteris was the son of Lady Margaret Charteris and was born on the 12th October, 1856. To commemorate his birth a fountain was erected in the centre of the town. This proved a boom to all. Until then they had to draw water from the river or from wells or pumps. The source of this supply came from a mountain area in the heart of Scarroughwood a few miles out of town.

Inhabitants along the route sought a connection here and there and this was in essence the birth of the waterworks. In 1928 the company built a new and enlarged reservoir complete with filter beds. It was a gravity fed system. A six inch pipe was laid down which carried pure crystal clear mountain water to the consumers. The water was a pleasure to drink. Nearing the town the mains were reduced to four inches, then two inches, one inch and finally half an inch. The water entering the reservoir filtered through thick old red sandstone taking approximately three months to reach the catchment area.

Over the years the demand for water exceeded the supply and there were times when the supply was virtually nil. As the town nestled in a valley, houses on the far upper regions were the first to feel the pinch. Consumers could not fathom why during a particularly wet spring, water was in short supply. Often irate they were mollified when it was explained how the overall system worked. Some years there was a problem with frogs. It goes without saying that this was not generally known. It happened occasionally that a consumer would report that the water supply had ceased suddenly. We would apologise and assure them that the matter would be attended to immediately. We would add that it was a 'gorf' problem affecting the stopcock. They were not aware that the word "gorf" was "frog" spelt backwards! The problem arose at source when small frogs occasionally

49

bypassed the filter screens and were carried along the mains until finally their head would block the stopcock. The maintenance staff would have the matter rectified in double quick time.

Fair Day was once a month when the streets were taken over by the farming community. Cows and sheep were everywhere. In no time at all the streets were covered with large cow-pats and sheep droppings, often in some part to a depth of a couple of inches. The smell was appalling particularly on a summer day. Foreign visitors, especially Americans, could not believe what they saw and there was the constant clicking of cameras to show the folks back home how dirty the Irish were. Shopkeepers and hotels had to erect barricades and bales of straw were used in public buildings such as banks and pubs, to alleviate the appalling mess. Many attempts were made to have a proper cattle mart built. Eventually one was built, but for years the townspeople had to suffer this imposition. Of course the local economy benefited but at what a price? The water supply was strained to the limit when it came to cleaning up the mess after the fair.

Part One

It was quite some time before consumers had their supply back to normal.

Many attempts were made to alleviate the situation. Col. Charteris wrote to the then Government Minister for Agriculture to see if he could use his influence in some way. His reply was a gem and was as follows:

Dear Colonel Charteris

Thanks for your letter of January 7th, which I would of course have answered sooner but for the fact that I have been ill and only got back to my office a few days ago.

Will you forgive me if I am quite frank on the subject about which you wrote to me? I know that my view is somewhat unorthodox, but I cannot help feeling that it has some merit to commend it. First, in this regulation-ridden world I have a horror of pushing people about, and having spent most of my life in rural Ireland, I know the irrational passion which small farmers have for showing their stock to what they think is best advantage. Comparing the background of the street with what to them seems the vast anonymity of the fair green, they instinctively believe that the former background presents a more flattering setting for the jewels they display. I am told that Hatton Garden diamond merchants sooner retire from business than display diamonds on any other background than black velvet, though in the last analysis they know that no skillful jeweller will suffer his judgement to be finally ruled by the first blaze of glory which diamonds on black velvet present. I am afraid that the railings on the square of Cahir are for the small farmers and their modest wares all and more than black velvet is to the merchants of Hatton Gardens.

You rightly surmise that the publicans secretly sympathise with this predilection of the farmers, believing that it brings grist to the mill. I have been 25 years a publican in a small Irish town whose public house has not been strategically situated and I know by experience that this intimate propinquity to the actual buying and selling is not so vitally important as those who enjoy it believe, but it is not a matter

51

of reason, it approximates to atavistic belief and, as St. Paul found so often in Corinth and Ephesus, reason without faith was rarely sufficient to overthrow inherited beliefs however irrational and exotic they may have been. Lastly, rural life in Ireland has much of tedium in it, and I am convinced that the monthly fair is for many of our people all that the spectacle of the Place de la Concord as one comes out from the Crillon is for those of us fortunate enough to have experienced this recurrent delight. I know that I should not stay at the Crillon nor indeed to be in Paris at all, because I cannot afford the one nor the other, but I do; and life would become well-nigh intolerable if prudence confined me [which it ought to do] perpetually to the four shores of Ireland. And so, I have never felt myself justified in denying to my neighbours on the grounds of unanswerable prudence and reason their irrational joy in displaying their wares everywhere they should not display them; in wasting fifteen pounds a month of the ratepayers' money washing streets that they should never have soiled; in glorying in their right to buy from itinerant "hand-me-downs" the raiment that they should buy from me in the respectable and orderly atmosphere that obtains in my venerable shop.

All this flight from reason seems to me the apotheosis of freedom, and all my annoyance at trying to drive my car through multitudes of bullocks and their proprietors evaporates in the realisation that in your country and mine there are no uniformed representatives of authority to push the people about, but rather that on this day they push me and I push them in friendly but vociferous assertion of exclusive rights which neither of us really have any title to at all.

I hope that this devotion to liberty at the cost of order will not shock you, but I know you will wish me to give you the facts as I see them.

With kind regards and best wishes for 1951.

Yours sincerely,

[Signed] James M. Dillon
Minister for Agriculture

I cannot recall exactly when that the monthly fair moved from the streets and resumed in a brand new purpose built cattle mart. Street fairs were a feature of Irish life for centuries and are now but a memory and a blurred one at that. Looking back, the waterworks and the monthly fair went hand in hand. They were finally divorced when the fair went to the mart and the waterworks was taken over by Tipperary S.R. County Council!

Chapter 14

THE HOUSE IN OLD CHURCH STREET

I was married on the 12th July, 1949 in Cork to Margaret. Following a honeymoon in the Isle of Man we returned to Cahir where we set up home. Houses of any sort were like gold dust and while a house went with my job, I was unable to take it up in 1944 when I started the job. Accordingly, it was rented out to someone else. I had arranged to rent a small flat, but as luck would have it, just three weeks before the date of our marriage, a tiny terraced house in Old Church Street became vacant. The management promptly allocated it to me.

The house had been occupied by an old man for many years and it had no water or electricity supply. The toilet facilities comprised of a tiny outhouse with a cesspit toilet. There was a shed for storing fuel, and the whole concrete back yard which measured about 16 feet x 12, feet was overrun by rats! The place was in an appalling condition. Seven large horse loads of rubbish were taken away, the house scoured and a water supply installed. This provided us with a tap and sink in the tiny kitchen and a flush toilet in place of the abomination in the back that had done duty for many years. Many of these small houses had cesspits over which grass and weeds grew.

The house design was simple. The front door opened directly from the street and a hallway ran through to the back door in a straight line. Half way along the hall on the left was the entrance to a tiny kitchen with an old open range, its chimney open to the sky. Illumination was through a very small window the glass of which was falling out of the frame. To keep the wind out we had to stuff it with rags. The front room off the kitchen measured nine feet by seven feet and had an open fire to provide heat. The floorboards were rotten in places and had hundreds of nails hammered in.

A decrepit stairway from the kitchen led to the upstairs accommodation. This comprised of the master bedroom, which was just big enough to take a double bed and a dressing table, both of which I had made in the local technical school at night. There was a tiny box room off the main bedroom and next to this was the spare room, which measured six feet by six and a half feet. Here hundreds of fleas jumped everywhere and it was a job to get rid of them.

Everywhere the floorboards had hundreds upon hundreds of woodworm holes. There were also cockroaches in the house and many a night we had to place saucers of Guinness in the rooms. This world-renowned product attracted the creatures and they either got drunk or drowned and were disposed of first thing each morning. The company papered the walls of the house and it was this that kept the plaster from falling off.

It was in this environment we started our married life. We were extremely hard up and like everyone else in those far off days we just had to make do as best we could. Covered orange boxes did duty as cupboards and bedside lockers. We had been given a wedding present of a dining-room suite comprising a table, four chairs and a sideboard cupboard. It was the cheapest of the cheap and was, in effect, simply plywood painted over.

Still, it was better than nothing. The only solid piece of furniture was an easy chair, given to us by my mother-in-law. That chair is still doing duty today, fifty-four years later.

Cooking facilities comprised of a Primus stove and a two-burner oil cooker. Paraffin oil was the order of the day. The floor of the kitchen was uneven and pitted but I covered it with a piece of cheap linoleum, purchased with the remaining few pounds that we had to our name. As we could not afford linoleum for the short hallway from front to rear, I resorted to a few yards of roofing felt which I laid down and dabbed with green paint to give a bit of colour. The first week-end we were actually on our own, taking it in turns to sit on the easy chair in front of a pretty miserable fire, we felt our spirits drop. All the excitement was well and truly over and we had to settle down and make the best of things. The rain, splattering against the front room window-pane, did not help us in our melancholy mood.

Suddenly our spirits lifted. On return from our honeymoon a personal letter of congratulations from Colonel Charteris awaited us. Inside was a cheque for £10! There and then we decided that we would use the money as a down payment on a Pye radio. The following Saturday we went by bus to Clonmel and bought a four-valve Pye radio which cost £17.17s - a fortune in those days. In common with so many others we bought it on the "never-never" - ten pounds down and ten shillings each month thereafter until the bill was paid. It put us to the pin of our collar to raise the ten shillings each month but we did. The radio was a godsend. Our home was filled with music and we were able to enjoy hearing the news, listening to documentaries, plays, light entertainment and all that went to make radio so enjoyable.

Looking back to the day we were married, I contrast our wedding breakfast with twenty-first century receptions. Ours was held in the Metropole Hotel, Cork and the guests numbered 36. There was not a drink in sight and the meal comprised of fruit cocktail, chicken and ham with vegetables, sherry trifle and a cup of coffee! Cost? Nine shillings and six pence - about £0.50 a head! We did have a few photographs taken on the roof of the hotel and then it was off to the station to catch the train to Dublin where we stayed overnight. The following morning we flew to the Isle of Man and so far as I was concerned it was the first time I had ever been in an aircraft! We enjoyed our ten days, but there was a scarcity of everything as the war had ended just four years previously.

Things like bars of chocolate were unknown and I remember one day my wife stood in a queue about fifty yards in length outside a pharmacy to buy a tin of blackcurrant pastilles. When bananas made a return to Ireland after the war none of the children had a clue what they were or how to eat them. Some thought they should eat the skin and throw away the centre. Hard to believe but true! For the first time in years household coal came on the market as indeed did many other items taken for granted today. The deprivations suffered by all and sundry during the dark days of the war and which continued for some time afterwards was a salutary lesson and taught us all to find substitutes for so many things. Coffee for example was unobtainable during the war years and so a concoction of chicory and sometimes acorns was used to provide an ersatz brew.

Shortages and learning to make do were additional lessons that had to be learned as we settled down to married life.

The railway viaduct over the river Suir outside Cahir

Chapter 15

MERGING WITH THE TOWN ACTIVITIES

By the time 1949 came around I was well and truly part and parcel of the community and got on well with everyone. To the best of my knowledge they in turn got on well with me but for one or two exceptions.

The previous four years were a learning curve as I came to grips with the running of the estate. During this time I involved myself in all the activities that went on in the town and made Cahir tick. I joined the local branch of Muintir na Tire [Family of the Land], the brain child of an inspirational priest named Fr. Hayes. He got his message across that the primary purpose of the organisation was to make people realise the power that collectively they enjoyed. By coming together as a unit, pooling the abilities and knowledge of each, great things could come about. The movement soon spread nation-wide.

In those times most towns looked dishevelled and unkempt with litter strewn around and weeds growing in every corner. Buildings too needed care and so the government set up The Tidy Towns Competition. This caught the imagination of many of us and as a result the Cahir Tidy Towns Committee came into being. The town was entered for the competition. There were cash prizes and trophies to be won. Every member of the committee worked with a will. Unsightly areas in the centre of the town were dug up and flowers planted in their stead. Railings were painted, signs were manufactured and erected on the main roads into the town bearing the inscription "Keep Cahir a tidy town".

A prime eyesore was the 1856 town fountain. It had a great deal of rubbish floating in it and the monument itself was covered with verdigris. My good friend Benny Peters and I volunteered to take on the work. We deliberately chose a Saturday afternoon when many people would be out and about. We knew that we were putting ourselves on the line for jibes and catcalls, but

58

working on the principle that one cannot have a circus unless there were at least two clowns, we went where angels feared to tread!

The fountain was surrounded by cars parked here, there and everywhere and this, on what was mark you, private property. Armed with buckets, scrubbing brushes and shovels we commenced what was not an easy job. Despite the taunting remarks made by passers-by we did not retort in kind, rather, we made a joke of the whole thing. One trader who ran a large hardware shop in the Square resented what we were trying to do. While Benny was local, I was an outsider and I think that this is what annoyed him.

He stood at the door of his shop smoking a pipe as he watched his assistant come across The Square with a torn, out-of-date cleaning powder of some sort. He laughed heartily as the assistant sheepishly handed us the box. Rather than get angry we pantomimed our thanks and covered the structure with the powder. Imagine our great surprise and the chagrin of the trader when the verdigris came away smoothly leaving a sparkling limestone fountain in its wake. What he did not know was that he had fallen into a trap and was hoisted by his own petard!

In addition to being the local radio correspondent for the national airways, I also wrote a weekly two-stick column for "The Munster Tribune" which was published in Clonmel. I 'phoned the editor and told him of my plan.

The following Thursday in large type the caption over my column read "Cahir trader fires first shot in Tidy Towns campaign".

The trader who was vehemently against what we were trying to do was swamped with people calling to his shop to congratulate him on his civic pride. Needless to report, all he could do was to say how delighted he was to lead the way. His sales increased and so the kudos paid off on the double.

Not to be outdone, another hardware shop donated five gallons of black and five gallons of white paint, with which we highlighted the corner curbs. The county council also made their contribution, by clearing the entire centre of the town around the fountain where they painted parking bays, so that for the first time ever, vehicles parked in an orderly fashion. The morning after the fountain clean-up, Sunday church-goers could not believe how much the face of the town had improved.

We tackled the litter problem by erecting wire litter baskets - 35 in all, hand-made by the indefatigable Benny who did Trojan work. He never charged for his time and barely accepted the cost of raw materials. We went and spoke to the school children urging them to pick up any litter they might see and put it in the litter boxes. Some small children confused the word "litter" with "letter" and a number of premises found waste paper in their hallways from time to time. Still really great strides were being made and the residents began to take great pride in their town.

The national competition covered cities, large and medium sized towns as well as villages. Competing towns were secretly inspected a number of times each year by a panel of judges and points awarded for effort, and so on. Then came the day the names of the winning towns were announced. We all held our breath and then a shout of joy went up when it was announced that Cahir had drawn first place in its category with Midleton, Co. Cork !

The win spurred everyone on to better and greater things and from this was born the Cahir Development Association. Many who were on the Tidy Town Committee were drafted onto the new organisation, which set off in dynamic fashion to really make the world at large aware that the town of Cahir was the place to be. An order was given to Faber Castell Ireland Limited in Fermoy, Co. Cork to manufacture and supply some thousands of attractive lead pencils bearing the slogan "Cahir the Crossroads of the South". These sold like hot cakes and swelled the coffers of the association allowing it to expand its operations.

Our first major effort was organising a Christmas Shopping Scheme. This necessitated the erection of Christmas lights. No matter how hard we looked at it there was absolutely no way that we would be able to raise the necessary wherewithal to illuminate the town. Then our in-built guru and stalwart came up with the idea that each trader, if asked, might agree to the erection of a minimum of ten coloured lights over the front of their respective premises, and bear the cost of the small amount of electricity necessary.

Most business people took up the offer and at a set time each evening all the lights were turned on. The centre of the town became a fairyland, the focal point being the illuminated Christmas tree in the square. The odd gap of darkness here and there singled out a trader who had not co-operated with the scheme. The subsequent loss of trade resulted in them being first in line the following year!

Every effort was made to get people to shop locally but the draw of the county town of Clonmel eleven miles away was difficult to overcome. The association printed and distributed attractive signs for every shop and meeting place bearing the slogan "Shop in Cahir for better fare". It must have done some good as soon other signs made their appearance and read "Shop in Clonmel and fare better"!

The association worked in conjunction with the railway company who ran mystery trains from Dublin and other cities during summer months. The cost of a ticket was nominal. On being advised beforehand the association organised private houses to provide ham salad meals, teas with bread and butter at an agreed price. We ran trips to the famous Swiss Cottage in Cahir Park, boat trips on the river and conducted tours of Cahir Castle.

An information centre was provided. No less than three mystery trains arrived from Dublin and disgorged 2,400 people. There were more people on the trains than the entire population of the town! It was an incredible sight with people milling here, there and everywhere. We were inundated but somehow or other we coped. A roaring business was done with shop tills clicking along merrily in competition with the boisterous singing that came from parched throats of those imbibing in the numerous hostelries. The hours passed until late in the afternoon when it was time for the trains to depart. The exodus from Egypt could not compare with the exodus from Cahir that Sunday.

One of the town's immortals, known as Patsy-the-Gag, had a field day playing his tin whistle for the multitudes. He received so many copper coins that the weight was instrumental - excuse the pun - in bringing his pants to below his knees. It was a day to remember. As far as I can recollect, there was a second mystery excursion to Cahir, but it paled into insignificance when compared to the first.

We also organised mystery bus trips for the townspeople that were hugely popular. The bus left at 7.00 p.m. for an unknown destination. The excitement of those on board was

Patsy the Gag
A loveable Cahir Character

frenetic as they guessed at where the destination might be. I did most of the planning for these trips and made sure that there would be a little café at the end where the passengers could have a meal. On the return journey I entertained the group with anecdotes and songs to the accompaniment of my piano accordion. They were happy days. Much good and public spirit was engendered both by the Tidy Town Committee and the Development Association.

Alas, all this came to an end for my family on the death of Colonel Charteris in 1961.

Some months later, I had to leave the town and the people I had come to love and return to my native city - Cork.

Chapter 16

THE SAWMILLS DEPARTMENT

As part of my estate management training, it was imperative that I visited different departments of the company. One of these was the sawmills, which was situated in New Church Street directly opposite the church of St. Paul. In comparison with the estate office I found the working hours very long. The sawmills opened at 8.00 a.m. and closed at 6.00 p.m. daily, and for good measure was open every Saturday morning for four hours. The estate office was closed on Saturdays.

I did spells of duty in the sawmills ranging from one to three months at a time. It was a challenge to learn about the different types of wood, costings and to work out the cubic capacity. I entered the strange world of donkeys and horses fellows - curved pieces of timber that went to make up the wooden wheel of a dray cart. Then there were stakes, fencing poles, T & G flooring, and so on. Naturally this linked in with the hardware business where I had more to learn about such things as the merits of plain and barbed wire, nails of all sorts as well as a myriad of other hardware lines. I dreaded the annual stock-taking.

When I first went to the sawmills, the power to drive the saws was supplied by a steam engine fuelled by all the scrap wood. A decision was made to install a diesel engine and a log band-mill. This was a mighty piece of equipment rather like a huge bacon slicer, which moved on what was tantamount to a railway track. It sliced through huge forest logs as easy as a knife through butter. To place this new equipment in its designated place necessitated the removal of a substantial quantity of clay at the right and rear of the complex.

This was long before bulldozers so one of the workmen, much to his disgust, was given the job. Using pickaxe and shovel he toiled for weeks digging up the sticky yellow clay, containing many stones of all shapes and sizes. There is no doubt, it was hard work, but Jack did not over-exert himself. As the soil piled up it was removed in a large horse-drawn cart by a powerful horse which, for many months, together with his master, ran a shuttle service from the sawmills to a dumping ground. Wet or fine "Jack-the-Rall "as he was known, toiled away.

One day there was great excitement. He had unearthed a human skull! This discovery was followed by some human bones. It transpired that during the terrible Irish potato famine a number of people had been interred there with no ceremony whatsoever. This led me to have an idea and jokingly I passed a remark to the sawmills manager to the effect of what would happen if something of significant value was found? He had a great sense of humour and, as he was annoyed at the very slow progress being made to level the area, he went along with my idea.

I happened to possess a number of old Irish copper coins, pennies and half-pennies, dating back prior to 1790, which I polished up. I also had a cheap onyx ornate box on the back of which I scored the date 1810. The manager found some thin tissue paper that was on its last legs and falling apart. We two conspirators carefully wrapped the coins in the paper and placed them in the onyx box, which we then muddied with the yellow clay. Each day at lunch time it was the practice of the manager to do his rounds and check if the saws had been sharpened correctly, the pits emptied of sawdust, driving belts secure, machinery oiled and all other safeguards in place. Working in such a dangerous place, one cannot afford to take chances. When satisfied that everything was in order it was his habit to see how Jack was faring.

Months had passed and Jack was heartily sick and tired of the job. The previous night the manager had careful selected a fairly big stone, the next to be removed, and tucked the onyx box beneath it. On this day of days I did the rounds with the manager, for I was not going to miss what was about to happen. Picture the scene - Jack leaning on his shovel puffing away at his pipe and delaying as long as he could before recommencing work after his break. Jack grumbled about how hard the work was and to show him that it was not so bad, the manager lifted a pickaxe and levered away the stone he had selected the night before. He lifted it and there for all to see was the mud-covered box!

A consummate actor and disregarding what the mud was doing to his trousers, the Manager was on his knees instantly.

"Buried treasure!" he exclaimed in a startled voice.

He opened the box and then it was my turn to sow a seed.

"They look like gold sovereigns to me," I said in hushed tones.

Jack was beside himself with rage and envy emitting curses and swear words right, left and centre, telling all and sundry how he had been slaving away for many months and all he could find was a skull, but then, at a moment's notice, the manager unearths a fortune and laid claims to it!

As if the box was the spoils of war, holding it high and appearing triumphant, we returned to the office. Word spread like wildfire about the fortune that had been found. All work stopped and customers left in abeyance as the entire staff crowded around the office door.

As fate would have it, the estate painter, whom I will call Dick Hallessey, was engaged in painting a property just outside the gate of the sawmills. He was better than any form of technical communication and the story of the gold coins went through the town with the speed of light, gathering momentum as it circulated. When I got back to Bleak House that evening, the value of the hoard had risen to £1,000!

It did not stop there and rumour reached a climax when a reporter from "The Nationalist" newspaper in Clonmel came especially to report on the find and spread the story to every corner of the county. We confessed to him the true story and apologised for having him make a journey for nothing. He did not feel cheated, adding that he had a top line anecdote for any after-dinner speech he might be called upon to make in the future. Up until the very last day I left Cahir, many years after this event, there were still people convinced that the manager and I had made a handsome profit!

The band-mill was finally erected and given its first trial run. In contrast to the circular saw machines, this was far superior. Huge dogs gripped the sixteen-foot logs commensurate with the thickness of the planks required. The machine was adjusted and set in motion. The long thick logs moved along the rails to meet the excessively fast-moving protruding teeth set in the four inch band-saw. The chief sawyer was in charge.

One day, while a colleague and I were inspecting stocks in a shed nearby, the air was suddenly filled with tiny pieces of steel flying in all directions at tremendous speed. The sawyer had misjudged the spacing and the metal dogs came in contact with the extremely fast-moving saw, shearing off the teeth in small fragments, any of which could have killed a person outright! It was all over within seconds.

As luck would have it, my colleague and I were inside the shed at the time. Had it been otherwise this narrative would never have seen the light of day. The large wooden doors were pock marked with the best part of a hundred deeply imbedded missiles. It was a close call. It was some time later before it dawned on me how lucky we had been. The experience brought with it a salutary lesson - the need for vigilance at all times. I had heard it said that it is cheaper to kill a man than have to continue to pay ongoing compensation for years following an accident.

As this story already shows, a sawmills can be a dangerous place. This next account will illustrate the danger even further. Timber for the mill was supplied from the large woods of the estate. One day a colossal tree stump was unloaded from the company's truck. The driver was a very reliable and conscientious employee and was always willing to lend a hand even when it was not expected of him to do so.

The task at hand was to split this huge solid oak tree stump, roughly six feet in height and five feet in width, down the middle into a manageable size. In such cases, the usual procedure was to make a deep cut on the top of the stump into which were hammered large steel wedges with sledgehammer blows. The purpose of this exercise was to widen the incision. As oak is a very hard wood, use was made of a ratchet-type piece of equipment. In essence, this was a long thick steel bar with adjustable clamps at either end. The centre of this implement was fitted with two steel wedges that, when held in position by the outer clamps, slotted into the incision at the top of the stump.

The operator stood on top and, by gripping a long lever and applying pressure, was able to expand the incision as the kingpin slotted ever so slowly into the grooves of the ratchet, thus widening the incision at the top, thereby encouraging the stump to split down the middle. Being a very strong man, the truck driver elected to operate the equipment. After expanding the stump by three notches he was unable to apply enough pressure on the lever to go any further. I witnessed one of the other workmen suggest tying a rope to the lever, which they would pull collectively. The theory was this would aid the man on the top to get a better leverage and allow the dog to move to the next ratchet groove. An old rope was procured and the plan duly put into operation.

Without any warning, a terrible thing happened. The rope snapped with the strain. The lever acted as a catapult and hurtled the workman on the top of the stump into the air. He somersaulted twice before crashing down, smashing the back of his skull on one of the steel wedges. It was an awful thing to happen and the memory of it haunts me to this day. The poor man was rushed to Cashel county hospital but died from his injuries. He left a wife and five small children. The estate's insurance company paid out the statutory amount under the Employer's Liability insurance policy which amounted to the princely sum of £600! It may sound callous, but as I said earlier, it was always cheaper for someone to die at work than have to pay ongoing compensation! However, the estate allocated a small pension to the man's widow and family.

Chapter 17

UNTO US A SON IS BORN

In January 1950, Margaret told me that she was pregnant. God willing, I was to become a father! While the thought was exhilarating, the responsibilities parenthood was going to bring in its wake frightened us. It was unknown territory. I took solace in the fact that many millions of fathers and mothers had gone down the same path we were now treading. My parents and in-laws were puffed with pride on hearing the glad tidings. When I brought the matter to the attention of my boss he immediately deemed it essential that a small kitchen and bathroom be added to the house. Also, the tiny window in the kitchen was to be removed and a much larger one put in its place; the same held good for the window in the front of the house. The worn out kitchen range was also to go and a new one installed. We were delighted at the news but months went by before any construction work began. The windows however were replaced and that was some consolation.

One day, my heavily pregnant wife had just moved out to the hall when there was a major rumble. The entire inside of the chimney had come crashing down, spewing bricks, mortar and blackened stone into the kitchen. Had she been there at the time it was likely she would have been killed or at least seriously injured. When the dust cleared, our small kitchen resembled a building site.

We lived in the house in Old Church Street for seven years. During this period we had transformed it from a dilapidated house into a small comfortable home. About the time of the major renovations it was discovered that the sustaining brick wall, supporting the upstairs portion, was in imminent danger of falling down. The bricks themselves had perished with old age. It took nearly a month for the wall to be rebuilt. The cross members supporting the floors in the rooms upstairs had huge mushrooms sprouting out of them and must have been secretly growing there for years.

I have always maintained that everything happens for a purpose. In this case, it spurred the company to start the proposed building work straight away. Overall the building job was a small one and in normal circumstances could have been completed in three months. Because of other commitments the work was not continuous but proceeded on a stop-go basis. We had to live and breathe dust and contend with sand, gravel and cement, rain water pipes, timber and slates for months on end. It was soul destroying and looking back I wonder how we stuck it out.

Our son Richard was born on the 23rd of October that year and he was seven months old when the building work was finally completed!

AN ANECDOTE:

The Cork Cycle Company was renowned for stocking a huge range of prams. The company also offered the facility of paying for a purchase by monthly installments, often referred to as 'the never, never!' (as the payments never seemed to end!). I need hardly say that this ten shillings down and a solicitor's letter every month facility was welcomed with open arms. We purchased the pram for Richard in 1950.

We had placed an advertisement in the "Cork Examiner" to let relations and friends know of Jean's birth. Imagine our surprise when we received a letter of congratulations from the Cork Cycle Company. They went on to say how they had had the privilege of supplying us with a pram in 1950 and specialised in refurbishing old prams. Bear in mind that there was no such thing as computers in use. It had to be the case that a member of staff operated a card index system and scanned the papers daily. Where appropriate, as in our case, the company wrote to the party concerned. I gave them full marks and also the job of refurbishment.

A popular story at that time concerned a young man who went into the store and said that he had come to pay the last installment on a pram.
"How's the baby?" the cashier asked.
"I'm very well thanks", replied the young man!

Part One

My mother-in-law was a midwife by profession and the number of babies she delivered in the Cork area was legion. She had therefore an especial interest as to how her daughter's pregnancy was progressing. As there was no maternity home in Cahir the confinement was to be a home birth. My mother-in-law came to give support but not to attend at the delivery. This was in the very capable hands of Dr. Dan Burke and Nurse O'Donoghue. Labour commenced and went on for over twelve hours. Constant supplies of water were kept boiling all through the long night. My mother-in-law was a chain smoker and nicknamed "Puffing Meb", her first name being Mabel. The doctor, dressed in his rubber apron, was up and down the creaking stairs and I knew instinctively that something was wrong. He would pass on some medical information to Mabel whose face took on a worried expression.

Finally, I was told that things were not going as planned and a decision had to be made as to whether to transfer mother-in-the-making and baby to the county hospital. Either might die so Dr. Burke opted to stay put. It was indeed fortunate that he had attained the highest marks possible in gynae-cology in his final year! His knowledge and skill coupled with Nurse O'Donoghue's care and prayers, not to mention our own, brought our son into the world at 10.15 a.m. His was a forceps delivery and I will never for-get the shock of seeing our blood covered son with a caput and wrapped in a shawl with but one leg protruding. In the state I was in I thought he had but one leg!

Mabel came into her own at this point and took care of the baby while the doctor and nurse tended to Margaret. She had gone through a very tough delivery and at one time had to have a special injection to strengthen her heart. That caused no surprise having regard to the trauma she had been through. The fact that the baby weighed 10 pounds 6 ounces was another large factor in every sense of the word. It is hard to believe in this day and age that the afterbirth had to be burned in the front room fireplace. I was in a daze as I ran to the telephone box at the end of Old Church Street to tell the family in Cork that the proverbial flag had gone up. There was great rejoicing and neighbours called offering congratulations, extending good will and offering advice. We were so proud of our first-born but felt dreadful when the poor child had to visit the doctor to have blood clots on his skull lanced. Our stalwart 'Nurse' Mabel returned to Cork and we were on our own. Somewhat frightening at first, but as the weeks went by we gained more confidence in spite of putting up with many sleepless nights. The months rolled on and wonder of wonders - the house at last boasted a bathroom. But a bathroom without any hot water!

In 1950 electricity was rationed. A consumer was allowed a certain number of units per week. Exceed the allocation and the supply was promptly disconnected. Hot water was needed each morning to bath the baby and this necessitated the use of a very large saucepan that contained nearly two gallons of water. This was heated on our Primus stove and then carried up the rickety stairs to the bathroom, which was on the left at the turn of the stairs. When our son began to crawl, the stairs held a fascination for him so I had to construct a solid gate to confine him to the small kitchen area.

One morning I was having a shave in the bathroom and for some reason was prompted to go to the bend in the stairs. I stood there with a razor in my right hand, the left side of my face covered in shaving soap as I watched my wife lift the boiling saucepan of water from off the primus, manoeuvre the pot and herself over the obstacle and start to mount the stairs. Richard followed and held on to the gate watching his mother carefully mount the steps one at a time. I had a premonition that something was going to happen. I stood there helpless. Suddenly she slipped and two gallons of boiling water cascaded down the stairs. The child gave a shriek as he disappeared in a cloud of steam. We both rushed to his aid full sure that he had been very badly scalded.

This was a crisis and without a moment's delay Margaret jumped on her bicycle and went to fetch Dr. Burke. He was with us in five minutes. All the steam had very nearly dispersed as he took the child for examination. We could not believe him when he told us there were only two or three tiny spots where the boiling water had made contact with his face. Then it dawned on us. Most of the boiling water had run down Margaret's left ankle and she had suffered a third degree burn to which she was oblivious as she went to fetch the doctor! In fact she did not even feel it - it was only on her return that she felt the agony. Over the following months she suffered dreadfully, to the extent that the bones of her foot were exposed. To this day the skin is paper thin and tender.

I wrote to the Electricity Supply Board reiterating what had happened, at the same time pointing out that if we had received permission to install an electric wall type geyser the accident would never have happened. I received a reply by return sanctioning the installation of a five-gallon hot water heater. An ample increase in the ration of electricity units came with it, so the bathroom became "alive" at last.

Chapter 18

FOR WHOM THE BELL TOLLS

I was an erratic church attendee. My upbringing had provided me with a surfeit of religion and while my own background was Anglican, as I previously explained, the family as a whole was a "mixum-gatherum" of faiths. All these divisions were anathema to me. It seemed ridiculous that Almighty God was in this box, that box, and so on ad nauseam.

Early on in my life I began to divorce religion from spirituality, coming to the conclusion that religion was man-made and spirituality God-made. Today I do not pay adherence to any specific church and have become a majority of one with peace of mind, peace of soul and peace of spirit. I will visit any church and take, from whatever form of worship I find, that which is consistent with my own personal thinking, and leave the rest. I am closer to Unitarianism, which I never thought of as being a religion per se.

My mind flashes back to the year we were married and the many Sundays we lay in bed listening to the bells of the respective churches tolling, calling the faithful to prayer. Peer pressure necessitated us putting in an appearance from time to time and parish activities, such as the social club and table tennis club, reached out their tentacles.

Our first-born was christened and, in view of the fact that our prayers had been heard, we became more regular members. I found myself, to all intents and purposes, being shanghaied into the choir. The ghosts of the past were coming to the fore and making their presence felt. I did not like it but in the circumstances found it best to go along with the flow.

It was a motley choir comprised of one bass, a baritone, two tenors and three sopranos. An organist who dealt lovingly with every note made up the balance. One of the tenors, an accountant in a bank in the town had also been pressed into service, but had little choice in the matter as his wife was

St. Paul's Church

the principal of the parish primary school. Occasionally he would show his displeasure by stopping singing where the voice of a tenor was essential to complete a given harmony. There was little harmony in the choir and little outside of it. Still, we dutifully turned up most weeks for the half-hour practice on Friday night in preparation for the Sunday morning service.

The teller, in the same bank as the accountant-tenor and was a musician – there was a bit of a spleen between them. The perfect squelch came from the teller who, when asked about the accountant's singing prowess, replied dryly, "he's not musical but he sings!" The Archdeacon, self-elected choirmaster [nobody else wanted the job] was prepared to go, in musical terms, where angels feared to tread! On one occasion we tackled "St. Patrick's Breastplate!" It was awful. 'Nuff said.

1955 was the year of a week-long Diocesan mission with Cahir parish church at the epicentre. Strange as it may seem, the two-manual forty-stop organ was not operated electrically but manually by the sweat of the brow of some parishioner shanghaied

St. Paul's Church

to do the needful. For good measure the ringing of the church bell was included. The finger of fate was pointed in my direction for first night duty. Very reluctantly I agreed to help out, never having taken on the job previously.

Cahir church was, and I presume still is, a beautiful edifice. The huge bellows was to be found more than half way down on the outside of the church to the right. The massive apparatus was housed as an adjunct to the building proper. As for the belfry, it was like undertaking a mountain climb. An outside door near to the pumping station led to a large gallery, which formed the right side of the nave. From here thick wooden steps were embedded into the wall which one had to climb to reach the lower part of the belfry. There was no handrail. From the ceiling high above was a bung hole through which hung a large substantial bell rope. It had to be substantial as the bell weighed about one ton!

That fateful Monday dawned and I reported for duty at 7.45 p.m. Even then the church was nearly full, to such an extent that the galleries had to be pressed into service. All the pews had doors - not seen in modern churches today. I was given explicit instructions that during the missioner's sermon I was to leave my outpost at the organ coalface and come into the church to hear what the man had to say. A vacant seat more than half-way down the aisle had been allocated to me.

I do not have a good head for heights and, with my heart in my mouth, climbed those unguarded steps to reach the bell rope. I had no experience of bell ringing but had been told to start to ring the bell at 7.50 p.m. for ten minutes. Picture the scene. I rubbed my hands together and took hold of the rope and pulled. Nothing seemed to want to happen. Then I felt a little "give" and there was a weak ding-dong. The next pull on the rope produced a much louder sound and I thought I was away on a hack. The bell pulling became hard work and I was being lifted off the floor if I did not take my hands from the rope in a synchronised fashion. Something was wrong; the bell was not ringing as it should and the bell rope had taken on a life of its own. It seemed to have become a serpent lashing around everywhere. It was out of my control when suddenly, like a rabbit disappearing into its burrow, the rope disappeared through the bung hole far above my head!

Threshing about like a mad thing the bell was ringing away, not "ding dong" fashion but "dong, dong, dong". All I could do was climb down the mountain and hurry to the main door of the church where I met the Archdeacon with his cassock on preparatory to commencing the mission.

"Who is ringing the bell?" he asked anxiously. I told him it was working away on is own! The clanging stopped suddenly and just as we thought all was well, off went the dong, dong, dong, once more. Just then it stopped, probably worn out from all its own exertion. As for me, I was like a wet rag as I hurried to my post outside the church to pump the organ bellows. I was met with this huge double size bellows with a massive wooden arm that had to be pumped up and down. I thought I was a galley slave!

The organist was unaware that I had not been in position with a full bellows of air for her disposal. With all the stops out, she commenced to play without enough air in the bellows. Instead of sweet sanctimonious sounds, came a sound like ten or more cats howling from the roof top! This was all too much for me. In order to steady my shattered nerves, I lit a cigarette while at the same time listening to the general confession of the congregation. I then heard coughs coming from members of the augmented choir. My cigarette smoke had passed through the thin division separating the choir stalls from where I was on duty. I was told afterwards that the smoke wafted partway down the church on the choir side, to such an extent that some people in the congregation thought a member of the choir was having a quick drag!

During the service, I began to inspect my habitat and noticed various scrawls on the wall put there by those valiant people who had manned the oar in times gone by. In one place a pertinent message read to the effect that if the oar of the bellows was brought to a certain mark on the wall, it would take about thirty seconds to come down to a given point when one took up the cudgels again. I tried it out, but as the organist had all the stops out yet again, there were more calls of the wild. At last it came to sermon time and duty bound, I left my post and as quietly as I could, entered the church.

Many stared at me full sure that I had deliberately missed half of the mission. I glared back as I went half way down the aisle to the seat that had been reserved for me. I opened the pew door, sat down and closed it again as if it was going to offer me some sort of protection. I had not a clue what the missioner was talking about as I was trying to overcome all the stresses and strains I had sustained.

I came out of my reverie just as he was saying,

"We will now kneel and while in this position sing hymn number something or other." I was aghast!

The organist was expecting to have air in the bellows and was unaware that I was not at my post. In the silence that pertained, I stood up quickly, opened the pew door and ran down the aisle at a gallop. I crashed through the door of the church, slipped on the gravel, tore my trousers and cut my knee. Despite it all I got to the pumping house in record time but all to no avail. On this occasion when the organist put her hands on the keys there was no sound at all. The choir began to sing unaccompanied. I suppose I should have left well alone but I started to pump and this brought about a battle for supremacy between the choir and the cats. I really do not know who won. After it was all over I informed the powers-that-be that no matter what happened, I would never again take on the challenge of the bell and the organ.

The whole debacle brought wondrous changes. Colonel Charteris donated the sum of five hundred pounds for an electric motor to pump the bellows, together with a device that rang the clapper of the bell as distinct from having to wrestle and struggle with the beast of a bell-rope.

As a tailpiece, the cause of the trouble was the one ton bell had come off its axis!

Part One

Chapter 19

THE BAND BUSINESS

I come from a musical family background on both sides. My father played the trumpet and coronet. My mother was an organist and taught pianoforte and violin. My sister Eileen and I were taught music professionally from an early age. I sat for numerous examinations where piano playing was concerned - and passed - while my sister concentrated on the intricacies of the violin. But when it came to classical music I was the black sheep. I found it nigh impossible to take to it overall but must confess that some classical music moved me greatly. Eileen went on to become a member of the Irish National Symphony Orchestra while I fizzled out from that scene and entered the world of jazz, swing and dance music in general - much to the disgust of my mother in particular.

In my youth the only way one could learn the latest hit was by buying sheet music or playing the melody by ear. I was a natural when it came to the lat-

ter while my mother, in contrast, could not play a note unless the music was there in front of her! This ability stood me in good stead all through life. I recall one day in 1936, when I was ten years old, I had managed to save up six pence with which I bought a copy of "The Sailor with the Navy Blue Eyes". This song was very popular at the time. As soon as I arrived home from the music store, I went straight to the piano and started to read, play and sing the song. I had just completed it a second time when the door of the front room burst open. There stood my mother with an angry look on her face as she blurted out, "stop playing that filth!" To say that I was taken aback is an understatement. It was just a simple song of yesteryears.

In my early teens I was permitted to attend a number of church socials, the music often provided by a lone pianist with drum backup. When the pianist broke off for a cup of tea and a sandwich, I often went on stage and did duty for the thirty minutes break. It gave me a good feeling; I felt that this was the line of country I should be in.

I was not living in Cahir very long before word got around that I was a piano and accordion player. Out of the blue I would receive a message from some small outfit or other stating they were short of a musician and would I like to fill the gap. Many a time I did and the experience was a revelation. I never knew what the line-up was going to be nor what the music was going to be like. In free-lance work like this one had to be versatile and it was absolutely essential to be able to busk in at least five different keys. Believe me it was good training.

However, I'd had enough of this when I was approached by a young musician, who also worked as a farmer. He told me that he was setting up an outfit called "The Southern Serenaders" and asked if I would be interested in joining up. It was a five-piece band and comprised of the drummer, trumpet player, saxophone player, myself, and an Hawaiian electric guitar played by the head man himself! This was a most unusual instrument to have lined up in those days and was played resting on the knees of the musician. Its sound was magical. There was a well-established dance band in the town; they received bookings from all over the south of Ireland. We certainly could not do them any harm as we were in demand only within a radius of ten to fifteen miles from base.

Our first engagement was about eight miles from Cahir. The hall was a small converted house that had lain derelict. The stage was high up at one end of the hall and could only be reached by climbing a ladder! When we were up we were up and that was the end of it. The stage itself was about six feet in width. The band's mode of transport was a five hundredweight Ford van as old as the hills. The original headlights were long since gone and taking their place were two lamps taken from a tractor. These were duly rigged on to the bumpers of the van. The door to the passenger seat - the death seat - was welded and could not be opened no matter what. The van had no hand brake and the main brakes worked hardly at all. The steering was very loose and, to cap it all, to turn on the headlights one had to lift the bonnet and connect the wires directly to the battery. In this contraption the five of us travelled for our first engagement. We duly arrived, climbed up the ladder and played, staying up on the stage for four hours from nine in the evening 'till one in the morning, in a fog of cigarette smoke. It seemed we would never get to the point of playing the national anthem and could go home.

It finally came to my turn to descend the ladder. Suddenly it slipped and, as it fell to the floor, scored and tore the inside of my left leg. In agony I held onto the upper rail, suspended in the air, while efforts were made to get the ladder into place so that I could reach the ground. It was weeks before the wound healed and the bruising departed.

To reach the passenger seat I had to climb over the driver's seat while the other three members of the band, together with their instruments, crowded into the back packed like sardines in a tin. We started for home. It was a moonless starlit night. The van's steering was very loose and as a result we tended to go from side to side of the lonely road.

We were in the centre of the road as another vehicle approached, lights blazing. I shouted to the driver to pull over to the left as we would surely have a head-on crash. The old van sluggishly responded. The driver of the oncoming car turned sharply to his left and in doing so sheared off the two lamps of our van. There we were careering along out of control and unable to see a thing. As we came out from under the overhanging trees, the starlight was just bright enough for us to see that we were going to hit a gully on the side of the ditch. The van seemed to have a life of its own as we ploughed along this small ravine for about a hundred yards before crashing into a tree.

I was knocked unconscious for a minute or two. When I came to I found the van was on its side and petrol was flowing everywhere. The lads in the back clambered out while I had to be helped out through the driver's door. We were all shocked, but all that seemed to worry the band leader was the state his van was in. Suddenly, the scene was lit up by the headlights of the car that nearly caused the fatal accident. As luck would have it, the driver was the first cousin of our bandleader. His was a brand new vehicle and his father had given him strict instructions not to take it to impress his girlfriend - but he did. The near crash had scored an indentation along one side from front to back. The old crock of a van was righted, the headlights collected off the road and driven home, fortunately not too far distant. We in turn were conveyed back the four miles or so to Cahir in the cousin's car.

Despite this initiation into the band business proper, I stayed with the outfit for a couple of years as I could do with the extra money to keep the home fires burning. It was very hard work for very small pay. Later, when I played with more professional bands, there was much more comfort travelling in ten-seated station wagons, but not much of an improvement where pay was concerned. I realised that beggars could not be choosers!

On one occasion our band secured a six-week contract to play every Wednesday night for - wait for it - the BBC! Buckley's Bakery, Cappawhite. Cappawhite was, and I suppose still is, a village somewhere beyond the town of Tipperary. Irish dancing was quite popular in the area and one of

the pieces we were expected to play was a Ballycommon Set. This set was in six separate parts but we did not know it at all. In order to fulfil the contract it was vital that we find a musician who did know the format of a Ballycommon Set. The Cahir area was scoured and we found a violinist - an albino, with a shock of snow white hair and pink eyes - known to all and sundry as "The Whitehead Boy". But he did not own an instrument. A search party was sent out and one was finally found. The snag was the bridge was not the correct size.

That first night with our augmented outfit we started to play a quickstep, in the middle of which the fiddler went to the microphone to do his bit. All of a sudden there was a twang sound and the bridge flew across the stage. The Whitehead Boy went after it, groping away on the floor until he found it. He was then ready for the next number, an old-time waltz with the song "Under the Bridges of Paris". Again our valiant violinist came forward with another rendition. All went well until he reached the "turn" of the song; there was another twang and another search. How he managed the Ballycommon Set I really do not know, for he sailed through that with no problem. As the night wore on the flying bridge was getting him down so he started to ram it into position. This resulted in the strings breaking. By the end of the night the floor was littered with violin strings and he finished up playing the National Anthem Japanese style - one string only!

I have to confess that, despite everything, they were happy days. The Southern Serenaders finally packed up and I went on to better things, playing with bigger outfits. On one occasion the band I was with at the time acted as relief to Felix Mendelhson's orchestra, which comprised of no less than sixteen musicians, not to mention dusky maidens from Hawaii. Another famous orchestra for which we acted as relief was that of Johnny Dankworth.

Playing with different outfits gave me tremendous experience. In those far off days it was quite common to have six-hour dances from 9.00 p.m. 'till three in the morning. Hunt balls were the worst as we had to play from 9.00 p.m. until 4.00 a.m. I had to carry a bottle of methylated spirits with me to rub into my fingers, which became bruised from striking the notes of the piano thousands of times. On a night like this one could expect to lose up to seven pounds in weight. As for my colleagues playing wind instruments, most of them died fairly young, as playing for long hours in smoky conditions was too great a strain on their heart. In truth, a book could be written about many more episodes – some sad and some hilarious.

It would be fair to say that all these experiences would make a book by themselves.

Chapter 20

JEAN IS BORN AND WE MOVE UP IN THE WORLD

Our daughter, Jean, was born on the 21st August, 1954 but not in the house. There was no way that there was to be a repeat performance of Richard's birth. The confinement took place in a nursing home in the town of Tipperary. When all the signs were showing, I ran to the telephone box and phoned Dr. Burke who now had his practice in the county town of Clonmel. He made the journey in nine minutes flat and took the expectant mother off to Tipperary, whispering in my ear as he went out the door,

"I'll have news for you around two in the morning."

He was spot on. He rang the door-bell at 2.45 a.m. to tell me that Jean had been born at 2.10 a.m. Everything had gone like clock-work, and mother and baby were in great shape.

Two years later our luck changed for the better. Colonel Charteris lived in Cahir Park House. It was a magnificent residence, regal in stature and stood in 1,000 acres of parklands, which was open to the public. It was beautifully furnished with no less than seven grand pianos spread throughout various rooms. There was a staff of twelve, which included the house overseer. He and his wife were provided with a house of their own, a fine building that at one time had been a coach house. It stood in its own grounds adjacent to Cahir Park House. This was the house that we were being allocated on the passing of the house overseer and his wife. We could not believe our good fortune.

The contrast between where we had been living and where we were about to live took our breath away. It boasted two large bedrooms, the larger of which had a bay window with a magnificent view of the river and the rear of Cahir Castle. A large glass-covered porch led onto a wide hall. Half way along the right side was the entrance to a sitting room, precisely the same size as the bedroom overhead. It too had a bay window. At the end of the hall was a substantial bathroom and store cupboard. There was a further big cupboard under the stairs. Next to this was a bright and sunny dining room. The light came through the two big windows strategically placed, one at either end of this eighteen by sixteen feet wonderful room. There was a substantial kitchen with a large wood-burning stove that provided massive amounts of hot water.

The great day dawned when we left our old home for good. In one way we were sad but in another, excited to the extreme. Our few possessions were transported across town. It was an extraordinary experience to pass through the huge wrought iron gates, opened by the gatekeeper, so that we could drive up the long tarmacadamed drive that led to Cahir Park House and now led to our new home.

It took some time for us to adapt to our new surroundings, especially the size of the house, which, incidentally was partly furnished. There was a substantial linen cupboard between the two large bedrooms. On the ground floor the sitting room had a fitted carpet laid by the famous firm of furnishers, Maples of London. This company had the contract to furnish Cahir Park House and obviously the overseer's home was included. The work, which was of superb quality, was carried out in 1917. There was an ornate fireplace complete with fire irons and fender, together with a chaise lounge and two easy chairs. In the dining room there was a most wonderful clock on the wall that boasted two peals of bells. At the time it was valued at £400. The floor was also carpeted but not to the standard pertaining in the sitting room. The kitchen, with hard-wearing linoleum as floor covering, had cupboards for glassware and others for pots and pans. We did not know ourselves. To crown it all, the sink had a draining-board, something we never had in the old house.

Outside, there was a huge purpose-built shed some little distance from the rear of the house. This stored vast amounts of firewood blocks, cut to size. While these blocks were initially for use in Cahir Park House, as a prequisite we were at liberty to use all the fuel we needed. This was in addition to a free electricity supply. All my hard work was being appreciated and paying off.

We had a sloping lawn to the front of the house, in the centre of which was a large jack-in-the-pulpit tree whose very enticing red berries were poisonous. There were some other flower-beds around the house. Thirteen peacocks and peahens patrolled the grounds. Their searing screech took some getting used to, especially in the middle of the night. At times, their continuous racket heralded rain in the offing. They could be seen all over the place strutting around as if they owned the whole demesne. To be frank, I disliked them intensely for whatever flower one might plant they came along and destroyed it. They were also costly to keep as they consumed considerable amounts of grain, which had to be purchased weekly. I know it was unkind of me, but I was not unduly saddened that in the five years we lived here, up to the end of 1961, the foxes killed off six of the peacocks. A seventh lost his life one day through vanity. The peahen lays but one egg per annum.

During the mating season, the male of the species struts around haughtily full plumage extended to impress the female. The day of his demise dawned. It was a lovely morning as Colonel Charteris, in a foul mood, walked along the river bank beneath the mansion. He invariably used a thumb stick - a walking stick that was vee-shaped at the top. Suddenly he came face to face with a peacock that was in love, and in all his glory decided to let out his cry. Close up the cry sounds distinctly like some one telling another to f-off! It hit a sore spot. Up came the walking stick and with one full powerful swing the colonel took the head off the peacock!

There stood the headless bird in all his finery. I never ate a peacock but I am told that it tastes very similar to turkey. The butler took charge, plucked and cleaned the bird outside – peacock feathers were deemed to bring bad luck if brought into a house. The bird provided a fine meal for his family.

We had been ensconced in our new home for about two weeks when we noticed that our two-year old daughter was missing. Try as we might we could not find her anywhere. We quickly enlisted help and a search began. Below us was the fast flowing river and something prompted me to search the river bank. Panic set in when I saw air bubbles come to the surface at one spot. I was full sure that the child had drowned. I scrambled up the embankment to seek help. As I reached the top, suddenly I heard our son Richard shout,

"I've found her!" I sagged to the ground in relief. We had searched everywhere except behind the huge shed where Jean sat placidly playing with some sticks and leaves.

There were fringe benefits living so close to the mansion. Every so often we were given the middle cut from a freshly caught salmon. My responsibilities along with my increment increased when, in addition to managing the estate office, I took charge of the household finances. It was an eye-opener to me to see just how much it cost to run a large house. I had to call to Cahir Park House at least once a week to discuss matters with the butler and other key personnel. The house boasted a really fine cellar of wines. Quite often the butler would ask if I would care for a drop of vintage port. Not wishing to insult him, I would be given a measure that would put one out on their ear. It was fortunate that the long way round to the estate office through the park was over a mile in length and gave me a chance to come up for air.

Our third child, Mark, was born in February 1960. Our faithful Dr. Burke had passed away at the early age of 45. He was greatly missed. If anyone had a dedication to the Hippocratic oath it was Dr. Dan Burke. Out in all weathers, he dedicated his whole life to helping others. For his pains he had a massive heart attack and died. His practice was taken over by another dedicated medical man, Dr. Henaghan.

This third confinement was to be in a nursing home in Clonmel. We did not have a telephone - very few did in those days - and Colonel Charteris arranged for an electric bell to ring in the home of the chauffeur. It was about two in the morning when it was necessary for us to press the bell. Promptly, the Rover saloon was taken out from the three-car garage.

Chauffeur-driven off we went in style to the nursing home. I returned to Cahir that night and before retiring to bed was offered another glass of vintage port.

Once, when rooting around and clearing out rubbish in the store room I came across a very interesting document, compiled by the house overseer. During the Irish Civil War, Eamon De Valera, later to be President of Ireland, took over Cahir Park House for a period of time. The document I unearthed listed all the foodstuffs consumed by Mr. De Valera's contingent during their stay. It embraced such items as milk, bread, eggs, butter, meat, poultry, vegetables and such-like. Believe it or not, the full cost of the foodstuffs was reimbursed about one year after the end of the Civil War.

One of the walls of Cahir Park House had been used for target practice and was peppered with bullet holes. To the best of my knowledge, Colonel Charteris refused to have the wall repaired and a large tapestry was hung to cover the historical wall. When Mr. De Valera was elected president he made a personal call on Colonel Charteris. I remember the day well.

Somehow or other word of the visit spread like wildfire throughout the town, yet I remained strangely ignorant of this impending visit. There was great excitement when the presidential car arrived in town and drove through the milling throng to the entrance gates. As soon as the president had driven up the drive the gates were closed shut. At that time I happened to have my father's car on loan. Unaware that the president was visiting Colonel Charteris, I drove down the drive on my way to town. I could not understand why so many people were congregated at the gates. My father's black Ford saloon was mistaken for the president's vehicle. A huge cheer went up from the assembled multitude as the gates opened and I drove through the crowds. I had been mistaken for the President of Ireland!

It took a long time for me to live that one down!

Chapter 21

POUND AVENUE

I remember a long, long time ago, when I was a small boy, my father taking from his pocket a ten shilling note. In those far off days that was a very substantial sum of money. It was more than enough to pay for food for a family for a week or a good night out which would include a meal, entertainment and transport. More often than not one came home with cash left over. In my young eyes it was a fortune.

Times were hard and, as I recalled previously, I can always remember my father telling me that he was still paying off the pharmacy account ten years after I was born. So you will appreciate my consternation when he nonchalantly tore the crisp red note in half and not in a straight line either! I was frantic and did not know what to think. This was my father's way of adding the word "indenture" to my vocabulary. He pointed out that the serial number of the note was printed on both the left and right hand side. In effect this meant that if a transaction took place between two people, each person held half of the note until the deal was done and the purchaser satisfied that everything was in order. Then and only then was the remaining portion handed over, sealed with tape of some sort and lodged in a bank.

It was many years later that I found this was a common occurrence at the monthly fair where the sale and purchase of livestock was concerned. But the notes used would be of high denominations ranging from £100 up to £500 in value.

In the legal world Indenture documents were common place. Before the advent of copying machines, or indeed the use of carbon paper, solicitors' clerks had to write in copperplate the terms and conditions agreed between the parties concerned. The document had to be transcribed twice. It was imperative that the initial twice-written portion came from the first sheet as this had to be indented, viz. cut with a scissors in an uneven way.,thus producing hills and valleys when separated one from the other. At any given time afterwards they would come together like a jig-saw puzzle, thereby proving authenticity. The amount of legal jargon and gobble-di-gook found in many old documents, and also some latter day ones, largely came about on purpose. It may not be generally known, but the clerks of the day were paid a fee for every 72 words they wrote! The longer the document the more was earned.

All legal documents had to be sent to Dublin to have the necessary endorsement stamped on them, thereby making them legal. I knew of a man who maintained the opinion that the authorities never read any document fully. To prove his point he incorporated three lines of "for the love of a duck, for the love of a duck" in the middle of a deed. It was sent to Dublin for endorsement. Back it came duly sealed, all present and correct!

As the company owned roughly 300 properties, I dealt with many documents. These would cover leases, yearly, monthly and weekly tenancies and caretaker agreements, not to mention eleven month lettings of arable land. Many of the small properties were in reality liabilities as they were controlled under the 1914 Rent Restrictions Act whereby rents could not be increased without very substantial work being done on the houses concerned. One such group of premises was to be found in Mountain Road. The estate owned forty-three houses here that were a chronic liability. One day I suggested that the company sell them off.

"Who would buy them?" I was asked.

"The tenants themselves," I replied triumphantly.

I was given carte blanche to handle the deal as I saw fit.

Some of the holdings were bigger than others, some had water supplies and sewage facilities while others did not. Rents ranged from as low as one shilling and six pence to approximately eight shillings a week. I decided to offer the houses to the tenants at one pound per house!

The sting in the tail, if one could call it such, was that everyone bought or the deal was off. The key to success was secrecy and surprise. As the estate office did not use a duplicating machine, I went to the local convent and asked for a stencil to fit a Gestetner machine. I was out of luck where correcting fluid was concerned so had to type the important letter ever so slowly so as not to make a mistake. This I did. Then with cap in hand I approached the cattle mart office seeking permission to run off 44 copies of my letter in secret - one for each for the tenants and one for the company files.

I gave the tenants the option of purchasing their property using an ordinary receipt that would cost them nothing or, alternatively, have the sale registered in Dublin Castle at a cost of six pounds ten shillings. The forty-three letters were mailed in one batch and duly delivered the following morning. None of the tenants went to work that morning. They were completely taken aback at the apparent windfall that had come out of the blue. They felt there had to be a catch somewhere and a deputation arrived at the office to see me. They all knew me well and I explained that there was no catch whatsoever. They would become house-owners in their own right. They left the office and went to arrange a meeting. Most of the tenants were all for purchasing their properties but there were others who did not want the old order to change.

After about a week, a further deputation arrived at the office to say that there were ten tenants who would not agree the deal. I told them calmly it was a case of all or nothing. That started up wheeling and dealing with those who were keen to purchase paying the reluctant ones hard cash to go ahead with the deal. Subsequently, all forty-three houses changed hands within the space of a couple of weeks. It was a load off my mind and that of the estate.

In turn, my own sense of pride was in direct proportion to that of the hearts and minds of the former tenants. They were now free to make application for grants from the county council for all sorts of improvements. It was not long before the appearance of the area improved dramatically. There was the touch of the wise and foolish virgins in that just over 60% of the purchasers had the sale registered. The remainder made do with the simple flimsy receipt, many of which were lost or mislaid so that proof of title went out the proverbial window. I am the only living person who could swear an Affidavit to put things in order, but I have never been asked! It is a very long time since I visited Cahir and while the Mountain Road is still there, many of us still fondly remember it as Pound Avenue. As an aside, I heard not so long ago that one of the houses sold for something like £60,000!

Few can say they bought their house for one single pound. The deal captured the imagination of the press and the story was carried nationally and even reached the USA. Mountain Road/Pound Avenue will never be forgotten but the name of the person that thought up the idea and saw the deal through will fade into oblivion.

That is of little consequence.

Chapter 22

SPREADING THE NEWS

As I have already said, it is my firm belief that wherever one works and earns his or her living, be it village, town or city, there is an obligation on that person to do whatever they can for that place and its people. In consequence of this tenet of mine I continued to strive to live up to my motto. Two opportunities came my way one after the other.

The weekly newspaper that circulated all over the county was 'The Nationalist'. It was a good newspaper and well entrenched with a sales figure of 500 copies per week in Cahir and its environs. While I am not too sure of the date, but I think it was in 1954, a new weekly paper – 'The Munster Tribune' - came on the scene in opposition. Its layout was fresh and contrasted greatly with the more staid and solid 'Nationalist'. The scene was reminiscent to that of David and Goliath! The circulation of 'The Munster Tribune' in the Cahir area was but four copies per week as against 500 copies for 'The Nationalist'.

One day I received a telephone call from the editor of 'The Munster Tribune'. He invited me to become their Cahir correspondent and the remuneration was one penny for each line published! It did not really matter how much the payment was, for I enjoyed the challenge and was very conscious of the fact that the pen was mightier than the sword. The Cahir news, until then, appeared under the caption "Cahir Roundabout" while my reporting of the local scene was entitled "Topics from Cahir." The battle commenced and it really was a great bit of fun.

I endeavoured at all times to present typical small town news in a racy and pepped up fashion, in contrast to the mundane reports that emanated from the opposition. My deadline was Tuesday of each week and on occasion there was a dearth of news. I sat at the typewriter with fingers on the home keys not having a clue as to what I was going to write about. It was at times like this, while in a vacant and pensive mood, that concepts and ideas would flash into my mind. I would write these down in a thought-provoking manner giving readers an opportunity for animated discussion. This often led to letters being written to the editor, which further stimulated local sales.

I always remember the advice one of my grandfathers gave me as a child. He insisted that after the Bible the most important book to have was a dictionary. He encouraged me to learn one new word every week. He was so right. It has stood me in good stead all my life. On average we use approximately 700 words daily in our dealings with one another. Our personal mental dictionaries contain between eight and ten thousand words. Winston Churchill, who was looked upon as being a virtual authority on the English language, knew 22,000 words. This seems a prodigious vocabulary to have but pales into insignificance when one comes to terms with the fact that there are over a million words in the English language.

Musing about this one day, two ideas came to mind. The first was to incorporate in my column an English word that it was unlikely the average person had heard previously. As the weeks went by, word got around [excuse the pun] about my column and stalwarts of 'The Nationalist' commenced to buy 'The Munster Tribune' in addition to the old reliable newspaper. Without realising it, readers were expanding their vocabulary through this weekly recourse to a dictionary.

A further innovation was the introduction of a tailpiece. This had to be short, crisp, humorous or serious. It did not take long to use up my own stock of this type of material. I had created a monster and searched frantically through all sorts of magazines and church publications to find an appropriate tailpiece. It is quite extraordinary that what is deemed newsworthy in a town, and passes unnoticed in a city, stands out in stark relief in country areas. This was often reflected when I found myself submitting a piece of news, as distinct from the weekly column, with a heading such as "Fox kills eleven chickens during night!" This was heady stuff. On three occasions as newspaper reporter I hit the front page.

The first time was when lightning struck the railway station causing structural damage. The second time was the tragic story of Paddy Kelly. He was a native of the town, well liked and a fine musician. The river was in flood when a child fell into the very fast flowing mill race. With not a thought for himself, Paddy dived into the raging torrent in an effort to save the child's life. He failed and instead, tragically, lost his own.

The body of the child was carried away by the floodwaters and was eventually located in Waterford city, thirty-eight miles distant. An appalling gloom came over the whole area. A fund was initiated by Colonel Charteris with a substantial donation. It was supported fully by all in aid of Paddy's widow and family.

The third and last time that I hit the front page was my report on the appalling train disaster. A runaway beet train, the brakes of which failed, came thundering down the five mile incline to Cahir from the direction of Clonmel. On the single through-track the night mail train was standing stationary at the platform. With continuous warning signals the beet special gathered speed. The signalman did the only thing he could do and changed the points transferring the runaway to the shunting line.

This short track was parallel to the through-line but stopped short at the buffers at the bridge over the river Suir. The beet train thundered through the station at high speed, swept away the buffers and careered on to the bridge where there was no track. The speed of the train and the weight of the wagons of sugar beet were too much for the bridge to support. The girders buckled and the whole train fell through into the river, eighty feet below, killing both the engine driver and fireman instantly.

In the morning light the disaster presented a grim spectacle. The engine was buried in the river while the remainder of the train hung suspended from the bridge. It was a terrible sight to behold.

The Cahir Estates Company was awarded the contract to remove the wreckage with heavy lifting gear and other equipment. This took several months and numerous axles and wheels were never found. They had sunk deep down under the river bed.

The readership of my column increased week by week and the circulation increased pro rata. The great day dawned when the weekly sales of 'The Munster Tribune' in Cahir exceeded those of 'The Nationalist'. The score was 500 copies for 'The Nationalist' and 504 copies for 'The Munster Tribune'! Shortly after this the old established newspaper bought out the younger upstart. I was asked to continue as a correspondent but refrained. My Tuesday deadline was a thing of the past and it took some time for my overall psyche to adapt to the change.

A few weeks went by when out of the blue I received a telephone call from the national radio station, looking for a local correspondent for the region. In those far off days it was known as Radio Eireann. Currently it goes under the title of RTE and embraces television as well as radio, and is a very effective and vibrant organisation.

At that time, after the ten o'clock evening news, came the feature "News from the Provinces". I was asked to fill one of the niches. The system of operation was simple. If I came across something that I thought was noteworthy [the editor of the programme might think otherwise] I simply made a reverse charge call to Dublin. A stenographer would take down the news item and then it was a question of waiting to hear if it was broadcast that night. If it was, a nominal agreed fee was credited to my account.

I was startled at the power of the written word and came to realise the inherent dangers that exist where propaganda is concerned. I always had to take great care that my facts were correct. Whatever the power of a weekly newspaper, the power of national radio blew my mind.

Shortly after my appointment I learned that a businessman, who was a dog fancier, was importing the first Italian greyhounds into Ireland. I phoned the man in question and he confirmed the report was true. I learned that they were called whippets but, to me, looked like overgrown rats. I was told by someone who knew these things that this was a worthy news item. I thought my informant was joking but as it was no skin off my nose I filed in the story.

I could hardly believe it when I heard the item being broadcast that night. I was delighted. Early next morning the importer was in touch with me. He sounded worn out, for after the broadcast he was inundated with telephone calls from all over Ireland, England, Scotland and Wales. Neither he nor his wife got a wink of sleep. During the following week the postal authorities were delivering mail by the sack-full. People from here, there and everywhere were anxious to purchase an animal. A substantial business developed by all accounts and all from a short news item on radio. My brief encounter with newspapers and radio taught me a great lesson.

I continued to act as radio correspondent until the programme was discontinued.

Chapter 23

THE PARFREY SYNDROME

I spent many years of my life undertaking family research. As a matter of interest, I was able to trace the family name back to 1140 A.D. but with huge gaps in between. By a strange coincidence (there is no such thing) Cahir Castle was built in 1140 A.D. To this day the two canon balls fired by Cromwell from the centre of the town can still be seen, embedded in the castle outer walls.

 Earlier records show that there had been some sort of fort on the site since around 600 A.D. The Irish name of the town is Cathair Dun Iasaig [pronounced Ka-her-doon-ish-key], a broad English translation being: "The town on the ford of the fish-abounding river."

Returning to the matter of the Parfrey syndrome, it can best be depicted as a game of Snakes and Ladders. The board on which the game is played is a family member's life. Having shaken the dice and come up with a six, one sets out hoping to climb the ladders and avoid the snakes. These bring one back to the starting point, or at the very least back quite a bit. In my research, time and time again I found this to be a common trait in our family. It goes without saying that I too was tarred with the same brush. For eighteen years of my life in Cahir I endeavoured to climb life's ladders and avoid life's snakes. I was relatively successful and hoped to reach the top and win the game. There are one hundred spaces on the board which, with a slip here and there, I traversed. Round about the 80th square, I metaphorically hit a snake and slid all the way to the bottom.

In real terms, Colonel Charteris died and with his passing my own security and that of others went out the window. His mother, Lady Margaret Charteris, in her will, had passed the estate to her son for a life interest only. I gather that his mother was anxious for him to marry a girl of her choice. However, he had other plans in mind and in 1930 he married an actress from

London's Drury Lane. Hence the life interest clause. On his death, the Irish estate passed to three family members who resided in England.

About a month after the obsequies I was asked to attend a meeting with the new owners. The meeting was short, curt and without sentiment. After formal introductions I was asked how long I had worked for the company. I replied that I had been employed for just over eighteen years. I was truly shocked to the core when I heard the spokesman for the group say,

"Well, we are afraid that we are going to have to do without you. After all, if you were run over by a bus we would have to do without you. So we ask you to clear out!"

I was given three months in which to make arrangements to pack up and leave Cahir for good. There was to be no compensation, no holiday pay and of course redundancy had never been heard of in 1961. [Three years after my dismissal I did received a cheque for £75 without comment!]

I broke the news on the home front and the question arose as to what we were going to do? Jobs were very scarce in 1961 and thousands of people were leaving Ireland every week, seeking work in England. On the face of it, I too was going to take the same trail. It took a couple of weeks for what had happened to sink in.

Referring back to Colonel Charteris' family, sadly his brother committed suicide shortly after he had married a woman from South America. She was of Aztec descent and a divorcee so far as I can recollect. She came equipped with one son. Again as far as I know, the son changed his name by Deed Poll to that of Charteris. The estate in London was huge and included property at Tilbury Docks and land or ground rent in connection with Guy's Hospital. During the war, over 2,000 houses were either damaged or destroyed. On one occasion I saw a document allotting rights of anchorage at a berthing site at a rent of £40,000 per annum!

Colonel Charteris' brother married on a Good Friday, of all days. In his will he bequeathed everything to his brother in Cahir, leaving his wife out in the cold. This lady was not welcome in Cahir. In fact Colonel Charteris would have nothing to do with her. Over the intervening years he mellowed somewhat and once she got a foot in the gate she seemed to be able to wrap the colonel around her little finger. He paid all her living expenses including the rent for her flat in Mayfair, London.

This galled me, for in addition to sending on the rent I had to arrange to send two pounds of butter every week as well as pay all bills, newspapers, magazines, foodstuffs and such-like. She came to visit about once every three months and never left without being entertained royally and given a cheque for at least one thousand pounds each time she departed.

Invariably there was a special dinner arranged when she was at Cahir Park House to which many VIPs and clergy of all the denominations were invited. On numerous occasions she went out of her way to insult her host in front of the guests. How he put up with this is anyone's guess. It was most embarrassing for all concerned. The climax of the relationship came when the two of them travelled to the Bahamas together and did not return for about six weeks. What happened there I really do not know.

From that time onwards she appeared to be in charge. While the Cahir estate was entailed, the capital of the company was the personal asset of Colonel Charteris and this he bequeathed to his sister-in-law after his death in 1961. By doing so, at one fell swoop he denuded the company of all its assets. The benefactors under the will of Lady Margaret Charteris had not the slightest intention of putting money into the company, which at that time had to be subsidised in numerous areas. The gardens department was one of these and was kept going simply for prestige. Upkeep of property including Cahir Castle itself made deep inroads. It is hard to believe that the woman who inherited the capital of the company was, about a year later, arrested in London for shoplifting!

My family and I were geared to leave Cahir just after Christmas. I assure you there was little to celebrate. My father had died in December 1960, the previous year and I missed him very much. Had he been alive he would

100

have been my central pivot in seeking employment in the city of my birth. I had been out of it for over eighteen years, felt very much alone and had virtually lost all contact. My father would have been an invaluable contact in the business world as he worked in a legal office and was an accountant by profession. Through personal circumstances he did not qualify as a solicitor but was renowned for his legal knowledge. My mother received over 450 letters and telegrams after his passing. She insisted that everybody be written a letter of personal thanks, which took quite a long time to complete.

One day in November I saw an advertisement in the Cork Examiner seeking the services of a manger for a small company. I applied for the position and was granted an interview. What I was being asked to take over and run was smaller than any of the twenty departments of the Cahir Estates Company. Although the salary was a pittance, I accepted the position and thus entered the drawing office and reproduction business. All the firm was short of was a notice which read, "Abandon hope all ye that enter here!"

It may not be generally known but, where a number of large estates are concerned, if an employee who occupied a house by virtue of his employment was in circumstances like I found myself, he was allowed to take whatever furniture and fittings that had been provided in the house in the first instance.

Though I was not to receive one solitary penny on leaving, I looked around and saw the old but good furniture, not forgetting the 1917 carpet that was in perfect condition. The outstanding piece that stood out was the wonderful valuable wall clock that hung in the dining room. I thought to myself that I would have at least the makings of £1,000 with which to start up again.

However, the Syndrome came alive! The inheritor threw the tradition out the window and I ended up with nothing. I was charged £3 for the threadbare carpet in the main bedroom and £7 for the carpet in the sitting room. She even commandeered the few walking sticks that were in the house! I came to Cahir in 1944 with nothing and I left in 1961 with nothing!

Part One

Nothing perhaps in financial terms, but the experience gained during my term of eighteen years was priceless. It stood me in good stead for the rest of my life. When it comes down to basics, no amount of money will make up for experience.

We put our furniture in store and the day came when we left our home in Cahir Park. It was with a heavy heart we turned the key in the lock for the last time, loaded up my mother's car with clothing and other essentials, and with tears streaming down our faces drove south to Cork city. We had said all our good-byes and there was nothing left but to go forward into the unknown. The next few years proved to be some of the most difficult in my life.

Chapter 23

A POT–POURRI FROM CAHIR

The strict meaning of the word that heads this chapter is, and I quote from the Concise Oxford Dictionary, "a mixture of dried petals and spices to perfume a room." To tell you the truth, the following pot-pourri of incidents helps to fill all the gaps in this narrative that have been omitted or forgotten.

Firstly, there was the local cinema, a proverbial stone's throw from Bleak House where I lived when I first came to the town. Full marks to the cinema management for providing a change of programme nightly. Outside of this there was only the pub, where one could spend an hour or two chatting over the day's events. Every once in a while the town would have a visit from a fit-up theatre. One of the best was that of Anew McMaster. The versatility of this troupe was extraordinary.

The first part of the programme included comedy, the playing of musical instruments, singing and all that goes to make up a good entertaining show. After the interval the very same artists would stage a play, often of a very high calibre. The fit-up theatre invariably drew big crowds to the parochial hall where the populace, sitting on hard seats and a cement floor was entertained for the best part of three hours. The shows were staged nightly and often for a week at a stretch with a different play each night!

In the field of entertainment the annual highlight was the visit of the famous Duffy's Circus to the town. Arriving at dawn, within the space of a few hours a huge circus tent was erected and people came from miles around to see acrobats, clowns, jugglers, tigers, elephants and high wire artistes; not forgetting the magnificent horses and their skilled riders. The circus brought with it a feeling of wonder, magic and thoughts of far off places. One day the circus was there and the following day it was gone! The visit was like a passing dream but a dream that was remembered until the next visit twelve months hence. There were however visits from smaller circuses. Though very good and entertaining, Duffy's reigned supreme.

The winter of 1947 was very severe. For weeks on end it snowed and snow-drifts built up everywhere. As the days went by the weight of snow on the roof of the old cinema proved to be too great and it collapsed. It was years later before a new cinema was built in another part of the town. In common with so many others, I really missed the entertainment the old cinema provided. I felt like a caged animal as we played cards at night whiling the time away.

One evening on impulse, I suggested to a friend that we take the 6.45 p.m. bus to Clonmel and return by the "ghost train" at 9.30 p.m. This was the night mail train that operated from Rosslare on the east coast to Waterford, and thence to Limerick via Limerick junction. Officially it did not carry passengers but there was always one unlit carriage to accommodate travellers of the night. The train was never on time for the fuel used was a mixture of cement and coal-dust. This produced massive clinkers and it was an horrendous job cleaning out the firebox every so often during the journey.

My friend liked the idea - at least it would be something different. Clonmel town boasted three cinemas but as we were caught for time we had to forego the pleasure of attending any of them. Suddenly our luck changed. We met a man from Cahir who was in the taxi business. He was like the biblical 'Good Samaritan'. He told us to go and enjoy ourselves as he would be returning at eleven that night and would bring us back to Cahir. Arrangements were made as to where we were to meet up and with light hearts off we went to the nearest cinema. The weather was miserable as we left the theatre. There was a damp cold rain drizzling from the sky. Neither of us had a raincoat.

We arrived at the meeting place - a shop - only to be given a message to the effect that our expected benefactor had been called to Waterford. He tendered profuse apologies for letting us down. At that time of night the streets cleared rapidly and we stood out in stark relief as we sheltered in a doorway and discussed our plan of action. We had very little money between us - certainly not enough to pay for a night's lodging and we did not fancy the eleven-mile walk to Cahir. To keep up our circulation we walked all over the town.

We were in a quiet suburban area when we were confronted by a Garda [policeman]. He looked at us suspiciously and asked what we were doing walking the streets at that time of night. I explained the situation but he did not believe me and told us in no uncertain manner to "get off the streets". Half-an-hour later we ran into him again. In an official tone of voice he said,

"I am arresting you on a charge of loitering with intent to commit a felony."

He marched us off to the police station. There was a large fire in the day room and we were so glad to see it. We sat around warming ourselves while other Gardaí attended to paperwork. Half an hour later a sergeant arrived and took in the situation. We did not look like criminals and I explained once again to the officer what had happened. He accepted my story especially when I told him that I was employed by the Cahir Estates Company. We were given some hot tea and offered accommodation in the cells for the night! I hasten to add that the doors were not locked. I undressed and, utterly exhausted, got under the blankets and was asleep in no time . My friend decided to sleep in his clothes, which was foolish as they were damp and he caught cold afterwards.

Next morning we were driven to the local bus depot where we caught the first bus back to Cahir. There was a degree of consternation in the boarding house when it was discovered that my friend and I had not slept in our beds. It was thought that perhaps we had had an accident. The landlady was about to report the matter to the local police when we arrived through the door. So ended my one and only brush with the police in my whole life.

There were many funny episodes over the years. One day an "in-from-out-there" arrived with his donkey and cart. (The phrase, 'in-from-out-there' is used when referring to someone who does not visit the town regularly). A large limousine was parked outside Cahir House Hotel. The "in-from-out there" visitor decided to hitch his donkey on to the back bumper of the car while he went to a nearby shop to purchase a few groceries. I was in Castle Street when the owner of the vehicle came out of the hotel. He slipped behind the wheel, gunned the motor and was off down the main street with the misfortunate donkey careering after him. It was a sight to behold and helped to make up a very good story for my column that week. It was the shouts and screams of passers-by near the castle that caught the attention of the driver. The poor donkey was none the worse for wear and one thing is certain, he never ran so fast in his entire life.

Thoughts flash back to the infamous monthly Fair Day. There were two small branch banks in the town. There was an unwritten law that no trader or private individual would do banking on that day. The farmers held sway. With inches of slurry mixed with gallons of urine the streets were an appalling mess. In order to protect the floors, thick layers of straw were laid down in each of the banks as well as in most shops and pubs. Three steps led up to the entrance of the then National Bank [now Bank of Ireland].

One Fair Day a heifer mounted the three steps and crashed through the swing doors scattering people right left and centre. The animal was obviously in a panic as were the customers and this resulted in the animal doing all she wanted to do all over the floor. The bank porter was doing his best to shoo the animal out when the teller shouted in a dry voice over the melee,

"Leave the animal alone; she's a customer; can't you see that she has just made a deposit!"

There was laughter all round. I think that the heifer saw the joke too for she walked placidly out the door of the bank with what I thought was a smile of satisfaction on her face.

Two doors away from the bank was a large wholesale and retail business. The manager of this firm would not conform to the unwritten law about banking on fair days. He insisted on carrying on as normal. In those far off days there was little chance of being robbed. He carried all the cash, a huge amount of which was made up of bags of coins in amounts of five and ten pounds, into the bank. On this particular day, his box was so full he could barely see where he was walking. Someone had hitched their donkey to the railings between his premises and that of the bank. The rope stretched across the path. Unable to see the obstacle the manager tripped. The box flew out of his arms and the many bags of coins split open. Hundreds of coins flew in all directions with high valued bank notes following in their wake. They all landed and sank into the inches-deep muck that covered the streets. A good time was had by all in retrieving as much trophy as possible. I leave the rest of it to the reader's imagination!

Every town has a character or two and Cahir was no exception. Punning is supposed to be the lowest form of wit. J.J. Carew was THE Mr. Pun! He was forever making puns. If one met him in the street he held on to you like glue as he punned away to his heart's content. In common with so many others, I did my best to avoid him but in a town the size of Cahir that was quite difficult. I seem to recall that at one time he was the reporter for 'The Nationalist'. He had concocted his own type of short-hand and was nearly always seen in the District Court month after month furiously taking notes. Whether they ever translated themselves into newsprint I cannot recall.

Typically Irish was the Cahir Central Bakery, which was not centrally located at all! It was situated nearly two miles outside the town. The bread was delivered in horse-drawn vans. One of the horses was a bit eccentric to say the least and was prone to set off at a gallop from time to time. There was a grocery and provisions shop at the corner of Castle Street and The Square, run by the Elliott brothers. One day the horse with no horse sense took off at a gallop straight across The Square and went right through the large plate glass window of the shop. Glass went flying everywhere and there was, in a word, bedlam. It was fortunate that there were no customers in the shop at the time. As luck would have it, J.J. Carew was just passing. He could not resist going in. The brothers were frantically trying to make some semblance of order out of the chaos. Addressing the distraught brothers, Carew calmly said to them, "Well, you're all right now."

"What do you mean?" exclaimed the eldest Elliott irritably.

"The pane you had is gone!" was the retort. Off went J.J. laughing heartily to himself, leaving the fuming brothers behind to get on with the massive clean up!

It was anecdotes such as these that made the town tick. Living in a small town is like living under a microscope. The smallest indiscretion or tiny innocent action could be magnified out of all proportion. As for a rumour, this could grow so many legs that it could turn itself into a centipede in double quick time without any trouble. Parallel with this, on the positive side one found that the metaphorical microscope could show up someone in distress. Perhaps a person had a very serious problem with which to contend and had been keeping the matter under wraps. In situations like this, the true mettle of the townspeople came to the fore. Old enmities - if they existed at all - went out the window. Invariably everyone rallied to do all they could to rectify a given situation.

As a tailpiece, I have to relate how on one occasion, late at night, I was visiting a wood ranger, who lived deep in the woods with his family. Walking in a forest in the dark with the moonlight shining through the tall trees is an eerie experience. I was glad to have had the wood-ranger as my guide. He and his wife had a baby about eight months old. Her sleeping pattern was not good. In the year 1947 a baby's four-ounce bottle was duck-shaped, with a teat at one end and a corresponding rubber stopper at the other. I learned something that night which I never forgot. If you want a baby to sleep soundly, half fill a four-ounce duck-shaped bottle with Guinness! It never fails! I suppose it is due to the child getting well and truly jarred!

No doubting the fact that one cannot beat people who live on mountains and have the forest as their home!

Chapter 25

DEPARTURE & TRANSITION

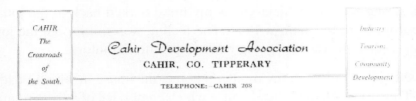

CAHIR
The
Crossroads
of
the South.

Cahir Development Association
CAHIR, CO. TIPPERARY

TELEPHONE: CAHIR 208

Industry
Tourism
Community
Development

TO: William Parfrey, Hon., Secretary,   23rd January, 1962.
Cahir Developement Association,
CAHIR.

On the occasion of your retirement as Secretary, we, the Members
of the Cahir Development Association, wish to pay tribute to the inestim-
able debt which the Association owes to you for your work as Secretary
and your tireless devotion and attention to all the affairs of the
Association. Your departure from our ranks is an occasion of sincere
regret by all members as you have been the prop and guiding light
of our Association from its inception. We hope you will accept this
wallet of notes as a small token of the appreciation and heart felt
gratitude of ourselves and of the citizens of Cahir for all you have done
for us, and we wish you every hapiness and success in the future.

Signed for and on behalf
of the Cahir Development
Association.

Chairman.

Letter of appreciation dated 23rd January, 1962 received from the Cahir Development
Association just before my departure from the town of Xcahir which had been my home
for eighteen years.

As we sped on our way back to the city of my birth, there was a lump in my throat and tears in my eyes when I looked in the rear mirror and saw the town of Cahir disappearing into the distance. The thought of the Holy family fleeing into Egypt flashed through my mind as we headed south. There was a strong feeling of 'deja-vu' as my mind harked back to the journey I made from Cork to Cahir in 1944. The feeling was similar but the journey was in reverse. It was like going backwards into the future!

We were going to live in my mother's home, the house in which I had been born. This was a small terraced house which comprised of a front room, dining room, tiny kitchen, a bathroom extension on the ground floor and three small bedrooms. There was a postage stamp size garden in the front of the house and a fairly long one at the rear.

My mother had lived alone since my father had died in December 1960. Now all of a sudden her home was being invaded! We numbered five. There was Margaret, eleven-year Richard, Jean, who was six, and Mark, who was nearly two years. We were so fortunate that my mother was able to provide us with accommodation. We arrived back to my starting point with nothing except for the princely sum of £10. It was a tight squeeze but we settled in and made the best of things. The sharing of the kitchen needed careful handling. We all had to adjust and were kept busy making arrangements for the children to attend the local school, meet new friends and start a new life.

It was not easy for the children as they had to accept that city life was completely different from that of the country town. The wide open spaces, the luscious countryside, the fast flowing river, the clean air, the sound of the peacocks, the view of the mountains were all gone. All to be replaced with having to live in cramped surroundings, learning to be wary of the constant flow of traffic and getting used to playing games on the streets. This whole new environment took some getting used to.

Luckily the local primary school was but a short distance from where we lived and it was arranged for our two eldest children to attend in the interim as we took stock of what we were going to do for the future.

A few hundred yards away from home was an open piece of ground where a ball could be kicked around and games played. This area did duty for all the other children who lived in the area. Of course there would be the odd inevitable row, another feature of suburban life. It was a real learning curve.

We were fortunate to be living near the area known in Cork as "The Lough". This is a large expanse of water, over one mile in circumference, and home to ducks, swans and all sorts of migratory birds. The lough was also full of roach and small fish known locally as "thorneens". These could be caught with a net, placed in a jam jar and brought home in triumph. The old pond, which my father had built in the back garden, became home to many and they thrived for years. Many happy hours were spent at the lough fishing and feeding the hundreds of birds that were so tame they followed anyone with a crust of bread in hand.

It was the 25th January 1962 that I officially took over the management of General Typewriter & Supplies Company. The firm was unlimited and privately owned. It had a chequered history and I was given to understand that it had been founded as far back as 1922 when it had no less than eight sales representatives on the road! In 1936 the company introduced the first dye-line printing service for architectural and engineering offices, which up to that time had depended on sun frames to reproduce copies of plans drawn on tracing paper. Stocks of drawing office instruments, such as scale-rules, technical pens, drawing boards and ancillary products were added to the conventional office requirements. The war did not help business and the company changed hands numerous times.

When I came on the scene it was in its death throes. After my first day in command I just simply wanted to run away. The company operated from the top floor of a building in the heart of the city. There were 49 steps to ascend up a dark uninviting staircase to the point of sale. On making an assessment of the company I found that the total stocks were valued at a poor £321.

This included a Rapidograph drawing pen which was stolen during my first week! The few pieces of equipment, including typewriters, were held together with wire. Staff wages were so low it was embarrassing and we got what we paid for! The reproduction machine was a museum piece. It was an old 1936 Nig Mason dyeline printing machine; the two movable arc lamps had been replaced with a battery of six 400 watt mercury vapour lamps.

In the reproduction room the heat was so intense that the thermometer often reached ninety degrees Fahrenheit! The sensitised paper had to be imported from England in fifty-yard lengths and had a shelf life of ten weeks. It was a nightmare getting the product through local customs, *and* finding the money to pay for the paper!. Making a copy of a traced drawing was a daunting feat. Three things had to be taken into consideration.

Firstly, the age of the paper; secondly, the state of the brushes in the electric motors; and last but not least, look out of the window to see if the street lights were on. Then by guess and by God one placed the drawing on the yellow diazo paper, fed the two sheets into the machine and prayed hard. There was a very large semicircular thick glass the width of the machine over which the drawing and diazo paper had to pass, guided by a thick canvas like something one would find on farm machinery. After what seemed an age the exposed paper and the original spewed out in what could only be called a cattle trough. There was a hand roller in a bath of developer through which the exposed print was passed. With bated breath one awaited the result. An inward sigh of relief indicated we had a copy. The company did not even boast a trimmer. A razor blade screwed on to a piece of wood about a foot in length was held against a long piece of squared up timber. This device was used to trim the finished product!

On the top floor there was a dark room. It is difficult to believe that in those days there were no Xerox or other photo-copying machines of that nature. Here was housed a 40" x 30" flat-bed photocopier. Making a copy of any size was a major operation. Firstly a gallon of developer and a gallon of fixing solution had to be prepared. A negative of the original produced, developed, washed and fixed. After it had dried off the same procedure had to be carried out yet again, this time to turn the negative into a positive. Taking time and cost of materials into consideration, in the majority of cases the company was in effect doing the work for nothing and giving away some money at the same time!

It took me about one month to come to the conclusion that the best thing that could be done was to close up shop, become unemployed, and sign on at the labour exchange. By adopting this course of action the very strong opposition with which we had to contend would have the satisfaction of beating us into the ground. They had everything going for them - a fine ground floor premises and new equipment. I did not know until I was in the hot seat that the manager of the opposition, who was brilliant in the technical field, had worked for my employer! He let him down and moved over to the opposition, taking with him price lists and all such pertinent data. This was my initiation into the tough field of business where it seemed that the maxim was, 'Never hit a person when they are down, kick the life out of them!' A whole new ball game so far as I was concerned.

During the first four weeks of working in the city word went out on the business bush telegraph that I, the son of my father who was held in very high esteem in professional circles, was back in town. I had lost contact with most people during my eighteen years sojourn in Co. Tipperary. Out of the blue I received two job offers. It turned out that the professional man who owned the General Typewriter & Supplies Company was subsidising it to the tune of about £1,000 a month.

I told him of the offers I had received and he said that if I left he would close up immediately. I hate to be beaten and have always been a fighter. We worked out a deal whereby if I got the business to a break-even point within the period of six months he would give me a one-third interest. There were no strings attached and I took up the offer. Thus began the next phase of a very difficult tough six months.

At the end of the agreed time frame I scraped past the magic break-even figure by a few pounds. I had created a monster! Any business, be it great, small or little is governed by two laws. They are Parkinson's Law and The

Peter Principle. Very simply the first law boils down to the fact that work creates more work. The Peter Principle states that in any given organisation a person will rise to the level of his or her INCOMPETENCE! I found out the hard way that these two laws are immutable.

Chapter 26

THE FIRST SIX MONTHS

Being back in the city took some difficulty adjusting. I was so used to bidding everyone the time of day up country I found myself addressing strangers on the street in like manner. I was receiving queer looks in return. It took a month or two for me to appreciate that I was no longer under the microscope! While I found this to be a relief in one way, it was coupled with a feeling of loneliness as it dawned on me that I was once again just part of a crowd. While this held good so far as the man in the street was concerned, unknown to me there were faceless people in the background keeping a close eye on my modus operandi in relation to the business. Most people thought I was going to fail as I had so much going against me.

Six people including myself, were employed by General Typewriters & Supplies Company and at least one of these – a key person – did not like me at all. Her allegiance was to her former boss who had gone over to the opposition. One evening I called the staff together and told them that while I was the boss I was also an employee. We were all in the same boat as Noah said once upon a time. Whatever I said made an impression and as a team we started to clean the place up. We threw out what was not required and did a 'feng shui' job as best we could. We gave the place a thorough going-over.

To give the illusion that we had plenty of stock on hand we put empty boxes on any shelves we could find. I picked up a counter top for a few pounds. This was our point of sale if anyone had the strength to climb the 49 steps upstairs. We took down the cobwebs, cleaned the windows and rearranged the desks. On reflection I suppose it was a con job but at least it gave the place a different appearance.

A new-type drawing pencil came on the market. It was called "Stabilo" and was a break-through in pencil technology. With very limited funds I travelled to Dublin to meet with Eric N. Webb & Company who had the franchise for the whole country. I was seeking nothing less than the sole agency to sell these new lines in the Munster area. When I was asked what my company could offer, I thought it best to be truthful and replied, "Candidly, nothing!" I will never forget the reply,

"We like the look of your face!" and with that I was given the franchise and a stock of over £500 [€634.87] worth of goods to be paid for on a sale or return basis. Utterly incredible!

My company did not boast a car and I did not have any transport of my own so I went around the south of Ireland by public transport, selling a few dozen pencils here and there together with the odd bottle of Indian ink and some accessories. It was hard going. I spent every week-end writing up invoices and making postings to the ledgers. In between I had to make a few pounds by playing my piano accordion and earned the princely sum of £5.00 [€6.35] by going with a busload of drunks to Bandon on a Saturday night. Included in the fee was a stipulation that I had to play from 3.00 p.m. to 10.00 p.m. on Sunday with a one-hour break. A cup of tea and a few sandwiches were thrown in for good measure.

There was no way that my salary was sufficient to survive so at least once a week I lugged my 56lb piano accordion to the station where I caught the express train to Dublin. Seventy miles up the line I was met at Limerick Junction by musical colleagues. My arrival completed the band's line up, which was quite a good outfit. There was both a male and female singer who were very popular – we numbered ten in all. Leaving Limerick Junction we would travel on to play in some hall or other in County Clare for at least four hours, sometimes five.

Around 4.30am found me drinking a hurried mug of strong coffee in the home of the band-leader. After passing Bleak House, I made my way to the main road to see if I could hitch a lift on a truck to get back and do another sixteen hour stint. Life was pretty hard, but when one's back is against the wall there is little one can do. Cope or go under was the order of the day.

In those days, Jacob's biscuits were running a nationwide campaign entitled "How do Jacobs get the figs into the fig rolls?" They employed Ireland's leading sleuth (!), Jim Figgerty to carry out the detective work. When he visited Cork, GTS was one of his stops.

Six months went by, at the end of which I found myself owning a third interest in the business. This was a further stimulus egging me on to greater efforts. My associate and his wife were very kind and were only too happy to have me on the board of management. Because my innovations had brought a turn-about in the fortunes of the company they were more than happy to listen to any further ideas I might have. I, in turn, listened to what they had in mind.

Being of an artistic bent they were conscious of the fact that at that time there was no art centre where a budding painter could display his or her work. Being outvoted on the proposal, it was agreed to open a gallery on the third floor. The date was set, a sherry reception arranged and invitations sent to those who would have an interest in the project. Some weeks before the official opening, word reached many artists in consequence of which there was quite an impressive exhibition on opening night. One exhibitor was Greta O'Brien; her painting was picked up for the sum of £20 [€25.39]. Greta O'Brien went from success to success and the purchaser of that paint-

117

ing in 1963 must be laughing all the way to the bank. The Gallery was short-lived. When we asked ourselves the question, 'What business are we in?' The answer had to be the supply of services to architectural and engineering offices. Exit the gallery stage left! Still, our efforts sowed a seed.

We survived. I was completely exhausted every Sunday night and then it was a case of nose to the grindstone again early on Monday morning. The company lacked or indeed had no image so far as the public was concerned. I gave an instruction that as soon as the telephone rang, instead of saying "General Typewriters & Supplies Company" the receptionist, my number one girl incidentally, would reply with a smart "GTS?" The public did not know what the letters stood for but the subtle point was they felt that they SHOULD know! This worked well for people were used to hearing ESB [Electricity Supply Board] and numerous others abbreviations that ran off the tip of the tongue. In any event, the company had not sold a typewriter in twenty years!

The company also specialised in circulation work and was under contract to a number of organisations to send out circulars as at short notice. I did a deal with the Roneo Company whereby they supplied me with a new duplicating machine and I, in turn, allowed them to demonstrate its capabilities to potential purchasers at any hour of the night or day. This deal meant we had a brand new machine at no cost to ourselves. If a sale was completed by the agent we could expect a bonus of 48 stencils, which was not to be sneered at.

In those days the installation of a telephone line was at a premium. The minimum time one had to wait, all things being equal, was three years! Hard to realise in this day and age. There were people "out there" - one-man businesses - who really needed a telephone. I saw an opening here that could bring a few more skills to the point of sale. I introduced the GTS 'Phone Call Service and set about placing small ads in the local papers. There were a number of inquiries. As luck would have it, the company had a second line so I devoted Cork 20933 to the service.

The system was simple to operate in the extreme. There was a standing charge of ten shillings per month and all incoming calls were charged to the client at six old pence each. When the service was up and running we had between fifteen and twenty customers. An individual clip was provided on the wall under the customer's name. Each call was logged with name and telephone number, together with the message. The person making the call had no idea that they were contacting an answering service. When they asked to speak with the person concerned, we invariably said that he or she was out of the office. We would add that the call would be returned. If the caller was simply making an enquiry we handled them in sequence.

The GTS 'Phone Call Service was a completely new venture for Cork. It turned the company into a whole series of illusionary firms, including grass-cutting, window cleaning, delivery service, car repairs, cleaning gutters, yoga classes, swimming instructors [three different and independent people]. The idea worked!

We did not make much money but we were putting GTS on the map slowly but surely. There was not a day passed without some problem or other and I worked long hours, often up to sixteen per day. Then there was the matter of the monthly accounts. We did not have an adding machine, so each month I hired one for a week-end. I worked all Friday, Saturday and Sunday at home endeavouring to finish the job about six on Sunday evening. There was no one else capable of doing the work and it was a long time before I was in a position to hire a person part-time to help out.

And so the years rolled on.

Chapter 27

WE MOVE ON!

The situation in my mother's house was becoming more difficult as the weeks went by. It was obvious that we had to have a place of our own. Here we were in 1962 walking on thin ice financially speaking, with no guarantee that we were not going to go under. There is an old saying that 'when we are at our weakest we are at our strongest'. Bearing this in mind we went house hunting. We chose the area of Beaumont in the Ballintemple district of Cork, which was being developed.

We found well-designed and constructed three-bedroom houses. The price? £1,750, peanuts today but a fortune in 1962. We spent three weeks making up our minds whether to choose one and working out how we might finance the purchase. While we debated the pros and cons, the price of the house increased to £2,000! This spurred us on. We were granted a loan from the Cork County Council and this, together with a deposit we scraped together, purchased our new home.

The day dawned when our few bits and pieces of furniture, in store in Cahir, arrived in Beaumont. There was something magical about owning our own home even though it was so sparsely furnished. It was seven years before we could afford to put a carpet on the floor of our front room. The bedrooms had to make do with threadbare pieces of this, that and the other thing. The area developed rapidly and we were very happy there. Our children attended the parish national school and thence to secondary level and beyond. With memories of the Cahir Development Association in mind I was instrumental in the setting up of the Beaumont Residents' Association - BRA for short [an uplifting organisation that was forging ahead and keeping abreast of the times!] From this a Ladies' section came into being, which went from success to success. There was a great 'esprit-de-corps' and good work was done for and by everyone in the district.

With the business in mind I made application to become a member of Junior Chamber Cork which was thriving at the time. It was part of the national organisation, which in turn was affiliated to the world association. It knew no bounds of race, creed, class or colour. This really appealed to me. Coupled with this was the fact that the programme embraced leadership training, debating, public speaking and community service. Before I was allowed to join, I had to be vetted by an induction committee who explained clearly and graphically what it was all about. It was made clear that, while Junior Chamber was a voluntary body, as soon as one signed on the dotted line it ceased to be voluntary.

One made a commitment. I learned that, on hearing what was involved, only three out of every five potential members were prepared to sign up. I never regretted it and revelled in all the various activities. In my career with Junior Chamber I became a council member and secretary of the national organisation, a post I held for a number of years. In recognition of my efforts I had the privilege of being awarded the highest honour that could be bestowed - I was elected a Senator of the international organisation. It was a momentous occasion for me and I was completely overcome. In 1971, I was elected Senate Chairman and took on the task of reorganising the Irish Senate and introducing a constitution, which was duly adopted in Kilkenny that same year. The friends and contacts made proved to be invaluable and led to a further business expansion.

Before leaving my mother's home it was important to do something to provide for her security. My father's advice had been sought by many and proved to be sound in every respect. It brought home the proverbial bacon. But he seldom, if ever, took his own advice so not much bacon came his way. The old adage that the tailor is often the worst dressed man in town was, in my father's case, metaphorical. He died a poor but honourable man, not even owning the small terraced house in which I was born.

Many years previously my father had asked the landlord how much would he be prepared to accept if he decided to purchase the house. "£350" came the reply. My father said he would be prepared to pay £300. "£325" said the landlord. My father would not budge from his offer of three hundred pounds and as the years rolled on he continued to pay the weekly rent. I could never understand this. After living in my mother's house for six months, before we moved out, I got in touch with the landlord to see if I could re-open the abortive deal of years long ago. There was going to be no argument on my part and a deal was clinched for the sale of the house for £525 with annual ground rent of £5. The problem I was facing was, where was the money going to be found? I approached the bank manager. I knew would be looking for security, so I thought up a plan.

Some years before my father died he wound up an estate of a client who had been left quite a bit of property. Part of this comprised of a row of six small cottages hidden away in an old part of the city. No one would buy them so my father made an offer of £175 for the lot. It was rather like shades of the sales I had negotiated when I was in Cahir. To get rid of the encumbrance the deal went through and my father became a landlord. The rents were small but when the rates were added [a feature of tenancy in those far off days] the income grossed somewhere in the region of twelve pounds per week. I suggested to the bank manager that the money accruing from the rents would be more than adequate to pay the interest on the proposed loan. He agreed and I promptly bought my mother's house in her name. I will never forget the look on her face when I handed her the deeds and told her that she owned the house, lock, stock and barrel. I think it was the greatest moment of her life.

Even though my father left slightly less than five hundred pounds in his will, excluding the six cottages, it was as if he was helping from the other side of the vale. Some three months into the drawing up of the loan, out of the blue, I got vacant possession of one of the cottages. I promptly put it up for sale and within ten days had it sold for £500, which paid off the bank. After this I sold three more houses at £500 each to three tenants. The remaining two I sold to a non-tenant for the nominal sum of £200. It just goes to show that when one door closes another one opens.

My mother passed away in May 1976. She was 79 years old. She willed the house to my sister and I. While it would have been lovely to have been in a situation of holding on to the house, sentiment had to go out the window as cash was needed for educational purposes. The sale of the house realised nearly £8,000. About twenty years later the house was put on the market again and sold for the sum of £100,000! Being adjacent to the University had sent the price sky high.

Another example of "The Parfrey Syndrome!"

Chapter 28

WE BECOME ESTABLISHED

By the year 1966 the firm was well established and, despite the opposition doing all they could to put us out of business, we became entrenched. Slowly but surely we gained the respect of our customers and also expanded to provide a collection and delivery service. The majority of our copying work came from the architectural and engineering drawing offices, most of which at that time were based in the city centre.

Our luck started to changed when the insurance company that occupied the ground floor offices was moving to larger premises. I promptly negotiated with them to buy out their lease, which had just two years to run, and was able to purchase this at a very low figure. This meant that when the lease expired GTS was entitled to a yearly tenancy, which suited us very well.

We raised some capital and renovated the ground floor and opened up a shop. Illuminated display stands were a must but the cost of the renovation work allowed us to purchase just three when six were really required. Still, it was a start and a mighty one at that. It was no longer necessary for our customers to climb the stairs - the staff had to do that as our old reproduction machine was still on the third floor. In a way there was method in the madness for while waiting for the copies to come to hand the client had an opportunity of looking at the stock we had for sale.

Within the space of a couple of months of being on the ground floor the increase in our cash sales, while not great, helped appreciatively to keep the bank happy. Though our shop was small I started to read up about retail selling and found some very handy tips about how the mind of an individual works.

Supermarkets today have brought this to a fine art. Any kind of shop window is invaluable and I soon learned how true this was. Our shop window was bow shaped and we made sure that there was nothing obstructing a potential customer from seeing what the inside of the shop looked like.

We learned that there should never be any form of psychological barrier so our place was open plan. We also learned that the average person passing any given shop window will look at what is on display for a maximum of ten days! All big stores are well aware of this fact, hence the change of window display every ten days or so. There was no way that we could afford this luxury so we had to be content with a monthly display. To compensate we endeavoured to be outrageous.

On one occasion we had a model of a full sized cow occupying most of the window space. It was so incongruous and the captions so good that people flocked to look at the window. Over the years we gained the reputation for unusual window displays and people often went out of their way to pass our premises just to see what was on offer at that time.

One of the best displays of all was simple in the extreme. It comprised of a very large sheet of white cardboard suspended in the window. On the card was printed a long black ink line about a quarter of an inch thick. The caption read,

"Where do you draw the line?" and this was followed with a large, "GTS!"

To this day, forty years on, from time to time people will say to me,

"Bill, where do you draw the line?" Powerful stuff.

Our business with Eric N. Webb in Dublin grew apace. The day dawned when they were able to supply us with a wet process photocopying machine. This was a small American manufactured machine called "Speed-o-Print" which stood on a desk and was simple to use. With this machine we could churn out crisp foolscap and quarto photocopies at a fraction of the cost of doing the same thing in the dark room.

We did not go overboard on our charges and had a steady daily trade that brought grist to the mill. We were making progress. Early in 1966 we formed a limited company - GTS [Sales & Services] Limited with three directors, I being one of them. Over the years we had often been asked what

GTS stood for. One of our customers who was quite a wag said that it meant that the girls were terribly sexy! We did not dispute this interpretation as it added an additional zing to our company image.

As I said previously, there were faceless people who were watching the growth of the business with interest. One notable observer was Mr. Hackett of J.D. Hackett & Company, Dublin. The director of this company had for a number of years been noting what was developing on the Cork scene. Later I learned that his company had been contemplating the purchase of General Typewriter & Supplies Company to expand their business in the south but ran the proverbial mile when their assessment was that such a proposal was a non-runner from the word go. During the years 1962 to 1966 we had been doing business with this company and on a personal level Mr. Joe Hackett and I got on extremely well.

My co-directors had reached the point where they wanted out. I negotiated a deal whereby they sold their shares to J.D. Hackett & Company for a very respectable sum. The firm of Hackett was becoming known nationally and internationally and was expanding significantly. Branches were opened in Liverpool, Manchester and London, England. In addition, the group set up a factory for the manufacture of Irish-made sensitised paper in the teeth of opposition from the English international companies. A further factory for the production of pre-printed tracing sheets came into being. The might of this organisation of which we were now part meant further expansion. The next-door premises came on the market and was promptly purchased. Our overall business increased in size as did our staff.

At the end of December 1969 I was unwell. I had been working flat out for seven years. After Christmas I went to see my doctor. He sent me directly to a surgeon and I found myself in hospital that very day. A week later I underwent a three hour operation. The hard slogging had taken its toll. I was barely out of hospital when I had to return because of complications.

As I lay there convalescing I could not take my mind off the matter of a new dyeline machine that was to be installed on the third floor of our premises.

Part One

The site had been examined by a structural engineer who gave us the green light. This necessitated taking out all windows on the floor in question. A huge crane was hired and with the co-operation of the police the street was closed to traffic at 8:00 am. The operation went off without a hitch apart from the worry that the floor would be unable to carry the weight! Our business was located in a one-way side street and when the lift had been carried out the huge crane was driven onto the main thoroughfare. The driver of a double-decker bus proceeding down the main artery certainly did not expect to see a huge mobile gantry suddenly make its appearance from a side street. There was one passenger on the upper deck of the bus sitting at the back. The protruding jib came in contact with the roof of the bus and peeled it off completely, as if opening an elongated tin! Apart from the huge fright experienced by the passenger, he was uninjured. As luck would have it, a press photographer happened to be passing at the very moment of contact and took a photograph that was published in the local press.

My sojourn in hospital took longer than I expected. One day I found myself shaking all over. My body was jerking and there was this peculiar feeling of tension in every cell of my body. At first I could not make out what it was. Suddenly the awful truth started to dawn on me that I was heading for a nervous breakdown. I would not wish this experience on my worst enemy. I returned to my job but I just was not right. I did not know how to handle the situation and would leave the office, go over to a bar and order a triple brandy! I had no idea why. Most of it would spill in any event and it did not do me one bit of good. As the weeks went by I got worse and worse.

A good friend came to my aid and when I felt an attack coming on I would telephone him and he would come right away. I would rant, rave and literally go mad! I was becoming a danger to myself and others. I was in the twilight zone when I signed myself into a mental hospital.

They were the darkest days of my life.

I was seeing coloured shafts of light shooting all over the place and was suffering from schizophrenia. The mental hospital was a private one and it was a horrible place. Four times without my permission I was given ECT treatment. In effect this is a controlled epileptic fit. It was a horrible experience and afterwards I could hardly remember my name. The course did not do me one bit of good and from that day to this I cannot remember names or numbers!

One thing I learned, one will never get well in a mental institution. Pills are shovelled down the red lane and these are expected to treat the cause but all they do is to treat the symptoms. The cause of my mental breakdown was twofold. Firstly, I had burned myself out endeavouring to survive and secondly, had to contend with the gift of Spiritual Healing that was developing on a subtle level at the same time. It took me six years to recover fully and I owe so much to my family, friends and the staff of GTS who stood by me and helped me in many difficult moments.

Chapter 29

SERVICE IS THE HIGHEST PRIORITY

In common with other businesses, the drawing office business was a very specialised one. To be successful, one had to know it thoroughly. By now we were part of a group of companies and had become a force to be reckoned with. We prided ourselves in knowing the business, the products and most important of all we knew that service to our customers had to be our highest priority. Without the customer there simply isn't any business. I was always very conscious of this fact.

In staff training I emphasised over and over again that the customer who came into the shop was the most important person we would meet that day. Customers were divided into two groups. There were those who came into the shop and those who wished us to bring our business to them. It was our policy to build up a strong relationship with all. This was achieved by providing consistently good service, getting to know people personally and treating everyone as we ourselves would like to be treated. Firm friendships were built up in this manner to the point where we were on first name terms with many.

As the years rolled by most of the drawing offices, traditionally located in the city centre, because of traffic and lack of parking facilities, moved out to the suburbs. In some cases offices transferred to nearby small towns. This necessitated a major review of how we were going to continue to provide a fast and efficient service. I drew out a large circle that represented a distance of fifteen miles from the hub. I then added similar circles inside the outer periphery. The finished product was like a shooting range target. Then taking the volume of business done with each company and the appropriate services required, planned calls were made on a twice-daily, daily, weekly, bi-weekly or tri-weekly basis. All this was depicted on the target board so that one could see at a glance how things were going at any given time.

Part One

To run the service we introduced a mini-car driven by a smart, efficient girl who made the planned calls. In addition, our customers were at liberty to telephone us for service at any time outside the planned schedule.

Long before mobile 'phones became commonplace we made use of an ultra-short wave communication system so that we were constantly in touch with our mini-driver. It is a recorded fact that on one occasion, as a result of being in a strategic position, our girl was with a customer within thirty seconds of his having laid down his telephone! His surprise and satisfaction can be left to the imagination.

This isolated case typified the standard of service we attained. Nothing was too small or too big. Over the years a reputation for courtesy, reliability, efficiency and service developed and GTS became a household word. The ordinary man-in-the-street also had his problems. Requests from this quarter were often bizarre in the extreme. Over the years we were asked to reproduce such items as the face of a clock, the palm of a hand, old coins, gold and silver jewellery, match boxes, keys, etc. And on one occasion the actual face of a customer!

To remain in the forefront of the drawing office business it was essential to keep abreast of all the latest developments. In this connection I travelled to trade fairs in England and on the continent of Europe, notably Germany. The Hanover trade fair was a "must". As it was a great advantage to speak the language, I started to study intensively.

Over a period of three years, for three hours weekly, I received individual tuition from a German lady. Though a difficult language to learn grammatically, I really enjoyed the tuition and spent as much time as I could in going over phrases and expressions one would never learn in an ordinary class. Many years have passed since those halcyon days but I can still make myself understood if the occasion arises.

GTS [Sales & Services] Limited continued to grow and expand. I made mention of the two famous laws, Parkinson's Law and The Peter Principle.

They began to come into play. Work was creating more work and the Peter Principle was slowly but surely pushing me up closer and closer to the apex of the principal's triangle. This is the point where the person who started it all faces either a serious nervous breakdown or, at the least, a heart attack. Over the intervening years the strain of running the company was beginning to play on my health and on a number of occasions I had to take refuge in a private hospital and go under sedation. So far as everyone was concerned, I was away on a holiday. I suppose they were not too far out on that point.

On the third floor of our next-door premises I had provided a coffee and tea-making machine for the staff. As I drank my coffee one morning I glanced out of the window, which was directly opposite a corresponding window in the bank premises across the narrow street. A man sat alone at a desk furiously working away and every few minutes he was on the telephone. He was without doubt a man under pressure.

Each day I watched him and I got it into my head that he must have a very responsible job working away in his own office. I took him to be a man with authority transferring vast sums of money from one side of the world to the other following world-wide interest rates in order to secure a fraction of a percent more in interest for the bank. I felt that his blood pressure was at a critical level and could see him getting a massive heart attack and die on the job. It would not take long for his immediate superiors to know that something was wrong and I could see them rushing to ascertain what was causing the hold up. Taking in the scene at a glance someone would push the body aside and simply sit down at the desk and carry on! It was this flight of fancy that made me realise I was not indispensable.

Early in 1977 I felt that it was time for me to go and I was going to have to pack up.

On parallel lines my healing gift was developing and the conflict that was going on within me was difficult to bear. Quietly in the background I had met a number of people who had more than a passing interest in spiritual rather than physical matters. We had ad hoc meetings. One night a small advertisement appeared in the local evening paper announcing a meeting of - wait for it - "The Society for the Research, Recording and Investigation of Natural and Unnatural Phenomena". A public meeting was arranged in a small hall in the Douglas area of Cork city.

Our small group went along. The organiser was a bit off the wall but at least he had started something. We attended other meetings he arranged but on some occasions he did not turn up at all. One night he asked me if I would take over. I agreed on the proviso that I had carte blanche to run things as I saw fit. He gladly passed the reins to me. I drew up a Constitution, called a general meeting and the Cork Psychical Society came into being, the original instigator having disappeared from the face of the earth.

In those early days we were up against bell, book and candle. We were causing a ripple - in a way, a breath of fresh air, and "the Church" did not like it. In our very early days we invited an English medium to Cork and provided her with accommodation. She was a lovely sincere woman of about 65 years of age. One night we had an open meeting in an hotel in Cork and forty people turned up. Unknown to us a Catholic priest in mufti was in the audience. No sooner had this lady commenced the meeting when she honed on to the priest and asked him why he had to come in disguise.

He was most embarrassed, particularly when she related some details about himself. He got up from his seat and left the meeting. The Cork Psychical Society did Trojan work during its existence and many of its activities are recorded in the next section of this book. We all have psychic ability - it is natural. Some people are more attuned than others and have experiences that they find hard to explain or even mention. The society was of great help to those in this predicament.

Chapter 30

THE END OF THE LINE

The day finally came on 25th January 1978, when I left GTS for the very last time. The second phase of my life was over. The previous night I had allowed my memory to go back to that fateful year in January 1962, when I took over General Typewriter & Supplies Company. I thought of all the happenings, good and bad. Faces and events flashed before me. I thought of the structures I had introduced, the job specifications, worked out for each staff member, ensuring that they synchronised and meshed smoothly so that the company could operate like a well-oiled machine.

I thought of our staff Christmas parties and of the wonderful staff I had who worked with a will. From tiny beginnings the company had grown and on the eve of my departure full and part-time members numbered 18. Incredible stuff. My co-director did everything he could to make me change my mind about leaving but to no avail, the die was cast. I had arranged a farewell dinner and we had a wonderful night never to be forgotten. I was deeply moved on receipt of a presentation. I always wore two hats, metaphorically speaking. During the day I was the boss and was known affectionately as "Mr. P.". As soon as business was finished for the day I became just plain "Bill". There was a great bond between us all.

My last day as managing director was a sad and difficult day as I said good-bye to the staff. A few tears were shed as I shook hands with everyone and then resolutely walked out the door for the last time. I tried to analyse my feelings. The nearest I got was the sense of a mother leaving the child she bore, never to see her offspring again. Everything was left behind and I felt very much alone. I started to walk and found myself heading to the Bon Secour hospital to see a friend who was a patient there. I was so emotionally upset I just could not go home. It is a four mile walk from the hospital to where I lived, and rather than avail of public transport [I had no car now] I thought the walk would do me good.

My decision to pack up affected my wife and to a lesser extent the family as a whole. I was now unemployed and was dependent solely on what I received weekly from the Unemployment Exchange, which was not much, together with what was being drawn from my limited capital each week.

I will never forget waking up the following morning and the awesome relief I felt as it dawned on me that daily business tensions were gone for good. It was really brilliant. For the next three months I wallowed in this luxurious feeling and then became conscious that it could not go on forever. While I received payment in respect of the shares I held in the company, for a number of reasons best forgotten, the amount bore very little resemblance to eighteen years of effort and the subsequent value of the company that I left behind me. After paying off the mortgage on my house I made a decision to travel to America to visit a pen friend with whom I had been corresponding for over forty years. We had never met but, all through the war years, he would send on some tea and other items that were unobtainable - subject to the ship carrying the goods not being sunk.

I was told that I could not afford it but this was the one and only time in my life when I would have enough money to make such a trip. We spent five weeks in the U.S.A. and travelled vast distances. New York to Philadelphia, then to Chicago, San Francisco, San Diego, Houston, Florida, Washington D.C. and back to New York. It was a momentous trip and I returned to Cork with the feeling that I had got something out of my system. Little did I think that the fates were to decree that I would visit the USA three more times!

Man proposes and God disposes.

It did not take me long to realise that I could not carry on the way I was going. Here I was commencing the third phase of my life with no job or income. I had to sit down and take an objective view of my whole situation. Survival was the name of the game so it was imperative that I concentrate on regaining a steady income. With few qualifications, let alone a degree to my name, I made a list of all the things that I was capable of doing, even small things like mowing a lawn. I was amazed at what I knew and the wealth of experience I had gained in life up to that point. There was no doubt about it, I was Jack-of-all-trades-and-master-of-none and what I did not know I could make up!

So I formed a new company and named it Pansolve Limited. The company's headed paper bore the slogan "we explore the world of ideas". One Saturday afternoon I stood in a pensive mood looking at GTS. My reverie was shattered when I heard a voice beside me saying,

"Admiring the edifice you've built up?"

Startled, I turned to see who was speaking to me. It turned out to be a former customer. He asked what I was doing since retiring from the business. I told him of my plans. He invited me to have a drink with him over which he informed me of an ongoing business problem with which he had to contend. In my new field of endeavour the use of the term "customer" changed to "client".

Pansolve Limited had its first client that Saturday afternoon. From there on the business grew. I ghosted reports, manipulated monies, acted as front man in deals, took on an agency here and there which I would then farm out. The list was endless. It was here that experience paid off. As the only employee of the company, I was like a juggler keeping all the balls up in the air at the same time. It was an exhilarating experience.

It confirmed one thing that I knew to be true. Sell the knowledge one has in one's head. Capital outlay is virtually nil and one can sleep at night. Contrast this with the buying and selling of goods, which can be a nightmare. I knew I was never going to be a rich man and that did not bother me in the slightest. The income was sufficient to pay the bills and have a little holiday now and again. Running concurrently with this work, requests for help in the field of healing increased, so my life was very varied.

At the outset I bought a Renault 4, which I named "The Yellow Peril". I found it to be a great little car. It was used for business purposes as well as making calls to those who were ill and seeking help.

And so life went on, but one never knows what is around the corner. The events to follow that are recorded here were profound and made a dramatic change in both myself and my thinking.

Grandad Cooney and I in Crosshaven

Chapter 31

THE STORY OF THE TEDDY BEAR

Although I am a sentimental old fool, I balance this with the knowledge that no matter how old we are, there is always the child within. We should never forget this. We pretend to be big but in reality we are all only small boys and girls pretending to be grown-up. Most of us had some cuddly dog, doll or such like as a child. In my case it was a small teddy bear. He had no name but went everywhere with me.

When I was seven years of age, way back in 1933, my father hired a large car together with the driver for a day's outing. Believe me this was a major event and in common with so many others at that time I had never been in a motor-car previously. This monster could seat about eight or ten people. In addition to the usual seating there were small seats that opened up. Hiring the car and Jerry the driver cost £10. An absolute fortune in those days and I have no idea how father could afford the fantastic luxury.

The day of the excursion to Co. Kerry came at last. The car was loaded up with sandwiches, lemonade, cakes, biscuits and other wonderful things to eat. The Primus stove, kettle and teapot were not forgotten as no one could live without a cup of tea. The excitement was intense. On board were my mother's father and mother, my aunt, my own parents together with my sister Eileen. Making up the group were two others. Although the mysterious mists of Kerry clouded the mountain tops this only added to the thrill of driving along the mountain roads and through the carved out tunnels.

On our return journey we passed through shady glades where a whole host of bluebells came into view. I confidently expected to see fairies and elves. It was decided that we all should pick some bunches of bluebells to bring home. We clambered over the rugged terrain and waded though magnificent green ferns and wild flowers. It was truly magical and I was lost in wonder at it all, as was my constant companion, my teddy bear. It was only when we arrived back at the waiting car, to my horror and chagrin, and everyone else's too, I found that teddy was missing. I was in a terrible state.

A search party that included the driver, set out to scour the terrain. We looked everywhere in the dense undergrowth but all to no avail. Teddy was lost and I had to come home without him. I was disconsolate and cried so much. Then one day a letter arrived addressed to me. It was written by my grandfather with an indelible pencil, on thin tissue-like paper. Ostensibly it came from the fairies. I still have the original letter, which comforted me a lot. This is what I received:

FAIRYLAND - TUESDAY - KILLARNEY

To our dear, dear Willie,

We, the Fairies are now all together assembled in our lovely Glen near Killarney. We were all hopping and skipping about when we saw yourself and darling little Annie, your sister, come into our wood to gather flowers. You had a great Big Man with you AND WE WERE AWFULLY AFRAID of him because he had great Big Boots and every time he made a step the twigs cracked like thunder under them and he killed fifteen thousand grasshoppers [our enemies] while he was there - that was good. We counted them when you went away and it will take a week to bury them properly; you see Willie WE ARE ONLY VERY SMALL - we fairies and if Big Man put Big Plop on us he would kill us too; he would not mean to of course but how was he to know so we held a meeting when he came too near us [oh, we were all trembling for fear he'd see us] and Mary Fairy said to us all the best thing to do was to call out all our soldiers - "THE TICKLERS" we call them; this we did and gave them orders to tickle Big Man hard on neck and hands so that he would run away from where we were. This they did and how we laughed - ha ha - when we heard Big Man shout loud and say something cross to our soldiers. When he got very cross Major-General Pip gave him a bite on the nose-top, so he confessed afterwards, but he said he was very hungry and Big Man could spare some.

Now Willie dear, we heard you crying last night because you left your little Teddy behind but cheer up. We will find him and bring him to your home and wait for your coming soon again.

We the fairies are sending Big Man another Teddy for you Willie, and now with lots of love from all of us here to you dear Willie and kindest regards to MUMMIE, BIG MAN [no Big Boots], Rene, Granny and Granddad and last but not least to your darling little sister Annie [to whom we have also written].

XXXXXXXXX

I am,

Your loving friend,

FAIRY MARY

P.S. Molly Diddlemass Fairy said that you grow and would soon have BIG BOOT LIKE BIG MAN because she said you killed 200 grasshoppers when you plopped 'round where she was hiding and she thinks when you and Big Man come again you leave Big Boots out on the road behind you and then the soldiers can't tickle your "foots" and you both will run all the faster, ha, ha. Of course we will tell our 'MIDGETS' to tickle you only - NOT BITE. Our soldiers went as far as Ballyvourney with you last night and had a fine supper on milk and cream before returning to Fairyland.

Good Bye Willie. Come again soon.

. FAIRY MARY

The loss of that teddy bear so long ago was like a bereavement. In a way I suppose it was. To this day, in my 79th year, I still miss that bear. Then some months after writing this the postman delivered a box to my door. It was from the National Geographic Society [my family subscribe to the National Geographic magazine]. I could hardly believe it when I opened the box for there nestling comfortably was a polar bear! It flashed into my mind that he was a reincarnation of the bear lost over seventy years ago. The replacement was more like an addition to the family and was given the name of Polo. I cannot account for it, but the sense of loss I have experienced all of my life has now disappeared! One wonders if it is a case of coming events casting their shadow afore!

Chapter 32

THE BLASKET ISLANDS

When one is in a vacant and pensive mood sitting in front of a warm fire, there in the flickering flames one may see people, pictures and images from the bygone years.

"Ah," one might exclaim, " I remember him", as if the flames produce an image of a long forgotten friend. The same holds good for places - home or abroad - which one visited for the first time in the dim and distant past. The memory is forever indelibly imprinted in the mind. Such is the case where I and the Blasket Islands and its people were concerned.

It was the year 1940 and the war was waging in Europe. As I have found throughout my life, nothing happens without there being a reason. Thanks to the grinding I received in the primary school, as I have previously mentioned, my knowledge of my native language was above the average of that of my fellow students in the secondary school. A new curate was appointed to the Cathedral parish of which I belonged.

Not only was he fluent in Irish but also spoke three or four other languages. He was also an authority on ancient Irish to boot. I came to know him and listened with rapturous attention as he told me stories about the Blasket Islands and its people. He had been a consistent visitor before the war and was known to all and sundry as Proinsios [The Irish word for 'Frank']. He had been there numerous times in the late thirties and had made many friends. It came about that he was planning a further trip in September of that same year and, in the interests of furthering my education, my parents agreed that I should accompany him on the trip.

It was a real adventure as I had never been in the west of Ireland before. As the crow flies the Blasket Islands are a mere 150 miles from Cork city but the journey took us three full days! Bags packed and bicycles at the ready we made our way to the Cork station. Due to the war, coal was at a premium and the fireboxes were fired with a mixture of cement and coal dust. There were but three trains per week and it took three engines to pull a relatively short train through the tunnel to Kilbarry station at the northern tip of the city.

Our immediate destination was Tralee, the capital of County Kerry. The journey was long with numerous halts to clear huge clinkers that built up in the fireboxes - extremely hard work. It was late in the evening when we arrived in the town. That night we booked a room in an hotel. Early next morning we travelled on the narrow-gauge rail line to the town of Dingle. The line snaked over hills and down into valleys at a speed of about twenty to thirty mph. It was exhilarating and eventually the train pulled into Dingle station.

Here we had to overnight once again. Through his church connections, my companion, Frank Hipwell, knew the rector of the small Church of Ireland congregation very well. We received an invitation from Canon Roycroft to spend the evening with him The Canon was also a fluent Irish speaker so the national language received a good airing. I did my best to follow the discussion and was relieved when we reverted back to English. He told us about Dingle and its people who earned their living from the sea. They were the salt of the earth. A strong community spirit prevailed, illustrated graphically when he told us a story of how on one occasion some dignitary of the church was paying a courtesy visit to the parish. The townspeople were aware of the dwindling congregation and on the occasion of the visit quite a number of those who were Catholics came to swell the congregation, despite the strict ban that debarred Catholics from stepping across the threshold of a Protestant church!

We slept well and next morning set off on our bikes for the village of Dunquin. The views were awe-inspiring as we trundled along, and after passing through Ventry the road winded around the mountainside as we started the climb. The sun shone brilliantly and it was not long before we began to sweat as we walked pushing our well-laden bicycles. A mountain stream was cascading down the hillside forming a shallow river as it tumbled down to the sea far below us. The water was cold and sparkling and tasted like nectar. We quenched our thirst.

Every turn in that narrow road produced a new vista. Clouds scudded across the sky forming patterns on the sparkling sea. The cry of the sea birds was the finishing touch. At last the road turned and we were confronted with the vast Atlantic Ocean. Standing majestically nearly four miles from the mainland was the Great Blasket Island. I could but stop and stare at the grandeur it presented with its family of smaller islands spread out to sea.

Leaving our bicycles in the care of someone Frank knew, laden down we made our way down the steep slope to the tiny inlet where we boarded a Currach or Nambhóg. These boats were sixteen feet long with tarred canvas stretched over a framework of thin wooden struts. When turned upside down and carried on the shoulders of the oarsmen they are like a huge black beetle. I looked at the craft and at the swirling waters of the Atlantic as fear gripped my heart. The thought of setting sail in such a craft was frightening, but I need not have worried. The currach floated on top of the water as if it was a cork. While the distance to be traversed was but three-and-a-half miles, the currents found in the sound were very dangerous. There was even a deadly whirlpool. Because of this the journey was not direct. It took the best part of three hours to reach the safety of the tiny harbour of An Blascaóid Mór.

The entire population of the island of three-and-a half miles in length, half-a-mile wide, was there to greet us - such a welcome. We made our way up the rocky path to the house of Maire Guiheen where we were to stay for three weeks. Thanks to an Atlantic storm we were compelled to stay on the island for an additional two weeks. Its terrifying strength is fearful to behold yet no islander liked to talk about storms; this seemed to be taboo.

The cluster of houses that nestled snugly into the side of the hill was therefore protected from the hurricane force of the wind. The storm we witnessed was of huge magnitude and gigantic snowballs of sea foam came sailing over the nine-hundred-foot peak of Croagh Mór. We were cut off from the mainland and had to rely on the resources the island itself could produce. There was but one cow on the island but she stopped producing milk. We had to learn to drink black tea. From that time to this day, I could never drink tea with milk ever again.

Maire Guiheen's house comprised of a large kitchen with an open turf fire, which was fanned with the aid of a bellows. Our bedroom was small and at the fire hearth side of the cottage. At the opposite end was a living room, seldom used, and another bedroom. Overhead were lofts used to store food-stuffs such as dried fish. In some of the houses animals were allotted space. The house was spotlessly clean and silver sand drawn from An Traigh Bhán [the White Strand] was sprinkled liberally on the floor and did duty as a carpet. Wooden settles lined the sides of the walls.

It took some days for me to adjust to a completely new way of life. Time did not matter. One went to bed when it got dark and got up again when the sun rose each morning. The focal point of the village was An Tobair [the well] where people gathered in the gloaming, exchanging news about the happenings of the day, told stories and in general had a few laughs.

On my first night at An Tobair I fell a couple of feet into the small pond area into which the crystal clear water cascaded from high in the hillside. I did not hurt myself but the comments were ribald and I had to ask my learned companion what was actually said. I cannot repeat the comments. So far as the islanders were concerned they were humorous innocent remarks but in print would take on an entirely different interpretation. At least I added a couple of new words to my Irish vocabulary!

The weeks flew by - the weather was perfect. We swam in the sea at the Traigh Bhán [White Strand] and needed no swimming gear, for there was no one to see us. The force of those mighty waves and the freedom of being really part of nature was wonderful. We climbed to the top of the island along the stony "road" called Both air De Valera and met some islanders leading a donkey with two panniers of turf being brought to the village to keep the fires glowing.

From vantage points we watched the gannets nose diving into the sea from a great height. Every time they came up with a fish in their beaks. We often spent as long as an hour rooting out the biggest boulder we could find. With all our strength we would stand it on its side and send it off down the mountainside, moving ever faster and faster until at last it careered into the sea with a huge splash. We traversed the length of the island to its most western point and gazed over the vastness of the Atlantic Ocean. Eight miles out to sea a lighthouse had been built on a small island. It must have been a prodigious engineering feat.

As we stood there looking at the magnificent sea we gained the impression of being the only two people left in the whole world. It was an extraordinary experience. Before wending our way back, we examined what could only be described as holes in the ground over which huge slabs of stone did duty as a roof. In these primitive shelters lived a group of monks who settled there in the eighth century. They must have had a most wondrous calling to eke out an existence with no shelter from the fury of the Atlantic.

Every day the islanders went fishing and we would join with others to await their return. It was always an anxious time and how happy everyone was on their safe return. They caught all sorts of fish, including mackerel. One day a currach arrived with a fourteen-foot long conger eel, lashed to the framework. Such a monster – I had never seen an eel so big. On the return journey the eel had bitten an oar in two! It could just as easy have been the hand of one of the fishermen. The day's catch was triumphantly brought to the respective homes where fresh fish was served that night. Unless one has eaten a large fresh mackerel cooked in its own juices on large tongs resting in red-hot turf ash, one has missed out on one of the finer things in life! The aroma cannot be described, only experienced.

The Government had built three or four concrete houses with slated roofs. One of these had been turned into a small factory where a number of girls made woollen stockings. As there was no electricity supply, the sewing machines had to be operated manually.

Peig Sayers

In the larger house lived the Queen of the Island - Peig Sayers. In 1940 she lived with her brother. The day we called to see her she was busily gutting rabbits. With a sharp knife, she would take a dead rabbit and with one deft slash cut the animal open. A gloved hand would take out the entire entrails in one movement to be thrown to the waiting cats and dogs outside the door. This work continued as she smoked her pipe. My friend had met Peig on numerous occasions but this was my first visit.

She spoke beautiful soft Munster Irish, which I was able to understand. Her brother sat by the open hearth smoking his pipe, lost in thought. We were invited to hear him sing and could not refuse. He sang his never-ending song [called in Irish, 'sean nós'] with his eyes closed. I could not understand one word. After about fifteen minutes he stopped and I started to clap my hands. As if it were a signal, his eyes closed once more and there was a rendering of the second part. It took over half an hour for the "treat"!

Every night we were reminded of the war as we listened to bombers flying out from their bases in England to attack German submarines far out in the Western Approaches. Many ships were sunk and wreck was often found. Once a huge quantity of bales of raw rubber was washed up. This was extremely valuable and found its way to the Dunlop Tyre Company to be turned into tyres of all kinds, bringing a bonus to the islanders.

On another occasion the mast of a large ship was washed up as well. Everything that could be salvaged was put to good use. The islanders could turn their hands to anything. I think it was in 1941, when I made a return visit, that a German Heinkel crash-landed on Innisvicilaun. I believe the crew numbered five, and having survived the crash they lived on rabbits for five days until help came from An Blascaóid Mór, eight miles distant. The islanders dismantled the aircraft and out of the aluminium nuts fashioned Claddagh rings. I used to have one of these but lost it, more's the pity.

A friend and I were to spend a third holiday on the island of Blascaóid Mór; the islanders themselves seemed to have become part of my life. Regretfully, owing to storm conditions it was impossible for us visit. We spent our holiday in Dunquin and stayed with the aunt of Maire Guiheen. The population of the island had dwindled dramatically and it was in around 1946 that the government transferred the remaining islanders to the mainland. Many years later one of the islands was purchased by the then Taoiseach - Charlie Haughey, who built a home there complete with helicopter landing pad! Every year just before Christmas my family and I made the journey to Dunquin to visit our friends and bring some Christmas cheer. Maire had got married and had two children of her own. The years took their toll and one by one all my wonderful friends passed to their just reward.

I never thought that I would set foot on Blascaóid Mór ever again in my life. In the year 2002 our national television station RTE was doing a documentary about the islands around Ireland and were seeking a person who had been on the island when people lived on An Blascaóid Mór. They found me! Despite the fact that I was far from well and was advised that if I made the trip, it would kill me. I retorted, "If I am to die on Great Blasket Island I will die there!"

We stayed overnight in the town of Dingle. The next day we went to Dunquin where we boarded a powerful sea-going vessel to bring us across the sound. I thought that I would never make it to the landing stage. As the little harbour was much too small to berth the vessel, we were compelled to disembark into a large rubber dinghy. That was extremely difficult.

Having to climb up the steep slope from the landing stage was really pushing it and I could feel my heart jumping all over the place. I was interviewed in Dunquin, on the journey across the sound and on the island itself. I thought that I would never get back to Cork that night.

On arrival in Cork, I had to be whisked away to hospital straight away and into ICU. The medical people told me that my heart might hold out for about three months and that was that. RTE got to hear this bit of news and whisked to the hospital an uncut copy of the film, together with a television, to enable me to see what the finished programme would be like.

In 2006 I am still on Spaceship Earth and have in my possession a copy of both the unedited and finished programme. It was broadcast a number of times over the intervening years under the title "Out of the Blue".

Chapter 33

THE CURSE

In all the years I was privileged to be a healer, out of a total of over 31,000 people, I came across only one who had been cursed! I was holding an open clinic in a city in the west of Ireland when one day a man, aged about thirty-five, came to see me. He was complaining of pains and aches in every joint of his body. Some days the pains would be external and on other days all the pains seemed to concentrate in his internal body muscles. He added that he had been to many doctors who were unable to diagnose his problem. My patient was a tough businessman engaged in the meat trade in a big way.

After listening to his story, I proceeded to clean down his aura preparatory to sending healing energies to the appropriate parts of the body as I was directed. To my astonishment, the energies bounced back at me! There was a complete tensile steel barrier debarring the healing energies from acting. I was confused. Suddenly, I heard myself blurting out,

"Did anybody ever put a curse on you?" With a surprised look on his face he confirmed that such a thing had happened. He added with venom, "and I cursed the man back!"

I found myself telling him that, until such time as he withdrew his curse on his business competitor and his opposition did the same, he would be plagued with his condition all of his life. He looked at me as if I had two heads. Snarling at what I suggested and stating categorically it was out of the question. He left the clinic abruptly. At the same time leaving me with much food for thought.

As I understand it, if a person puts a curse on another, ultimately the curse comes back to the initiator! Every action has an equal and opposite reaction. As regards the case with which I had to contend, both parties had put a curse on each other! I wonder to this day what was the final outcome. Did one

"Poor Ren"

neutralise the other or both continue to suffer the consequences?

Coming nearer to home, I had an aunt named Irene Cooney - affectionately known as Ren. She was a beautiful baby [see photograph] born in the year 1912, and developed into a lovely young girl, vivacious, kind, affectionate and very intelligent.

One day, when she was twelve years old, she and her mother were shopping in the centre of the city. Suddenly from one of the side streets a thin tall gaunt woman wearing a long black cape approached them. She had all the appearance of a witch complete with a pointed nose. All she was short of was the proverbial broomstick! Completely taken aback, my aunt and her mother stood transfixed. Pointing a long boney forefinger at Irene, the woman said to my grandmother in a squeaky voice, "That child is too beautiful to go through life so pretty. I will see that she does not."

She placed a curse on my aunt. From that day onwards "poor Ren", as she became known, went through a litany of accidents and happenings of all kinds during her sixty-two years on Earth.

One minute the witch was there and the next moment seemed to disappear into thin air. One week after this weird experience poor Ren fell from a milk cart and flattened her nose into her face. She had barely recovered from the surgery, which left her so disfigured, when she fell and split her forehead wide open. Worse was to follow. Disregarding many minor mishaps, all of which were painful, one day while playing with other girls she tripped over a skipping rope and broke her kneecap. From this she developed poliomyelitis. Two years later she contracted the disease in her other leg.

The years rolled by and Irene did her best to make as much of life as she could. She could just about walk with the aid of two sticks. We all loved poor Ren and did whatever we could to see that she was involved in family activities. She seldom complained but suffered in silence. She knew the names and melodies of virtually all composers of any piece of classical music she heard on the radio *even though she never had any musical training!* She had a passion for crosswords and puzzles of all kinds. Her prime hobby was to know every single thing there was to be known about film stars the world over. It was the year 1935 and in those days it was common to purchase two newspapers a day, "The Cork Examiner" and the English publication "The Daily Mail". The latter publication had huge sales and often ran competitions with the princely sum of £1,000 as top prize.

In 1935 this was a colossal sum of money and indeed hard to visualise. One day this huge prize was offered to any reader who could name a given film star just by recognising their eyes. This competition was right up poor Ren's street. But it was no easy competition. First of all one had to purchase a jigsaw puzzle containing nearly one thousand pieces. This had to be assembled - a mammoth job - and all the eyes depicted had to be ciphered to ascertain which pair of eyes belonged to which film star. The puzzle was duly ordered and everyone fretted waiting for the package to arrive from England. At last it came to hand. Could the jigsaw puzzle be assembled in time?

All the family and friends were pressed into service. We worked through the night hour after hour and it seemed like a lifetime before bits and pieces of the puzzle began to come together. Two days and two nights later the job was done and poor Ren went to work deciphering all the different eyes. It took days for everyone to recover from the Herculean task but we basked in the knowledge of a job well done.

At last the entry was ready for posting. My Uncle Tom, poor Ren's brother, was given the task of seeing it safely dispatched. To this day I still see him putting the entry into an inside pocket of his jacket. Two weeks later the results were published. To the chagrin of all, there was no outright winner.

A bomb seemed to explode when poor Ren screamed at the top of her voice,

"My entry was one hundred percent correct!" We were taken aback and came to the conclusion that it was either of two things: the promoters had slipped up or that the entry did not reach its destination by the deadline set. All eyes turned in the direction of Uncle Tom. His blanched face told the whole story. He had forgotten to post the entry, which was still in his inside pocket! Out of all the thousands upon thousands of entries poor Ren was the ONLY competitor with an all-correct solution! From that day onwards never again did she go to a cinema and all interest in film stars vanished like virgin snow. The curse was still working. She was twenty-four years of age.

Living with her father and mother up to the time of her father's death, she attended a secretarial course. Her father [Granddad Cooney of the Fairyland story] was a chronic asthmatic and he finally succumbed at the age of 73. With his army pension terminated and poor Ren unable to secure any permanent position, finance was at a premium. As luck would have it, an old bachelor living on his own in a small terraced house was seeking a housekeeper. Poor Ren and her mother took on the job and in return were offered accommodation and food. This arrangement carried on until the death of the owner of the small house. They were facing eviction when my father came to the rescue, raised some money and bought the house thereby becoming their landlord! He really could not afford to do this, but desperate diseases require desperate cures. In those days the amount of money involved in today's terms was laughable, but not so in those sparse and difficult times.

Concerning my grandfather's illness, an on-going bill remained with a local pharmacy. My grandmother was doing her best to pay it off in dribs and drabs. The Irish Hospitals Sweepstake was very popular in those days but the chance of winning anything was millions to one. A small huckster's shop had an agency for the sweepstakes and one day another aunt of mine bought an eighth share in a ticket for Granny Cooney. Lo and behold and against all the odds it was drawn in one of the many small consolation prizes and netted £25. This was like the proverbial manna from heaven and went a long way in helping to reduce the medical debt. Three months later my aunt bought a similar share of a ticket in the same tiny shop. Again Lady Luck turned up trumps and provided a further £25. This was more than ample to clear the outstanding debt. The third time she attempted the same feat she found that the shop had closed down!

With the war being waged, rationing in full force and fuel in short supply, things just became much too difficult. Poor Ren and her mother [Granny] had to move to the house in which I was born and where Granny passed away. My mother, being a widow, was left with her sister who was progressing downhill rapidly. Poor Ren's physical body was unable to bear all that was happening to it. She became incontinent, confined to a wheelchair and the whole situation was just appalling.

I sought help from the authorities and found myself caught between two sections of local government who were at loggerheads. My misfortunate aunt was the pawn used in the fray! I decided to go to the top so I sought a meeting with the Lord Mayor of Cork. He had given Trojan service to the afflicted and was responsible for the setting up of the Cork Polio and General After-Care Association. In common with many others, I worked tirelessly for one year raising funds not only in Ireland but England as well.

As if by magic, all practical problems disappeared. Poor Ren found herself in the Cheshire Home in Tivoli. It was very difficult to persuade her that leaving the apparent security of my mother's small house was for the best. The break was made and it was only a short time before she settled in and found herself with friends, themselves in worse states than herself. Well-versed and after the Bible, a dictionary was her next essential reading. She wrote letters for other inmates, joined in the fun, the parties and outings that were arranged. It was like one big happy family. Every Tuesday without fail I collected poor Ren and brought her to my mother's home for lunch.

My mother, having learned to drive a car at the age of 65, set off in a 127 Fiat car each Tuesday afternoon with poor Ren, taking their packet of sandwiches and flask of tea with them to "Cat Dell" or "Fairy Grove"- names given by them both to little places they visited together. A Guardian Angel was at the wheel at all times otherwise they would never have arrived at their chosen destination or made a safe return journey. Late that evening I would collect poor Ren and take her back to the Cheshire Home. Yes, she used the word "home" for it was here that she had found her forte in life. Her life of pain, anguish, disappointment, painful illnesses, trials of all sorts, all of which afforded her the opportunity to set an example and help to so many others.

In common with many bizarre things in the Parfrey/Cooney clan, poor Ren when able would attend ceremonies at different churches. To a degree, she followed the music rather than the ritual. So far as the Cheshire Home was concerned she was looked upon as a Catholic with which she had no problem, but she had never been received into the Catholic Church. Every Sunday a priest attended the home to serve Mass. He was a kind and considerate man and knew how to deal with all the inmates with their different problems and concepts. One particular Sunday, the usual priest was ill and a young man came in his stead. He was of the fire-and-brimstone brigade and told the inmates that their respective problems were due to past omissions and sins.

Poor Ren took this to heart in a big way and searched in anguish for the sins that she was purported to have committed to warrant a life of pain and suffering. At this time her physical health had deteriorated to an alarming degree. Amongst other complaints she was suffering from were hiatus hernia, gall stones, diverticulitis, cancer of the uterus, kidney failure, excessive losses of blood which necessitated constant blood transfusions. The list was endless.

Her death certificate lists eight causes of death. Poor Ren was frightened to die. We prayed with all our might that she would pass to the world of Spirit. One night she experienced the frightening never-to-be-forgotten sound of the Banshee (the fairy woman, harbinger of death) outside her bedroom window. Her Soul at last had freedom to leave the wreck of a once beautiful body, cursed by some unknown person. Poor Ren was buried in the Catholic side of St. Fin Barre's cemetery although she had never been a member of that faith. Spiritually she was wise far beyond our and her years. I have endeavoured to follow her example.

After the obsequies, I went to collect her few possessions. In 62 years she had accumulated a dictionary, a Rosary Beads, a poem or two she had written and a few prayer cards. Total value? Probably under €4.00.

Poor Ren was a very advanced soul. I thank God for her being my aunt.

Part Two

Part Two

Chapter 01

THE PSYCHIC WORLD AROUND US!

We come to this part of my book where we have to say a few words about Psychics.

Now, when we come to this subject and we ask the ordinary man or woman in the street if they know anything about the subject, the chances are that their retort will be,

"Surely, you don't believe that rubbish!"

Press the subject further and inquire as to what they have read about the subject and one draws a blank! A further question, "Did you ever speak to anyone that has had a psychic experience?" and, again, the answer will, invariably be, "No". It is amazing how ignorant people can be.

The fact of the matter is that everyone has an interest in the subject without realising it! Just look at the many people that dread the number 13! There are those who are afraid to walk under a ladder or open an umbrella in the house! The breaking of a mirror - seven year's bad luck! What about the Ace of Spades - the Death Card? Throwing salt over one's shoulder. The list is endless. Again, you are probably one of the countless millions that read the Horoscopes in the daily papers and glossy magazines.

People love ghost stories or hearing about haunted houses or places. Again, people flock to fortune-tellers or palmists. All of the foregoing superstitions etc., and countless others come under the heading of "Psychics". Adding further leaves to our "Psychic Tree" we may include Clairvoyance, Clairaudience, Clairsentience, Astral Projection, Numerology, Crystal Gazing, Psychometry, Divination of all kinds, Precognitive Dreams, the use and misuse of Ouija Boards and the "Spirit Glass'. From a life time of study of the subject I have found that "The Psychic Tree:" [which in reality is ourselves!] comprises of a minimum of 77 leaves which, in turn, are connected to the twigs which are connected to the branches and thence eventually connect with the tree itself, viz. OURSELVES!

The truth of the matter is that we are ALL psychic for what we are talking about is something that is NATURAL! The gross material way in which most of us live our lives dims our personal psychic spark to such an extent that we are, in most cases, unaware of our other sensitivities far and away beyond the conventional five of sight, hearing, taste, smell and touch! On this score, Dr. Deepak Chopra states we have an ADDITIONAL thirteen senses. I have come to KNOW that Psychics are the tools of Spirit! In consequence, the more one strives to develop one's psychic abilities the greater the instrument one can become to serve the CREATOR by helping one's fellow human being.

The "Psychic World" is often looked upon by many as being "Supernatural." To my mind the word is a misnomer which could be deemed the night sky of our minds, the shadow side of our mental daylight of reason and hard fact. Like the night, it contains mystery, beauty, enchantment and horror. It has a powerful attraction and all, in one way or another, are involved in it.

We often talk about the modern age as a time of materialism, reason, technical and scientific advance but the supernatural, which I like to refer to as "super-normal", still plays a vital part in the world in which we live.

Many people, still, are religious. Many people still believe in Astrology, Palmistry, Cartomancy, Crystal Gazing and any of the other seventy-seven "leaves" that go to constitute the "Psychic Tree." It is nigh impossible to live for very long without acquiring an interest, however reluctantly, in the matter of life after death and each of our minds has its shadow side where old terrors mingle with old truths!

The Supernormal surrounds us at many different levels; in churches, synagogues, mosques; in dreams, in the antiseptic corridors of Parapsychology laboratories where experimenters test the strange powers of the mind; in experiences induced by drugs; in newspaper reports on witchcraft, the black arts and the desecration of churches; on poltergeist activity and exorcisms; in all forms of Healing, in the increasing interest in ancient religions and magic.

In the history of occultism in the West the last 150 years has been the most flourishing period since the 17th century. We have seen the rise of modern study in comparative religion, the modern interpretation of mythology, the attempts to test objectively such phenomena as ghosts and telepathy and the application of modern psychology to belief about the psychic world in general.

In the following chapters I will relate some of the experiences that I had and it is up to you, the reader, to accept or reject what happened. In the final analysis I do not really care what you think, for to me it WAS. But reality to one person can be the complete opposite to another.

On the matter of "Reality" I have come to the conclusion that it is, in fact an illusion! The illusion being so great we take it to be reality! But more on this subject later on.

You know, writing this book is much more difficult than I thought it would be. I am no great writer so my story is being written rather as a letter to all and sundry and perhaps in this way it will have more effect. The biggest problem is to know where to start! I can hear you saying, "Well, start from the beginning", and that is what I have tried to do.

If you have stuck it so far, you will have read the first portion of my book which dealt with my early life and I can tell you now if that infamous Fairy Godmother came back this moment and said, "I can wave a magic wand and put you back fifty years or put you forward fifty years!" My reply would be, "Put me forward fifty years as fast as you can!" And so, I better start writing about the many and varied experiences, as distinct from the third part of the book, that deals with the most important part of my life which was dedicated to acting as a channel for Healing.

Chapter 02

PSYCHIC INHERITANCE

In my own life I was blessed [some may say "plagued"] in that both sides of my family were psychic. The earliest example of this that I can recall with accuracy was the case of my Grandmother on my mother's side. Granny Cooney was her name and I loved her deeply. She was an English woman and married my Grand-father, who was Irish and served in the British Army.

To complicate things further, Granny Cooney was an Anglican and my Grand-father was a Roman Catholic. Her father objected to the marriage, not on religious grounds, but he felt, and I quote, "His daughter was marrying beneath her station!" He had a small Hatter's business in London and felt that his daughter was worthy of something better. However, they married and came to live in the British Barracks in a little place called Crinkle, just two miles outside of Birr, Co. Offaly, Ireland.

One day, Granny was resting in her bedroom, [this was in 1895 AD] when she was expecting the birth of my mother, Eileen. The curtains were drawn as she rested and at 3.00p.m., Granny, half asleep and half awake, became conscious of her father standing beside her! From the time of their marriage, her father had never spoken to her and then, suddenly, in that bedroom in the barracks in Crinkle, here was her father standing beside her at 3.00p.m.in the afternoon! He was REAL and said, "Annie, will you forgive me?" In a little bemused state she replied, "Of course, Dad, I forgive you. With that he disappeared!

Many hours later she received a telegraphic message to the effect that her father had passed away precisely at 3.00p.m. that same day! He had a fistula in his rectum and refused to undergo the operation that would save his life!

(Around 1898 Grand-dad Cooney was transferred to Collins Barracks in Cork and he and my grandmother, took up residence at 22, Alexandra Villas, St. Luke's, on the north side of the city.)

Granny Cooney was a good and loving person and would help everyone that came her way. Around this time there were numerous Indians [India] who eked out an existence by selling shoe laces and other such cheap items from door to door! One day, in the year 1899 one of these poor traders called to the house and asked my Grand-mother to buy some of his wares. She took pity on him, as indeed was her want, and took him into the kitchen where she fed him with tea and sandwiches. My Grandmother always believed in the sharing with others that which she had herself.

As he left the house, he pressed a gift into her hand which turned out to be a small Crystal Ball which she placed on the hall table. At that time, her brother was with the British Army in South Africa fighting in the Boer War.

One day as Granny walked past the crystal it "lit" up and she "saw" her brother who was an officer in the British Army being assassinated by a Boer! Two days later she received a telegraphic message to the effect that her brother had been killed just the moment that she saw it in the Crystal!

This experience frightened her as one can imagine and she packed the crystal away.

Her youngest son, Tom [my uncle, affectionately known as "Custard Pants"] was in the British Army as a young bands-man. He was sent to the trenches in Flanders around 1915/1916. His chances of survival were pretty small and one day Granny took out the crystal ball and it suddenly "glowed". Through the glow she could see my Uncle Tom pacing up and down some muddy trench. Immediately she wrote a letter to her son asking him what he had been doing or experiencing at that precise moment. Some weeks letter she received a letter through the Army Postal Service advising her that precisely at the time she "saw" him in the crystal he had been pacing up and down the trench!

I never heard anything else about the crystal and have no idea to this day what became of it.

Shortly after this, one day, my Uncle Tom had, with so many others, to 'go over the top!' I cannot imagine the fear that all those young men experienced as they faced the wrath of withering machine gun fire with the big guns in the rear adding to the carnage. In a very short time Uncle Tom was blown into a shell hole! Battered and barely conscious, he crawled out of the hole only to be shot at by a German soldier. The bullet went through his left wrist! At the same time another shell exploded and once more he was blown into a shell hole.

He lay there, battered and bleeding, blinded by the shock. Somehow or other he crawled out. An "Old Sweat" [a professional soldier] miraculously came to his aid! "Lay your good arm on my shoulder and I will lead you to a first-aid post", he commanded. He led my uncle through "No-man's Land." With machine-gun fire, shells exploding, mud, parts of blown-up soldiers lying all around him [fortunately he could not see the carnage] he arrived at the first-aid post where he was treated. When he had recovered to some degree, he asked one of the orderlies if he could thank the old soldier that had brought him to apparent safety. Looking at him queerly, he was informed that he came into the first-aid station ON HIS OWN - there had been NO old soldier to guide him to safety!

Uncle Tom lived to be 94 years of age and his birthday was the same date of mine, viz. 23rd September. He never drank alcohol or smoked in his life. He often told me the story, adding that he was sent back far from the front line to a hospital where, believe it or not, surgeons inserted rabbit nerves to do duty in place of those that had been damaged by the bullet! I often saw the hole that was in his wrist as he played the piano stretching his right hand as far as he could to strengthen the muscles in his hand and fingers.

I have often heard the Story of "The Old Soldier". Was it his Guardian Angel or some Spirit that came to his aid? We will never know but Uncle Tom's experience fits in, perfectly, with all that went on in our family.

Chapter 3

SPIRIT COMMUNICATION.

This is going to be a long chapter for what I am endeavouring to compress into a few pages of a book would, itself, comprise a book on its own! It is a subject of unique importance and vital for everyone without exception!

It is nigh impossible to cover the whole gambit of spirit communication, and all I can do is to touch, lightly, on one or two points, but even these should be more than adequate to stimulate animated discussion.

The reader must bear with the fact that what I write must be "assumed" to be the truth as I see it, pending one's own individual research into this fascinating and absorbing subject.

We are all familiar with the "Here" but it is the mystery of the "Hereafter" that takes pride of place. After all, at some time or other we are all going to go there whether we like it or not!

What is the other world like?

Do we continue to live on?

The logical thing to do is to listen to what those who live there have to tell us!

Those that live in the Spirit World are NOT dead! From time immemorial, communication from the World of Spirit has been received by people who are commonly called "Mediums." As an aside, the Bible, both the Old and New Testaments, is full of accounts of Spirit communication).

A Medium is usually described as an agent or intermediary through whom communication may be transmitted between the physical and spiritual worlds. Precisely what constitutes a medium is not known [but I stand to be corrected on this point]. He or she differs from others in that they have super-normal faculties, due, apparently, to a condition of semi-freedom or detachment of the subconscious mind or spirit which enables it on occasion, to obtain knowledge of external things otherwise than by the usual sense organs. Not all mediums have the same degree of attunement.

I should state at this point that there is a huge difference between a person that is a Medium and a person that is a good Psychic! A Medium possesses psychic ability. A Psychic does not but often claims to do so! A Medium depends, entirely on their "Spirit Control" found in the Throat Chackra while a Psychic is often extremely good at "reading" the Aura of a person.

In my opinion, there are many good Psychics and far less good Mediums!

An example of what I am trying to convey can be illustrated by the following hypothetical sitting.

The Psychic, who can genuinely feel that he/she has Mediumistic abilities says to the sitter,

> "I have here, a man about 70 years of age.   He is Grey-haired and his hair is closely cropped.   He has a club foot!"

> "Yes, yes," exclaims the sitter,

> "That is my Uncle Tom, you describe him graphically."

At this point the sitter should ask of the Psychic/Medium,

> "What is my Uncle Tom's second name?" and in ninety-nine cases out of a hundred back will come the reply,

> "I am afraid he does not give me that!"   The retort should be,

> "Well, you are no way in touch with my uncle for he would certainly know his own second name!"

A trained Medium has to learn to divide the mind into three sections.   The "front" is the part that is used for speaking to those attending an open demonstration, the "back" of the mind is used as a receiver, the information being directed by the Medium's Controlling Spirit, while the "centre" of the mind is where the information is compiled and then given to the person in the audience who is the actual recipient. It is important to know that Spirit ALWAYS COMES WITH THE MESSAGE PREPARED. An inexperienced Medium can often embellish an actual message with thoughts, which are coming from the Ego and NOT from Spirit.

The subconscious mind of a Medium possesses psychic receptivity, i.e. it is accessible to instruction from foreign spirits, discarnate or incarnate, which can impress, instruct on matters of which he or she knows nothing and also can produce Automatic Writing. The influence may be compelling or otherwise. In the latter case it is known as "inspiration." Very many painters, poets, musicians, scientists and inventors owe their best work to direct inspiration, and have recognised the fact and admitted it to be so. The suggestion that Shakespeare was an inspirational medium would explain the mystery of his learned writings, for he was un-travelled and practically uneducated!

One cannot command of Spirit. All communication comes FROM Spirit.

From time immemorial there has been communication from the Spirit world to the Physical. The Bible is full of many accounts. One such episode is well worth reading, that of King Saul who sought the help of Samson after his passing. The portion to read is First Book of Samuel, Chapter 28! This illustrates what I have said, we cannot COMMAND of Spirit!

TAILPIECE

It is a truism that a prophet is not without honour save in his or her own country. This is well and truly borne out in the case of Cork woman, Geraldine Cummins.

She came from a wellknown family that lived in the Glanmire area early in the 20th century. Her brother was Dr. Bob Cummins who was legendary in providing medical help to the poor of Cork. Geraldine was a Suffragette and around the year 1918 she fought for the right of women to vote in parliamentary elections. She went so far as to chain herself to railings in the Cork suburb of Blackpool and I think was actually force-fed when she went on hunger strike.

She possessed a most amazing ability in the field of Automatic Writing through her Spirit Guide named Astor. With the help of this guide she wrote a large number of books, including "Paul of Tarsus," "Swan on a Black Sea" and "The Fate of Colonel Fawcett" which was last printed in 1940. There were numerous other books together with an amazing compilation of papers containing information from the World of Spirit. She was very famous and in 1947 was presented with "The Spiritualist of the Year" award. On her death she bequeathed to the city of her birth – Cork – no less than thirteen tea-chests, full to the brim with a huge selection of of her books, both published and unpublished.

All of this priceless material is housed at the Cork Archives Institute centred at Blackpool, Cork 3. Tel: 021-4505886. I doubt if there is more than a dozen Corkonians who are aware of this deep well of information right on their proverbial doorstep!

If you wish to get an idea of the amount of information available on Geraldine Cummins, just enter 'Geraldine Cummins' into Google on your computer.

Part Two

Chapter 4

EARLY PERSONAL EXPERIENCES:

As far back as I can remember there was always the feeling that we were close to those that had departed this life. My Grandmothers on both sides of my family were quite psychic as indeed were other members of the family.

In August 1976, my aunt Amelia Keziah Turpin [my father's sister] wrote to me and I quote her letter:

"Grandmother and Grandfather Parfrey died in this house [86, Hibernian Buildings, Albert Road, Cork]. My mother was staying up one night with my Grandmother Parfrey who was very ill, when she said she heard Grandfather Parfrey who used to shuffle along, coming up to the bed and she (Grandmother) said, "Fred, I am coming." When she looked, Grandmother was dead! When my mother's first child, Fred, two years of age, was in a cradle by the bed, sick, my mother woke and said to my father, "Fred is dead! I just saw my father come and take him out of the cot!" I thought you would be interested, so my mother must have been like you!

"Strange" incidents such as this were taken as being quite normal in my family. [What is 'normal' you may well ask?].

When I was a youngster, every Monday evening I went down to Granny Parfrey for my tea. Her husband, my Grandfather, died in 1932 and I fondly remember his visits to my home when Dad would show him what was growing in the garden. Our garden produce kept us in vegetables and, as my grand-parents did not have a garden, they delighted in ours.

After tea, Granny would give both my cousin, Billy Turpin and me one shilling   That was a lot of money way back in the thirties and, on reflection, I am sure that Granny found it left her short for the week!   Billy and I would always go to the cinema which cost nine pence for a long evening show.   Afterwards we were able to buy a huge bag of French fries each for one penny!   The remaining penny was used for the bus fare home.

Granny had a friend - we'll call her Ann Thornton.   Ann would often be visiting on a Monday.   She was a very friendly person, and to me, quite old. She had a very distinct way of speaking so that her voice sounded shaky and went up and down slowly. At times I wondered if it was her voice at all! She wore a battered old hat and her face sported a number of long hairs. She was quite psychic and her forte was reading the tea leaves!   Never would she drink tea from a cup!   It always had to be from a slop bowl!

Many a time I saw Ann reading the dregs of the tea leaves left in one's cup. How she did it I really do not know, but she could "see" shapes from which she could make deductions and each of the tea leaves seemed to tell her a separate story. When compiled into one these stories could turn out to be a saga.   The number of times her predictions were correct was astonishing. At that early age I was just fascinated.   The thing I recall the most is her greeting on seeing me.   In her peculiar voice she would exclaim,

"Well, Willie, you have got a fine looking boy, God bless you."

I can remember that voice to this day which is in the month of October, 2004!

Christmas Eve was always something special.   We visited Granny Parfrey and the family.   The house was tiny but that did not deter our enjoyment. In the small front room was the large traditional Christmas candle.   Home-made Christmas decorations festooned the small rooms and hallway epitomising the spirit of the feast of good cheer.

For my sister and I, it was imperative that we be home in bed before midnight, otherwise we would miss the visit of Santa Claus.   There would be all sorts of stories told many of which related to ghosts and strange happenings!

I was about ten years old when my mother's father, Grand-dad Cooney died. About a year after his passing there was quite an extraordinary happening.

One day there was a knock at the front door. A man stood there and said that he had a message for my mother from her deceased father! Though my Mother was a little taken aback, the man's demeanour made it quite obvious that he was sincere. He was invited into the house. I was there as he entered our small sitting-room. As soon as he crossed the threshold, the lid of the piano banged shut. Then a picture fell off the wall!

He sat down and over a cup of tea and, told an extraordinary story.

He went on to explain that he was very interested in Mediumship and attended a Development Circle on a weekly basis in London. At one of the sittings Grandfather Cooney came through and "spoke" to this man asking him if he would be prepared to bring a message of love and comfort to his daughter, Eileen Cooney [my mother]. The only further information relayed was that his daughter lived in Cork city!

With this flimsy bit of information that man [whose name I do not know] travelled to Fishguard and sailed on the "Innisfallen" to Cork where the next morning, he disembarked at Penrose Quay. He had never been in Ireland, let alone Cork, in his entire life and did not know where to start to find my mother.

At the foot of Summerhill, a short distance from Penrose Quay, he entered Cudmore's shop and said to one of the girls serving behind the counter,

"I have never been in Cork before and I am trying to find a woman named Eileen Cooney. I do not even know if she is single or not!"

Believe it or believe it not one of the assistants said,

"I knew a Cooney family that lived at 22, Alexandra Villas, St. Lukes."

Thanking the assistant and armed with directions he arrived at the address, just over a mile away from the shop. He knocked on the door of number twenty-two and enquired of the lady who answered his knock if she knew anything of the Cooney family. He was told that the lady had no idea. By a coincidence [in fact there is NO such thing as a coincidence] the woman who lived next door was of the Ryan family who had been there for generations. Overhearing the conversation, Mrs. Ryan told the man from London that my mother was married and that her name was Eileen Parfrey. She was also able to give him the home address which was 16, Vincent View, College Road, Cork.

Within the space of two hours the anonymous man from London, who had never been to Cork in his life, who neither knew whether my mother was married nor where she lived, was guided to our home!

The conversation with my mother (which I was not privy to) went on for a couple of hours, after which the man left and returned to England on the "Innisfallen" that night. He was never heard of again!

This was the kind of world I grew up in. From a very early age, I was conscious of the World of Spirit.

In September, 1944 I left home to take up a position in Cahir, Co. Tipperary. It was quite a wrench leaving my parents and my sister Eileen and the comfort of my small home to take up residence in a gaunt three storied lodging house in which some rooms had electricity and others none. ["Bleak House" was only trotting after it!] My sparse room was at the top of the house and was illuminated by a small oil lamp. There were no curtains, simply wooden shutters. As well as a hard sheet-less bed there was a small wardrobe and a dressing table upon which stood my cheap alarm clock.

One evening in May 1946 I was in my room and the evening sunlight was streaming through the window, giving a warm glow inside. All was quiet in the room and the only sound to permeate the silence was the tick tick of the clock. Having nothing else to do, I started to sort out a pile of cards I had received the previous year for my birthday and Christmas. There I sat on the floor going through them all when suddenly the clock stopped ticking! I heard my Grandmother [on my mother's side] speak, quite distinctly and say,

172

"We are all very happy here, we are all very happy here. We send our love, we send our love, we are very happy here!"

Immediately the clock started to tick loudly once again!

I was not frightened but instead felt this wonderful sense of love. I looked at the card I was holding - IT WAS THE LAST CARD I RECEIVED FROM GRANNY COONEY BEFORE SHE HAD PASSED TO THE WORLD OF SPIRIT!

I never felt at ease in that house and after spending over two years of my life there, I was glad to leave. The house had a strange feeling about it and I often had to pluck up courage to mount the stairs in the dark to reach my bedroom.

During my stay there I had two terrifying experiences. The person whose job I had taken over had been suffering from cancer and died of the disease a few months previously. He was a man in his early forties and, as luck would have it, before his marriage he had actually lived in "Bleak House" where he occupied the same bedroom I had been allotted! I had never met the man but I had a distinct uneasy feeling every night I went to bed.

One night I returned to the "digs" around 10.30 p.m. and "ran the gauntlet" of the dark stairs. I went to turn the knob of my bedroom door but it would not move. As none of the rooms in the building had a door key, I knew that the door was not locked! Try as I might I could not open it. In the end I gave up and knocked on the bedroom door of another lodger, George. George did not take too kindly to being awakened and when I told him that I could not open my bedroom door he thought that I had been drinking. Grumbling to himself he put his hand on the door knob and it opened without a hitch! He went back to his room as I lit my small oil lamp and sat on my bed wondering if I had been having a dizzy spell!

As I thought the matter over I got the distinct impression that my predecessor resented my being appointed to his position and, what's more, occupying what had been his room for a number of years! I climbed into bed and drew the blankets around me [we were not given the luxury of sheets], turned out my light and began to settle down. I must have been asleep for over two hours lying on my back when suddenly I felt as if a heavy-set person was lying on top of me! The pressure mounted and literally I had to struggle and fight off my ghostly adversary. Shaking with fear and my hands trembling, I attempted to strike a match to light the lamp. On the third attempt I managed to do so and the warm glow coming from the candlewick pushed back those dark shadows. It was impossible for me to go to sleep after the episode so I lay awake, more than ever convinced that my surmise was correct.

For many a night afterwards, I made a point to keep my oil lamp burning all the time. One night I decided to sleep in the dark and on that very night I was "attacked" by the same force!

That finished it and I set about searching for another place in which to live.

Chapter 5

Further Experiences

I was a young teenager when I first encountered "The Spirit Glass." "The Spirit Glass" does duty for an Ouija Board or Planchette used in contacting those in the World of Spirit. From my experience, fooling around with these means of communication while not knowing what one is doing can bring untold problems for those involved. Often this very serious subject is looked upon as a party game. Such was the case where I was concerned.

I had been invited to a party in a private house in Cork and there were about ten people of my own age in the group. During the evening, after we had eaten our fill, the mother of my friend who had invited me took over. As part of the night's entertainment she was going to try to make contact with spirits. I thought this was hilarious and watched as she set out the letters of the alphabet on a polished table to form a large circle. On the left side of the circle was placed a card with the word "No" and on the right a card with the word "Yes."

We all sat around the large table as our hostess placed an inverted tumbler glass smack in the middle of the circle. She then placed the forefinger of her right hand on the glass asking one of the onlookers to do the same.

"Is there a spirit there?" she inquired.

Again, "Is there a spirit there?"

She repeated the question quite a number of times. There was giggling going on when suddenly the glass began to move! We looked on in amazement as slowly and surely the glass moved over to the right side and stopped at the word "Yes." We were dumbfounded.

"What is your name?" was the next question and slowly but surely the glass moved from letter to letter spelling out a name. Though astonished I was full sure that our hostess was directing the glass along herself. It took ages for a full message to come through which was to the effect that the communicator had come from Cork but lost his life in South America round about the year 1766.

Each of us was given the opportunity to place our finger on the glass and when it came to my turn, to my astonishment, I felt a force of some kind move down my right arm and the glass moved at a much faster speed. I was informed that I had a lot of psychic energy but at that time I did not understand what it was.

About an hour later, our hostess said,

"Now, watch what will happen when I castigate the Spirit".

She started to ridicule the Spirit and as she did so the glass started to move around the table at an enormous rate, BY ITSELF!!! Suddenly, it jumped off the table and stayed suspended in the air near the ceiling for about three seconds, when an invisible hand hurtled it across the room where it broke into a thousand pieces in the corner! We were frightened out of our wits and the party ended there and then!

For days and weeks I could not get the experience out of my head. Despite the scare, I started to experiment at home but received a message to the effect that I should desist and this I did on the spot.

Many years later I was discussing the episode with a young man whom I knew well, and who had psychic abilities, let's call him Jack. He told me of his frightening experience with an Ouija Board. ["Oui" is the French word for "Yes" and "Ja" is the German word for "Yes" so one could call it a "Yes-Yes Board." The board also contains numbers, and words such as "goodbye" and comes equipped with a triangular cursor standing on three legs embracing a small circular magnifying glass so that one could see the letters clearly]. Believe it or not these dangerous items were sold in shops as toys! They were ultimately taken off the shelves because of the effect they had on many people!

Jack related his story. One evening he and a companion were experimenting with an Ouija Board and were getting nowhere. The letters being spelled out made no sense. (It should be noted that messages can come in ANY language as well as English and indeed messages may come with spelling reversed). History repeated itself when the two got fed-up and decided to call the Spirit names. The cursor went mad! They gave up and retired to the bedroom of my friend who lived with his elderly mother.

There was a sofa in the room and Jack's friend sat on it, while Jack himself sat on a chair. Just as the guy on the sofa had picked up his guitar to strum a few notes, the bedroom door slammed shut! Next, the lights in the room went out so that the room was only dimly lit by a street-light. Suddenly, the street-light went out and the two companions found themselves in stygian darkness. Both were sure that there had been a major power failure, but such was not the case. To steady himself, Jack ran his hands down the legs of the chair and just when he should have touched the floor, to his utter consternation there was nothing!

He shouted to his companion but could not utter any sound. His mouth felt as if it was stuffed with cotton wool! He sat transfixed when suddenly in the pitch darkness a big red eye was staring at him! The eye rushed towards him getting bigger and bigger until it was close to his face! Then, just as quickly, it receded at speed, only to come towards him once again! Back and forth it went for what appeared to be an eternity. Just as Jack was about to go unconscious, the street-light came back on, followed by the lights in the room. He looked across the room and there sat his friend absolutely ashen and still clutching the guitar. He too had undergone the same terrifying experience! Without saying a word they ran from the room downstairs to the kitchen where they found the lady of the house fast asleep in front of the TV. Five hours had elapsed!

What could be the explanation one may well ask? In reality there is NO answer but it is an example of what can happen when a person is so foolish to go where angels fear to tread.

Chapter 06

ON THE MATTER OF APPORTS

Seeking out charlatans does nothing to help those who are genuine! People who KNOW the truth as they understand it are ridiculed and, indeed hounded, to such a degree that they keep their mouths shut and say nothing This is the easy way out. But there are others, like myself, who are pre pared to tell the truth as THEY understand the truth to be! There is an old saying, and a true one at that, which I quote, 'The speed of a convoy is based in direct proportion to the speed of the slowest ship!'

Shakespeare put it another way when he wrote, 'Some are born great; some achieve greatness and some have greatness thrust upon them!'

I will take the liberty to paraphrase this quote in the following manner "Some are born psychic, some achieve psychism ad some have psychism thrust upon them!" This epitomises the writer!

Some of you may know of the word "Apport" and understand to what it per tains. The Concise Oxford Dictionary defines the word as follows: "The production of material objects by supposedly occult means at a séance. An object so produced."

In the cases I am about to relate, there was no séance!

Years ago, when I was the MD of a company in Cork, those in the world of Spirit came to my aid. It was a dirty and very wet Friday night when I closed up both of the premises for the week. Due to persistent break-in attempts, the main shop was like Fort Knox, with numerous locks and bul let-proof glass. I went to lock the premises next door and as I went to turn the key in the lock, laid my soft leather briefcase on the window ledge.

The weather was atrocious and I had offered a lift home to one of my employees who was already sitting in the car. With water running down my neck I got into the car and sped away, completely forgetting my briefcase. It was only as I was having my evening meal that I remembered it. Such a shock it gave me that it was missing. It was not the value of the briefcase that concerned me, but what it contained.

I had collected very important papers dealing with company plans and projections, which would have been a gift for my opposition. As I was due to send a final report to head office on the following Monday, I had intended working on these over the weekend. To make matters worse, THERE WERE NO DUPLICATES!

Panic stricken, I drove at speed into town but I need hardly tell you the brief case was gone!   I went to the police and told them what had happened. They asked me had there been any money in the case. I replied £30.00.

"In that case," came the reply, " in all probability those that took the briefcase would be interested in the money only and the briefcase would have been thrown away."

I was promised that they would give the whole district a going over but would concentrate on one particular area. I went home and waited anxiously for a telephone call, but none came.   During the following three hours I telephoned police headquarters but there was no news.

On the off-chance, I visited the employee I had driven home and asked her to recall precisely what I had done before driving off. She told me that due to the heavy downpour she had not been able to see clearly, but could recall me leaving the briefcase on the window ledge. That was enough for me!

I spent a sleepless night, tossing, turning and going over the implications of what was going to happen when I reported that the documents were gone!

Saturday dawned and all I could think about was Monday morning looming and what I was going to do.   I think I must have had a brainstorm or something, for I persisted in going into the office two, three or four times in addition to telephoning the police.   I actually started to search my home - every nook and cranny, under the stairs and up in the attic. It was the antics of someone not right in the head.

Another sleepless night and on Sunday morning I was mentally and physically exhausted. I just sat like a zombie. Then, an amazing thing happened! My eldest son had bought a Sunday newspaper which was lying open on the sofa. I gave it a cursory glance and saw that it was opened at the page "What the Stars Foretell." I do not know to this day what prompted me to look under my sign which, incidentally, is Libra, and there I read "Something you have mislaid is right under your eyes!"

I couldn't believe it but I KNEW it was a message for me from Spirit. Again I set off for town leaving my wife with a confused look on her face. As it was Sunday there was virtually no traffic and I was able to park the car right outside the door of the main shop. An inner voice told me to go into "Fort Knox" but for the life of me I could not see the sense in doing so. I opened all the locks and entered the shop. No sign of the briefcase anywhere. At the far end of the shop was a passage which led to my private office. I was prompted to go there. The office was small and contained a desk, a steel cabinet and a four-drawer filing cabinet. I took one look and

to my astonishment noted that the top three drawers were firmly closed but the fourth and lower drawer was slightly ajar! I was taken aback for on Friday night I had double checked to see that all the files were locked properly.

A strange feeling came over me as I bent down to pull the lower drawer out fully! As long as I live I will never forget what I saw. There inside the drawer was a "nest" of newspaper cuttings dealing with the subject of Psychism which had been formed by some invisible hand and nestling snugly in the middle was the briefcase!

I was staggered! Overwhelmed by feelings of relief and thankfulness, which engulfed me to such a degree, that I had to collapse on the chair to deal with a flood of tears – tears of joy I might add.

There is no point in my embellishing the story. Take it or leave it! I KNOW that it happened and that is all there is to it.

Recently, on the subject of Apports I had a remarkable experience. It demonstrates once again the awesome power and indeed majesty of the power of God who allows everything to come about. This latest experience occurred on the morning of Sunday 6th February 2005. My sister Eileen was on a visit to us. We got to talking about our childhood and all the ups and downs we experienced over the years. We were discussing our father, how good a dad he was to us and of the many difficulties with which he had to contend in his relatively short life. He died when 62 years of age.

In 1938 when my sister was eight years of age, Dad took her on a three day voyage on a liner from Cobh to Le Harve and back to London. Believe me that was some experience for, truth to tell, that kind of thing did not happen in the normal course of events. I vaguely recollect that it was a sponsored business trip so Eileen landed on her feet! As we continued our conversation we became quite nostalgic and this brought us closer together.

It was four in the morning when I dragged myself to bed and fell asleep. I awoke suddenly. On the carpet beside my bed was what I thought was the stalk of a bunch of grapes. I bent down to pick it up and to my utter astonishment it turned out to be a cuff-link. The picture depicted was of the liner Georgic - the very liner on which my father took my sister to France! It was obviously a souvenir from the year 1938! I was completely taken aback at the awesome experience. I felt my father's presence ever so strongly and this coupled with the smell of the tobacco he used to smoke – and killed him in the end – brought the most wonderful feeling of comfort and solace.

Sometimes an Apport will disappear just as suddenly but so far this treasured item has not done so..

I had never ever seen the cufflink before in my life and it certainly was never in my possession. I have indeed been so fortunate to have had so many experiences in my life.

Chapter 07

FURTHER EVIDENCE OF APPORTS

Numerous people experience evidence of Apports but are afraid to mention the matter in case of ridicule or worse!

I can recall a Dublin woman appearing on The Late Late Show many years ago relating to the famous Gay Byrne, about an experience she had. She went on to tell the audience and the country at large that her husband whom she loved deeply, passed away after a long protracted illness. She had been at his bedside constantly and after his funeral she was induced by family and friends to take a holiday either in Spain or Majorca. This she did.

One morning while on holiday, when she awoke, there on the bedside locker was a cigarette lighter. She was flabbergasted to see it there for it was a special lighter she had given to her husband as a present. She had not brought the lighter with her so how did it travel from Dublin to Majorca?

The Power of Spirit dematerialised the lighter and transmuted it as a demonstration of the love her husband had for her and to bring her comfort, which it did in no uncertain terms.

In my own career I was once shown an object that had been placed in the coffin of a loved one. Spirit had dematerialised it and brought it back to a solid form!

In 1973 my wife and I spent a holiday in the small town of St. Anton in Austria. We were on a package holiday and were billeted in a small typical wooden Austrian chalet. The house had two bedrooms, one which we occupied while the other was taken by a young married honeymoon couple from Dublin. They had never before been south of the River Liffey and here they were in Austria! As I spoke some German they latched on to us for advice and help with communication. As it was the summer months there was no skiing, and apart from going up the mountains in a ski lift every so often, there was little to do except to wander down the long main street from one end of the town to the other. This became a regular feature each day where we ended up at a little café where we enjoyed scrumptious cakes and coffee.

One day while returning back to base, to his consternation the young husband found that his wedding ring had slipped of his finger [it had been a little loose]. He and his wife were very upset as we speedily retraced our steps to the café. The ring was not there! We searched the pathways as we slowly walked back to our chalet hoping against hope that one of us would see the ring glinting in the sunlight. It was not to be.

We were passing the local church complete with its "onion" when I suddenly exclaimed,

"This is St. Anton".

In other words the church of St Anthony!

"Why not go in and ask him for help in finding the ring!" Though not very religious he went and sought the help of St. Anthony. Shortly after this we continued to wend our way to our chalet to get ready for our evening meal.

My wife and I were in our bedroom for a few seconds when we heard a loud shout coming from the room next door. We rushed out thinking that something serious had happened. It surely had! There on the window ledge was a beautifully formed circular nest of tissue paper and right in the centre was the wedding ring!

The most startling and extraordinary case demonstrating the power of Spirit to produce Apports is illustrated graphically in the following account.

I have already made mention of the two buildings from where I managed a business. The business dealt in architectural and drawing office equipment as well as all forms of reproduction work. The accounts department was situated right at the top of one of the buildings, under the attic.

I had retained the services of two brothers, to run and control the finances of the company. Both were retired but had a very good grounding in accounting. The elder brother was a widower who had married when he was about fifty years of age. He and his wife suited each other down to the proverbial "T". They were married but ten years when tragedy struck.

One day, while enjoying a holiday in a mobile home near Rosscarbery in West Cork, [let us call him Eddie] went shopping. On return, to his horror he discovered that his wife had had a heart attack, and had somehow fallen into the sea and drowned!

As this tragedy unfolded, Eddie could not get over his loss and grieved enormously. One day his world was filled with happiness and joy, and the next, the light of his life had gone out and with it, meaning and purpose. The job he had in the accounts department started to do duty for his loss. In fact he loved his work and it was as if the "Powers-that-Be" gave him this love of his work to compensate to some degree for his heart-felt sorrow.

We became very good friends and I had to learn to wear two hats, in that between business hours I was the boss, and afterwards a friend. This was a policy I adopted with all those who worked under my management. I worked on the principle that everyone should be treated as I, myself, would like to be treated.

I had from time to time visited Eddie in his semi-detached home. After his wife's passing everything in the house was just as she left it. Even the clothes she wore were still hanging in the wardrobe for ten years!

She enjoyed gardening and had, shortly after they were married, planted two flowering cherry trees, one in the front of the house and the other at the rear. These grew bigger and bigger and each year in the Spring there was a prodigious display of Cherry Blossom - it was as if it was a symbol of their love for one another.

One Friday evening as we were closing up shop for the week Eddie said to me that he was going to have to do something about the size and height of the Cherry trees.   One, growing in the back, was debarring light from entering his dining room. The tree in the front was blocking off the light from the sitting-room.   There was nothing for it but to have the trees cut down and that he had engaged a man to do the work on the following day, Saturday.

The weekend went by and bright and early on Monday morning, Eddie informed me that the trees had been chopped down and the whole house had become so much brighter as a result.   He was very pleased and happy.

Tuesday morning dawned, but the bright and glowing Eddie of Monday had changed into a man with a confused and bewildered facial expression.   I thought at first I might have upset him by something I had said while in the boss mode and I asked him outright if such was the case.   "No," he replied, "It is nothing like that."

"Well, what is it?" I exclaimed.   He paused for a short time as if he was trying to find the right words and then it came out!

"Bill," he said, "I have to tell you an extraordinary story!"   And "extraordinary" is the word for it!   He continued,

"When I got home at the usual time around 7.00 p.m. I put the door key into the lock to open the door.   There was a strong resistance, as if something was jammed against it.   I pushed harder and managed to enter the hallway. I stood back aghast and dumbstruck for what was stopping the door from opening was masses of Cherry tree blossom!   The hall was filled, both the sitting and dining room as was the kitchen, the stairs, the bathroom and, for good measure the three bedrooms."

He sat down as he paused for breath before continuing.

"I was at a complete loss, for what I was seeing with my own two eyes was away and beyond my comprehension.   I did not know what to think or indeed what to do.   Then I started to gather my failing faculties together and said to myself that the first thing I had to do was to start clearing these masses and masses of Cherry Blossom."

He had to get help and after many hours the last of the blossom had been carted away to a dump leaving an empty feeling in the house.

At this time I was Chairman of The Cork Psychical Society holding the position since I founded the organisation ten years previously. Having had an interest in the subject area Eddie, too, was a member. He turned to me for an explanation.

"Eddie my good friend," I said, "This is the most momentous example of Apports that I have ever come across and I do not expect to see the likes of it ever again as long as I live!" I continued,

"As to its meaning, there can be but two. The first and most likely one is that your wife was expressing her great undying love for you in an awe-inspiring spiritual manner or in the second interpretation she is telling you that she was annoyed you cut down the trees she planted! I think that you know in your heart and soul that the first explanation is the correct one!"

Eddie agreed!

Chapter 08

OBEs & NEAR DEATH EXPERIENCES

I suppose it is hard to come to terms with the fact that we "die" every night! We have what is called an OBE [Out-of-the Body Experience] which is just about first cousin to a Near-Death Experience!

As the Bible tells us "we are fearfully and wonderfully made!" Most of us just see our physical body, which in effect is worth about 60 cent, made up of 80% to 90% blood and water while the remainder is carbon and trace elements. Without going any further the truth of the matter is that our bodies are "slowed down energy". In addition to our physical "diving suit" we have a further six bodies "behind" us and these are the Etheric, the Astral, Lower, Intermediate and Higher Mental bodies and finally our Spiritual! The wonderful thing about all this is that we cannot die! We are Spiritual Beings with Physical Bodies and NOT Physical beings with Spiritual Bodies. We are Spirit now, we always were Spirit and we will always BE Spirit!

We travel in our Astral bodies every night when we sleep. We can travel anywhere in the world and indeed into the world of Spirit. Thanks to the fact that our Physical/Etheric body is connected to our Astral body by what is called "The Silver Cord" no matter how far we travel our life-line is always there. It is only when this life-line is severed at what we call death does our Soul travel on to higher climes.

Research into the matter of sleep and dreams has shown that on average each of us turns in our bed over forty times during the night. Now, let us say one goes to sleep lying flat on one's back, the Astral body will "take off" on its journey from that position. If in the morning the physical body happens to be lying on its side, on awakening, the Astral body will return and settle into the position it left! Result? We wake up "out of sorts" due to the fact that the Physical and Astral bodies are not in alignment! To overcome this feeling, all one has to do is to recall the position in which one went to sleep, lie in that position for about ten minutes and the feeling will pass as the bodies synchronise one with the other.

Many people have "flying dreams" on the Astral planes which can be quite exhilarating and exciting. Everyone has had the experience of falling from a great height and wake suddenly with a jerk [not necessarily their husband or wife!]. Seriously, the general consensus of opinion is that the heart missed a beat but in Astral terms it is more likely that it was what is termed a "bad landing!" You see, when we are "out" our Silver Cord stretches and stretches and is literally our life-line.

While on the Astral Planes, should the physical body prove to be in any danger, a signal is sent to the astral body with the speed of light with the message - "Come back!"

It is the sudden return that gives the shock.

On the other hand, Conscious Astral Projection using the Fire, Air, Earth and Water symbols is extremely dangerous and can result in serious damage to the brain. It should not be attempted at any time.

Despite this, Astral Projection is an extremely interesting subject. Books to read on the subject would include "The Phenomena of Astral Projection" by Sylvan Muldoon and Hereward Carrington. "The Techniques of Astral Projection" by Robert Crookall, and "Astral Projection" by Oliver Fox. To my mind, the book that should be at the top of one's list is "Journeys Out of the Body" by Robert A. Munroe. To me, essential reading.

In the Cork Psychical Society there was a sub-committee who studied this interesting subject and on one occasion the members were asked to take part in an experiment - not Conscious Astral Projection I hasten to add. Those taking part [and I was one of them] were asked to concentrate on making a journey in the Astral to a selected point in the centre of Cork City and see if they could remember the trip in the morning. We were instructed to repeat a mantra which went something like this:

189

"I will travel in the Astral to-night and remember my trip in the morning."

This was to be repeated about twenty times before going to sleep. At the Society's next meeting at least three members could recall the trip!

The success of this experiment resulted in a further experiment. This was much more difficult in that a member, sworn to secrecy, made a journey to a given point on a country road about ten miles from the city and there, by a field gate, placed a large square-shaped boulder. This time, those taking part were asked to travel to the given spot and report what they found at the gate, first of all having been told where the site was but no description of the object was given. Two members out of the twenty taking part found the site and described the stone!

In my own life I cannot recall doing any Astral travelling but I did have numerous experiences which were very vivid and real to me. These experiences are described below.

I was married in 1949 and by the year 1957 was the proud father of two children, a boy and a girl, struggling to make ends meet in common with everyone else. In April 1957 I was struck down with "Asian Flu" from which I contracted Rheumatic Fever. For months I lay in my bed in agony, all the joints in my body were swollen, and I was unable to do anything for myself. Three years later I could walk only with the aid of two sticks!

One morning early on in my illness I had the most extraordinary sensation. I felt that I was sinking into the bed and the deeper I sank, the more the pain eased until finally it left me! I could not believe it. Then it hit me! I was NOT sinking into the bed BUT RISING OUT OF MY BODY! It was at that moment that I realised that I was actually dying!!! The sense of comfort was overwhelming and I just wanted to continue to rise and rise! It was then that I thought of my wife and children. As if one threw a switch I stopped rising and back came all the awful pain. I had this experience TWICE and I have to confess that it took a tremendous effort of will not to give in to it.

All my life I have held firmly to the concept that the test of a person is the fight that person makes. And believe me, I DID have to fight.

When I travelled to the city of Westminster in Pennsylvania on a business and pleasure trip with a group of others, little did I realise that the Rheumatic Fever had left me with a damaged heart muscle and a leaking heart valve.

One morning, our delegation was being received by the Mayor at City Hall. While in the presence of such august company I began to feel distinctly unwell. On leaving City Hall and walking down the main street I experienced a violent pain in my heart. As luck would have it we were passing a public park and in the company of a colleague, I managed to lie down on the grass. The sun shone brightly as the pain in my chest became worse. I loosened my collar and tie and my friend said that he would go and get help. I did not want to go to hospital but in my heart of hearts I knew that I would have to do so. I was rushed to the A & E and from there to the ICU. One evening the pain in my chest became very bad. Two nurses came to my assistance and administered injections.

Suddenly I "shot" out of my body and there on the opposite side of the private room stood my maternal grandmother, Granny Cooney, to whom I have already made reference. She smiled at me as she stood beside a tunnel! At the end of the tunnel I could see a brilliant light which issued an amazing sense of peace past all understanding. Granny "told" me that I was to enter the tunnel, which I did. I knew instinctively that this was the door to the next world. I went down the tunnel but a short distance, when I thought of my wife and what would she do in America without me! Instantly I found myself back in my body. It was a profound experience.

Everything happens when it is meant to happen and it was in that hospital that a Doctor Neghana diagnosed that I had a leaking heart valve, a damaged heart muscle, blocked arteries and I was suffering from Wolffe-Parkinson-Whyte Syndrome [WPW]. Believe it or not one in 2,500 people can have this syndrome and I had to be the one that drew the short straw!

After a period of recuperation in the home of a friend, I made the difficult journey back to Cork.   I went into hospital immediately for further evaluation. This was the forerunner of all my heart problems from that day onwards.

I managed to stay free of them until February 1989 when I was struck down again and from that date to this [June 2006] I have been in and out of hospital dozens of times!   In my innocence in February 1989 I thought that I could have a bypass to clear my blocked arteries, but no.   I was told that my heart would become progressively weaker, and so it has.   As my situation worsened I had to go to hospital about once every eight weeks.   Things reached a climax in March 2002.

I had a strange experience that month which has a direct bearing on my next brush with crossing the Great Divide.

One morning I was seated at the breakfast table, the sun was shinning through the window when, suddenly I saw about ten most beautiful Bee-like creatures flying about the room.   They were about three times the size of a Bumble Bee and were made up of all the colours of the rainbow.   They were definitely not of this world.   I looked at them in awe and said to my wife,

"Look at those beautiful creatures; what could they possibly be?"   SHE COULD NOT SEE A THING!   They continued to fly around for about a minute and then disappeared.

A couple of weeks later I became very seriously ill with kidney and liver failure and was rushed to Intensive Care.   Now, I had a most wonderful and saintly friend Sr. Loreto and who had passed away a couple of years previously.   We were very close and though she is in the world of Spirit, the bond is still and always will be there.

One morning, I saw, suddenly, about a hundred of these creatures flying around the ICU. It was like recognising old friends.   Then the wall opposite my bed opened up and there was an inviting path before me at the end of which was my good friend Sr. Loreto with her hands extended in welcome.   She was surrounded by thousands of these heavenly creatures.

Perhaps they were a form of Angel - I do not know. I was so happy. I made an effort to rise from my bed and join Sr. Loreto but, to my chagrin, the "door" closed.

Sister Loreto

Obviously the tunnel as seen in America and which I did not go through was the same one! Again I was not being allowed to travel instead it appeared to signify that I was still to stay on Spaceship Earth for the time being!

Here is a frightening account of an OBE:

A very spiritual experience [as referred to in part 3 of this book] can transfer the Spirit to very high climes. Conversely, one can find oneself in the lower realms of the Astral world where one can come across entities that thrive on fear. If under the influence of drugs or alcohol, one can see all sorts of things like rats, spiders, faces of gargoyles and all sorts of similar dreadful creatures, it comes under the category of a Bad OBE!

I little thought that I would have such an experience, but I feel compelled to record what happened to me, as what I have to tell may be of value to others. I still get nightmares when I think of what happened but I feel that I should come clean with the episode.

It happened in Germany when I, with two friends went down the Rhine Valley to enjoy the Wine Festival, in the town of Andernach. I had been in Germany once before on business to attend the Hanover Trade Fair. When I went to the Fatherland for the first time, I knew about ten words of the language but after six month's study my knowledge had improved slightly.

On the first night in Andernach the three of us went off the beaten track and into a local bar for a drink. I had heard of a drink called KORN, which turned out to be a potent spirit. As the measures were small, I ordered them in lots of four in a glass. The evening progressed and I did not feel inebriated. However, unknown to me, one never drinks Korn in quantity but interspersed with one of those wonderful German beers.

I got back to the hotel and early next morning decided to visit Koblenz - some twenty miles away. It was a crisp cold October morning as I hurried to the train station. I began to feel "queer" and on arrival at Koblenz I began to feel more strange as a most awful pain developed in my stomach.

Saturday morning, and as I walked along the deserted business section, suddenly I found that I was out of my body! Walking beside me was my Doppelganger - my other self! Without warning a large gold picture frame appeared on the path and the "two" of us were compelled to step through the frame. A short distance further on another similar picture frame, half the size of the original, made its appearance and bending low "we" managed to get through. Horror of horrors, a third picture frame appeared fifty per cent smaller than the previous one! We were down on our knees crawling and forcing ourselves through. I knew what was happening but did not know what to do. I could not go to a pharmacist and try to explain what was going on, even in English. I was far from hungry but something told me to eat. The "two" of us entered a supermarket and bought bread, cheese, biscuits and mineral water. I was really frightened and nearly in panic. Somehow we reached the station, and returned the to Andernach-am-Rhine.

How I got back to the hotel I really do not know. I went to my room and working on the principle that desperate diseases require desperate cures, I took a large measure of brandy with a few pills. I went out like a light. Some six hours later I came to and found that my Doppelganger had slotted itself back into my physical body.

The experience shocked me to the core and never, ever again did I touch Korn or anything like it. The following morning I learned authoritatively I had given myself alcoholic poisoning! I had nearly killed myself!

Chapter 09

FROM ONE WORLD TO ANOTHER!

It was in June, 2002 I was back again in hospital very seriously ill. My heart was taking a terrible pounding and I was having WPW attacks one after the other. I knew inwardly that it could not go on and that I would be "dead" within a month or two. This was confirmed by my heart specialist who informed me that unless something could be done to relieve the syndrome I would not have very long to live. I asked what could be done and was informed that there was a procedure whereby my heart could be stopped for a short period during which time a Laser beam would be directed through the organ to "blow out" the syndrome. I asked about the risks involved and the chances of success.

"1,000 to one you could end up completely paralysed, 50,000 to one you might die and 90% chance of success but no guarantee that the Syndrome would not return," came the reply.

It did not take long to make up my mind. All I said was, "Where do I sign?"

It was quite an emotional time, particularly as I had to take cognisance of the fact that I may not make it. The family were brought together and I told them how much I loved them.

After this I had to make contact with a firm of Undertakers. Many years previously I had donated my body for medical research. It had always been my ambition to go to the University and as I was unable to do so in life, I was making sure that I would when I died! Despite the seriousness of the situation I laughed to myself at what others might term "black humour." The Undertaker was an old friend of mine and when I rang him up I said, "Val, there is a good chance that you are going to get me at last!"

I ordered a cardboard coffin which at that date was £269. I suppose it would be £1,000. today. I certainly did not want an elaborate box for my remains, as this to me was tantamount to placing an empty package worth 60 cents in a very expensive ornate container.

Down in the ICU four silver disks were placed on my chest and I was told that I might have a couple of burns after the procedure. I did not care. The anaesthetist, for good measure, added that I might find myself a little sick. I did not have time to think for suddenly I went out like the proverbial light and there was my old friend - the tunnel! I shot down this with the speed of light and on this occasion CAME OUT AT THE OTHER END! What a staggering sight I saw. No words could be found to describe the scene. It was simply awesome, beautiful and wonderful in the extreme!

I found myself in a beautiful flat landscape with the most luscious and magnificent lawns one could ever hope to see. The lawns were in the form of triangles and circles. All were surrounded with continuous rolling gold which radiated out the love of God, Sanctity, Security, Forgiveness.

No dictionary could contain the adjectives necessary to describe what I was experiencing. There were beautiful walks between the lawns. Away in the distance one could see a magnificent range of blue mountains, from my left side, came a gentle warm zephyr from some sea I could not observe.

"Thank you Almighty God", I said to myself.

There were people there - men and women - but I was unable to differentiate between them as they were all dressed in long-flowing robes of beautiful grey silk material. They were walking in twos and threes along these staggeringly beautiful paths absorbing all the pulsating heavenly Spiritual Energy that was being radiated out. I stood there endeavouring to comprehend the majesty of it all, suddenly a woman approached me and said, not unkindly, "You are not to be here!" I replied, "I am here and I am staying here!"

Again she told me that I was NOT to be in this wonderful domain. I remembered arguing with her but she kept repeating insistently that I could not stay.

196

Then, for some reason, I turned my head to look over my shoulder and there, about one hundred million miles away I could see a minute speck of light which was my temporary home - THE EARTH!   I could see the cord that was linking my physical body to my Spiritual Body and came to realise that the "tunnel," in effect was my own Silver Cord!

From this vast distance I heard a voice say to me, "Bill, come back!"   "No, I won't" I replied.   The voice repeated the request and I again replied in the negative.   Then came the question, "What about your family?" to which I retorted, "My family can manage perfectly well without me."

No sooner had I said this when a terrifyingly strong suction took hold of me and with the speed of light I sped back down the tunnel and found myself back in my body.   I WAS DISGUSTED!

Sometime later a nurse brought me a cup of tea and some sort of a fry.   I started to laugh and everyone in the ICU thought that I had gone round the bend.   I was laughing at the incongruity of being asked to eat some food and drink and a very short time previously I had actually been in another world!

Chapter 10

THERE IS NO SUCH THING AS DEATH!

Many thousands of people like me have had similar experiences but are often too shy to speak about them in fear that they would not be believed and have to go quietly when the men with the white coats came!

I have found through a long life that everything happens for a purpose and no one has the right to say they are wrong!   Many people will not agree with this statement but what one feels inwardly to be true IS true.

The following story will bear out what I have just stated.

Because of my heart condition I have to visit my hospital practically every two weeks for blood tests.   It is a drudge but a necessary one and I have to rely on the kindness of neighbours to take me there and back.   On one such visit I had a lift to the Pathology department of the hospital but none for the return journey.   As I shuffled along the path aiming for the hospital proper to 'phone for a taxi, I heard a voice in my head say, clearly, "You are going to be offered a lift home!"   Straight away I heard a man's voice behind me ask, "Can I offer you a lift home?"   Extraordinary.

I turned to see the smiling face of a well-dressed middle-aged man awaiting my reply.   I thanked him profusely and had the pleasure of being transported back to base in a brand new Mercedes.   My benefactor enquired as to where I lived and when I told him he said that as he did not know the area in question he would follow my directions.

I noticed he drove rather slowly and it seemed strange that every traffic light we met displayed red.   As we drove along he told me that he, too, had to attend the Pathology Department on a regular basis as he had a quadruple heart bypass sixteen years previously but now was having serious trouble yet again.   He asked me what was wrong with me and I reiterated my long saga of constant hospital visits.   With a questioning look he asked, "Did you ever have any peculiar experiences during all those illnesses of yours?" I knew immediately to what he was referring and said off-hand, "You mean Out of the Body Experiences?" "Yes," he replied and I told him of my experiences. He listened intently and when I was finished he exclaimed, "Thank God I have found someone to whom I can relate my experience!"

Taking a deep breath, he continued, "For sixteen years I was keeping my experience secret. I was sure that people would think I was crazy if I told them."

He then told how, while on the operating table, he found himself leaving his body. From the height of the ceiling he watched the surgeons work on his heart. He saw a nurse he knew enter the operating theatre and speak to one of the surgeons. He then found himself going through the roof and as he rose he could discern the area around the hospital. He rose higher and higher increasing speed all the time. Then he could see the whole country and so it went on, Europe, the world which was getting smaller and smaller until he, too, found himself in a place very similar to that which my Spirit visited. Taking the words out of my mouth, he said that he believed that everything happens for a purpose and our meeting was not chance or coincidence. He was so relieved to have found a person who related to his experiences.

Truly God moves in mysterious ways His wonders to perform.

One last word. An experience such as has been described in this chapter, takes ALL fear of death away.

Chapter 11

"COMING EVENTS CAST THEIR SHADOWS AFORE!"

Omens or signs, natural and super-normal, which hint and in some cases predict coming events, are common to humankind the world over. Take for example the farmer who can look at the sky and tell what the weather is going to be like by "reading the signs."

Coming down to the family unit, many people have experienced the sense of a pending bereavement, tragedy or accident. On inquiring as to how they knew that such and such was going to happen the usual reply is, "I just knew!"

Many families have inherited certain definite signs which foretell coming events, especially where bereavements are concerned. In my own family birds are of great significance. If a bird comes down the chimney start getting the black clothes out right away. The sudden "death" of a house plant which one day was blooming and the next was withering away. Numerous signs and portents are associated with us and these include knocks on the door, a picture falling from the wall and many other such occurrences.

My father died just as he was nearing his sixty-third birthday. He had been ill in hospital with heart trouble, like myself, except I am still here at seventy-eight years of age as I write this chapter. He had been in a coma for three days before his Soul decided it was time to leave when he suddenly came out of the coma for a minute or two and said to my mother who was at his bedside,

"Tell Billy that I am sorry but the writing is on the wall!"

I regretted, bitterly, the fact that I was not present at his transition as a short time previously I had, on the command of my mother, left the hospital for a snack. Just as my father passed away the private room in which he occupied was filled with the sound of birds flapping their wings! None could be seen but the sound of the flapping wings was loud and clear. On returning to my mother's home later the sound could still be heard but much more muted. I often thought that the sound might be coming from the wings of Angels for, as we all know, they are God's messengers.

When it came to the time that my mother was departing this life, she did so in her own home! She always said, "When my time comes I want to die in my own home standing on my two feet!"

And that is just what happened!

In the garden attached to the house there was a misshapen lily pond built by my father with the help of a friend. It was rectangular in shape and about three feet deep. In the centre an "island" had been built where the water lilies took root. The pond boasted two goldfish that had been there for at least thirty years. They had grown big and as the years rolled by the gold was showing patches of white!

In the garden stood a Christmas Tree! I experienced my first Christmas in 1926 when I was but three months old! My parents had bought a little Christmas tree in a pot. After the festive season, my father planted the little tree at the top of the garden and over the intervening years it grew higher and higher until it was taller than the house! During the war years fuel was very scarce. I was sure the tree would have to come down and be used to keep us warm for a few days. But no! The tree was left standing.

I have always loved the birds and would feed them just as my mother did. A few days before my mother passed away three extraordinary things happened.

All the birds disappeared! What was utterly extraordinary was the fact that the two old goldfish, that had been swimming in that pond for thirty years, vanished! No cat could have taken them, and, to cap it all, the Christmas Tree which had always been healthy with beautiful luscious green branches died overnight! There it stood dead – every bit of it had turned brown!

My mother's sister, Agnes, lived in Bristol and even though she was informed right away of my mother's passing, a letter she had written before my mother died arrived in the midst of the obsequies. In part of the letter was a paragraph, which I cannot quote verbatim, but it went on to report that a blackbird had come down the chimney of Agnes' bedroom! She added, "You know what that means, Eileen!"

In or around the year 1999, I was once more very ill in hospital ensconced in the Cardiac department. I shared a ward with six other heart patients. One afternoon a pigeon flew through the window at the end of a small corridor and all attempts to get the bird to move failed. Over the door of the ward was a transom and nothing would stop the pigeon from flying there over and over again. I was seated on a chair wrapped up in blankets and here was this fat pigeon staring at me all of the time. It was most disconcerting and I had the distinct feeling that the bird was coming with a message for me to pack my bags. After a considerable length of time the bird flew off down the corridor and out the window without any encouragement. I can tell you that I said an extra prayer that night and at the same time asked the night sister to double up the sleeping pills!

My mother passed into the World of Spirit when she was 79 years of age. Despite umpteen medical problems during her long life - including Cancer - her tenacity to keep going was extraordinary and she never felt old! That was until the time that she was struck down with Static Asthma and was in hospital for quite a number of weeks.

How she survived I really do not know. One day before she was discharged from hospital she said to me, "Do you know Bill, while in the oxygen tent I saw a white line. I knew that if I crossed that line I would move into the next world. Tempted to do so, I resolved not to cross."

While in hospital she had lost a tremendous amount of weight and after a short period of recuperation insisted on returning to her own home. It was obvious that she would be unable to manage on her own but so far as she was concerned this tremendous willpower of hers made her believe that she could carry on as heretofore. Truly was it a case of the spirit being willing but the flesh weak. It was "last breath time" and her Soul passed on to pastures new.

One night, approximately three months later, at about 3.00am she came back to me! There she was sporting a new hair-do and a new overcoat and appeared as if she was 54 years of age.

"Mum, you're dead", I exclaimed!

"Indeed I'm not dead" she retorted, "I am very much alive!"

With that I put my arms about her and as if we were Peter Pan we "flew" in our Astral bodies to the old home We arrived in the small kitchen and I distinctly remember her looking at the old sink and the cracks and blemishes she had painted over so many times for forty years. She looked at the old gas cooker and said, "Did I cook countless meals on that stove during my lifetime?" I replied in the affirmative. With that she "took off" like the proverbial rocket and I never heard a word from her from that day to this!

It may seem strange that my mother who had passed away aged 81 should appear to me as if she was in her early fifties. This is accounted for by the fact that, when we pass into Spirit World, we regress to when were twenty-one! If I had no knowledge of this my mother would have appeared as she was at eighty-one years of age!

This experience came about through Love. Love is the bond between us all and, no matter what happens, this never dies!

Part Two

Chapter 12

POLTERGEIST ACTIVITIES AND PERSONAL EXPERIENCES

The word "poltergeist" is defined in the Concise Oxford Dictionary as "a noisy mischievous ghost, especially one manifesting itself by physical damage [from the German poltern - create a disturbance + Geist Ghost].

Over the many years of my life I came across poltergeist activity of all sorts, some benevolent and some quite the opposite.

Aside from the episode related elsewhere there were numerous other strange happenings. As I told you, I founded the Cork Psychical Society way back in 1965/66 and was chairman for ten years. One of our members, a very dignified and cultured lady, had a keen interest, particularly since she constantly had Poltergeist activity in her home. She lived in a large house in a suburb of Cork - an old house that boasted a basement, as far as I can recall, and was three stories in height. Sometimes our monthly meetings were held in the homes of various members and on this particular occasion our meeting was held in the home of Mrs. Ambrose [not her real name].

The house had a comfortable feeling about it and the lounge where we conducted our meeting was large with a bay window. We had known that there was poltergeist activity in the house and on the night in question Mrs. Ambrose asked us all to remain silent.

After a few minutes we could hear, coming from the draped bay window, the sound of "twittering voices." Straining our ears, try as we might we could not distinguish any words. It was as if someone was speaking twenty times faster than was humanly possible to speak. Mrs. Ambrose went on to explain that this phenomenon was a daily occurrence and then went on to relate other quite extraordinary things that happened regularly.

On the large mantle-shelf were numerous pieces of Jade - quite valuable - and on occasion when Mrs. Ambrose left the room, on her return the Jade would be found on the floor over ten feet away from the mantle-shelf! No damage would ever be caused to this delicate work of art. There were two pets in the house - a dog and a cat. The cat was very old while the dog was in his prime. On leaving the house for a few hours to do some shopping, Mrs. Ambrose would leave the dog OUTSIDE of the house and the cat INSIDE.

On her return she inevitably found that the cat was outside the house and the dog inside! Once, during the summer months she returned to find that the central heating was turned on to its highest level, despite the fact that the whole system had been turned off for the summer months!

Mrs. Ambrose had an interest in cooking and had a very large cookery book in which she pasted any recipe that took her fancy. It was quite a tome and had pride of place on a shelf in her kitchen. One day it disappeared! There was a big gap on the shelf where the book should have been. She searched the house from top to bottom but there was no sign of the book. Months rolled by and one day for reasons best known to himself, her son - a mature adult in his thirties - visited the large attic. There, under the eaves of the roof was the missing cookery book!

Some schools of thought suggest that a girl at puberty can emit a kinetic energy that can shatter an electric light bulb or cause some other similar happening. There have been many instances of such happenings.

In a personal capacity I had numerous experiences of Poltergeist activity. One such experience was in connection with cheap ballpoint pens of all things. They simply disappeared! When I was earning my living working as a Private Business Consultant ["Jack-of-all-trades-and-master-of-none and what you did not know you made up!"] I was engaged by a small company involved in advertising and design work. About five or six people worked for the firm and my contract required me to be available on three afternoons a week. I was allocated a small office in which to work and I always carried a black and red pen. A couple of times per week if I left the office, when I returned my red pen was not on the desk! This happened so often that it was the stock joke of all the staff including the wife of one of the directors who punched in some hours each week. Every one thought the disappearance of the red pens was a prank but as the months rolled by it became quite obvious that such was not the case. One day the wife of the boss gave me a relatively expensive red pen, adding the rider,

"I don't think that will disappear!" It did!

I had a small office at home. One evening to my utter astonishment I found a cluster of red pens in my desk! I knew without a shadow of a doubt that I had not put them there, but there they were! Another peculiar thing in connection with red ballpoint pens is illustrated by the following example.

Let's say I wish to take a red pen out of a box which contained pencils, markers etc., and none was there. I found that if I kept rustling the contents long enough, suddenly a red pen would appear out of the blue! This sort of thing was a feature of my life and I got quite used to it. Things would disappear never to return! In other cases the missing object would return.

I was a staunch member of Junior Chamber International and made my mark on the local, national and international levels. For my efforts, which in effect was a labour of love, I was awarded the highest honour of the international organisation and was made a Senator. World-wide, Senators are looked upon as elder statesmen and though an honourary title, I wore my Senator's pin proudly. I took great care of it, especially if I had to send my jacket to the cleaners. On one such occasion, I carefully wrapped up my treasured emblem and placed it in the left hand corner of my dressing table for safe keeping. A few days later after collecting the jacket in question I went to retrieve my badge of honour! Yes, it had disappeared!

Four years went by. One day it was necessary to shift a fitted bed. After it was pulled away from the frame for some reason I ripped back the carpet a distance of approximately four feet. To my astonishment there was my Senator's pin! How or why it should be there I have never understood, but I KNOW there is a reason for everything that happens in our lives.

Part Two

There were many such instances but the highlight of them all was associated with a small one and a half inch high metal statue of the Blessed Virgin Mary which had been given to me by a friend. A very strong bond and affinity built up between me and the little statue which I always carried in the top pocket of my shirt. Over the years I began to notice that the statue would disappear for a few days and then suddenly reappear. It was as if the Virgin Mary wanted to be by herself - and who could blame her! She always came back!

I remember on one occasion a friend of mine invited me to a Presentation Dinner in a big hotel. I had to dress up for the occasion and, as usual, my little statue travelled with me. On my return, as I undressed for bed, to my chagrin my statue had disappeared! I thought I had lost my friend but then remembered all of the other times that she had gone her way only to return so I did not feel too badly.

A few days prior to the function I had sent a pair of pants to the cleaners and now as I was hanging up my suit after the function I decided to take off the cellophane covering my cleaned trousers. As I did so, I felt something in the right pocket! Wondering what it was but, at the same time KNOWING what it was, I drew out the statue!

On another occasion I was getting ready for bed and I placed the statue together with a crucifix on my small dressing table. Suddenly the Virgin Mary "hopped" off the dressing table top and fell into a full waste paper basket . I went to retrieve my statue but this necessitated placing newspaper on the bed and taking out all the rubbish piece by piece. I was just at the bottom of the basket and there was the statue resting on two twenty Euro notes and one ten Euro note! Only for the fact that my constant companion decided to hop into the basket the fifty Euro would have been thrown out with the rest of the rubbish in the morning!

Do I really have to say more? "Trust and Know and all will be well!"

Chapter 13

PRECOGNITIVE DREAMS

From the beginning of time everyone has been and is a dreamer! We can have good and bad dreams. The good ones we want to go on forever and the terrifying ones to stop in their tracks. Dreaming has always been a never-ending source of wonder and often inspiration - and terror! For the majority of us the process of dreaming can be described as an extraordinary kaleidoscope of visual images which come to us during sleep, yet involve EMOTION and SENSES. We seem to hear sounds, smell pleasant or unpleasant odours, actually laugh, cry, talk, sweat and walk because the CONTENTS of our dreams which, by waking standards are devoid of logic but at the time often appear to be making perfect sense.

Some people dream in colour all of the time but for me, except on very rare occasions, I have to fall back on the good old black and white. Once in a blue moon I get a glimpse of Technicolour. Strange as it may seem, even though 99% of my dreams are in monochrome I would KNOW what colours are being depicted! It's sort of weird. The same thing holds good for my clairvoyant abilities.

Dreams are often seen as signs and omens. The Bible is full of warnings coming from God to His people. The one that stands out above all else is where we read that God told Joseph to leave with Jesus and His mother, the Virgin Mary and flee into Egypt!

Since time immemorial humankind has been interpreting dreams. One has only to glance at the myriad of dream books to realise they are the descendants of writings consulted by our ancestors. Clay tablets found at Ninevah, that belonged to the library of the Assyrian King Ashurbanipal who reigned six centuries before Christ, contain material dating back to 5,000 BC!

At the end of the 19th century, Sigmund Freud saw dreams as KEYS with which to unlock the door of the unconscious. The famous Dr. Karl Jung, who once was a pupil of Freud, wrote many books including the book entitled "Man and his Symbols" which is a "must" for those interested in this fascinating subject. One thing we all have in common is that we have had dreams of flying, falling, death, being naked in a public place. The list is endless.

Then there is the Precognitive dream - dreaming of an event before it happened! In my life I had three such dreams. The first of these was when I dreamt that a very popular bank official had died. He had been in perfect health and I was shocked to the core the following morning to learn that he had passed away during the night! Why should I have had that dream? I just do not know. Did anyone else have the same precognitive dream? I never found out.

My second precognitive dream pertained to an air crash in Scotland. I cannot remember the year but it was sometime in the fifties or sixties. I remember waking in the morning, turning on the radio and heard the report. I just could not believe it.

The most vivid and extraordinary of the three was associated with the Cork Psychical Society. As I am not at liberty to give place names or mention specific people, what I have to relate is couched in such a way that it should be impossible to pinpoint the area or people involved. Despite this, what I relate IS true.

Mrs. Ambrose, to whom I have previously made reference, brought to my attention an article that had appeared in a daily paper making reference to a place on an estate in the south of Ireland that was reported to be haunted. It appears that the owner of this estate hundreds of years ago had put many people to death at the haunted spot. Mrs. Ambrose was chairperson of the Society's committee which dealt with haunting, ghosts, etc. She asked me, in my capacity as Chairman, if I would make inquiries of the current owner if permission would be granted to visit the site. This was very kindly grant-

ed and the delegation was confined to three people, Mrs. Ambrose, our photographer [who was an atheist by the way] and myself.   It was on Monday
that I received word that our visit was arranged for the following Saturday
afternoon.

That night I had a very vivid dream.

I found myself in the countryside in front of large black entrance gates. A
driveway lead to a very large square type house, which was obviously very
old, surrounded with trees all of which were waving in the wind giving the
whole atmosphere of the place a distinctly eerie feeling.   I found myself
indoors facing a large wooden staircase, the timber of which was nearly
white from hundreds of years of scrubbing.   I went up the stairs and found
that the house boasted eight bedrooms, one of which had three wooden steps
leading up to it.   I went up the stairs and found myself in a huge bedroom
which must have measured thirty feet by twenty.   I noticed that the room
boasted three large multi-paned glass windows, through which I could see
the trees blowing and hear hear the hedges rustling in the wind.

I looked down the long room and at the end saw a large white marble fireplace. Above it was a painting of daisies of every hue imaginable including
purple! I walked down the room to examine the picture further and as I did
so, I became conscious of the sound of clocks ticking. I looked around and
thought it strange that there should be no less than eight clocks of all shapes
and sizes ticking away merrily.

Standing and looking at this strange daisy painting, I noticed on my left ,a
door that stood ajar.   For some reason or other, I walked over and closed it.
No sooner had I done so, when it opened again.   Three times I tried to close
the door, but to no avail.

It was at that point I turned to look back to the windows on the opposite side
of this large room and it was then I saw the ghost!

There, in the middle of the room, standing beside a very large old period bed
and highlighted by the dwindling winter evening light was this thin woman.

She was very tall, nearly six feet in height I should think, dressed in a long full length cotton nightdress, her thin hair strewing down to her shoulders.

I was completely taken aback and after the initial shock told myself that, as I had never seen a ghost before, this was an opportunity for me to meet one in the "flesh" so to speak.   My heart beating I walked towards the apparition and when I came up close to touch her, my hand simply went through nothing and that was it!   Getting over the shock I resumed observation of the bedroom taking in chairs and various other pieces of furniture.

I woke with a start.   Never in my life did I have such a vivid dream.

It was a wet, gray and depressing October Saturday as we set off on our journey.   It took us a little time before we found our destination.   As we turned a corner I was completely taken aback to see the portals - the very ones that I had seen in my dream the previous Monday night!   We drove up the long drive and stopped at the front door of the house, a large rectangular building, just as I had seen in my dream.   I had a distinct deja-vu feeling as we rang the front door bell, which we could hear reverberating through the house.   We were greeted courteously by the owner who also had an interest in the paranormal.

Well wrapped up against the inclement weather, our hostess conducted us to the infamous spot where so many had been put to death.   I did not feel one bit comfortable as we observed the spot while our photographer took some pictures.   It would be more correct to say that he ENDEAVOURED to take some photographs BUT THE CAMERA WOULD NOT WORK!!!

We were invited back to the house for afternoon tea and were so glad to sit in the large drawing room with a roaring fire in its large grate.   It goes without saying that conversation was centered on all aspects of Psychics but on haunted places in particular.   Our hostess told us that there was a haunted bedroom in the house and no one would stay the night there.   Straight away Mrs. Ambrose asked if it would be permissible to see the room and with the answer in the affirmative we went towards the stairway.

Again I had this strange deja-vu feeling for the stairway we were about to climb was just as I had seen in my dream! I mentioned this to the lady of the house and also went one further and related my dream experience. At the corner of the wide wooden stairway there was a distinct very cold feeling. Again our photographer tried to take a photograph but to no avail. There was nothing wrong with the camera for it had worked in the drawing room. We entered the haunted room. As soon as we crossed the threshold I, for one, just wanted to bolt out of the place for without the shadow of a doubt there was an "evil" presence in the room.

Once again, the camera would not work and as the two members of our delegation returned to the warmth downstairs I was given the conducted tour of all the rooms to see if I could recognise the bedroom I had seen so clearly in my dream. One room after the other was visited and each time I was asked the question,

"Well, is it this room?" to which I had to reply in the negative.

I could see that I might be pressing my luck too far as there was irritation in the voice of the hostess as she exclaimed rather crossly,

"Well that leaves only the master bedroom."

As we rounded the bend in the corridor, there were the three steps leading to the room! Excitedly I said I was positive that this was the room at last! My heart beat faster as we went up the short stairway and missed a beat as I gazed on what was a familiar sight. But something was different, it took a moment for me to come to understand that everything I had seen in my dream was a reverse of what I was then looking at! Rather as if one had been observing a negative and then handed a positive print.

I sought permission to stay on my own in the room for twenty minutes and, with a "Join us downstairs when you are finished," I was left alone.

I looked about the room and noticed that there were but two windows, as distinct from the three I had seen in my precognitive dream. As if a play-

212

back, I did all the same actions as I had in my dream. I went down to the far wall but the white marble fireplace was not there, nor indeed was the daisy picture. It was obvious however, that the original fireplace had been taken out and replaced with a smaller one. Over the mantel was a large round mirror mounted in an ornate black metal frame on which were paint-ed daisies of all the hues I had seen!

As I marvelled at all this, I turned my head to the left and there was a very large walk-in wardrobe and the door was ajar! [I learned subsequently that the door in question was originally another exit door]. I went to close it, but it would not stay closed. After the third attempt I gave up and being con-scious of the part of the dream where I saw the ghost's silhouette, with eyes closed I turned around. I have to confess to being a little frightened and then said to myself that I would chance one eye! To my disappointment and chagrin there was no ghost! What a let down.

This was more than compensated for when I realised that there were clocks ticking away everywhere [collecting clocks was the hobby of our hostess!] From memory I think I counted ten clocks in that huge bedroom, which also sported a full length dress mirror. I decided to use the mirror as a form of crystal allowing the plain painted wall opposite to act as a screen. Using my clairvoyant abilities I let my eyes diffuse and after about ten minutes I "saw" a man with vicious features, a large bandage going around his head and covering his left eye. He was lying on the huge bed! That was enough for me and I left that room post haste to join the others downstairs.

I recounted to the extended group what I had experienced. Our hostess gasped and said in a subdued voice,

"The man you saw was the infamous man responsible for all the killings. He had recuperated for three weeks in that bedroom after losing his left eye in a shooting accident!!!

Chapter 14

PSYCHOMETRY

The word "Psychometry" is defined in the Concise Oxford Dictionary as "the supposed divination about facts, events, people etc., from inanimate objects associated with them."

Countless people have the ability to "see" events from the past, the present and, in some cases, the future, simply by holding an object in the hand! Few people realise that EVERYTHING they handle daily vibrates. Take for example the strings of a piano, the lower register being produced by a small built-in hammer striking a thick slow vibrating string. In contrast the higher notes of the top register are coming from the hammer striking the thin taut strings! Inanimate objects such as pencils, pens, rings, jewellery, trees, flowers, stones, buildings of all shapes and sizes, old castles, modern structures, the list is literally endless. And we need not confine ourselves to any of the billions of solar systems and galaxies that go to constitute our Universe seen and unseen. We are ourselves, a vibration!

"Maybe he will go quietly when the men with the white coats come?" I hear some people say!

It is they that should "go" for they do not appreciate that above the normal five senses there are, as already mentioned, at least eighteen more senses above the normal five! A person can learn to use some of these and when they do, a whole new world, in fact, whole new worlds are open to them. .

Physical Science has its place but for me it is IMPOSSIBLE to prove something that is non-physical by physical means, yet that is what physical scientists continually endeavour to do. At the same time they are seemingly unaware that THEY ARE NON-PHYSICAL THEMSELVES!

The only person or persons that can "prove" something are those who had a unique experience. When they try to convey their experience to others they are unable to do so for the simple fact that no one can "get into" the mind of another!

For example, a good friend suffers a bereavement and one tenders sincere and deep condolences. They are, in effect, but words! While they act as a solace, in reality they mean nothing!   Hard to say this, but it is the truth! Wreaths, Mass Cards and flowers of all types are but symbols and, dare we say it, an ease to our conscience!

Everyone is familiar with their "Sixth Sense."   The phone rings and YOU know who is going to be on the line!   Similarly, the door bell rings and again, you know who is there before YOU open the door!   How is that done? Think about it!

One can practise to develop this sensitivity which we ALL possess. On the off-chance that someone is interested in developing this skill the simple way to start is by picking up a well-used and worn pencil but before doing so, wash the hands to clear the countless vibrations picked up during the day from such actions as shaking hands, handling notes and coins, reading a letter or even a bill received through the post!

Sit down quietly in a comfortable seat and subdued lighting.   Taking the battered pencil in your hands examine it closely and see how many imperfections you can spot.   For instance note where the paint has flaked away, the number of teeth marks made by the owner chewing the pencil while he or she was thinking. Note the name of the manufacturer and how many letters are missing. Carry on doing that sort of thing.   Stick with it for about half-an-hour and lay the pencil aside.   It is a good idea to jot down all the things observed. Two days later carry out the same procedure and note how many other imperfections you did not observe first time round.   Carry out the same procedure a third time after another few days and again endeavour to spot imperfections you missed on the first two periods of observation.

By this time you are heartily sick and tired of the pencil and you will notice that you can see the wretched thing with all its imperfections in your

215

"Mind's Eye!" Your powers of observation have impinged the image of the pencil in your brain. On your third time round the course you are ready to pack up and then, suddenly, it dawns on you that you never thought of looking at the graphite itself! Lo and behold you note that through the sharpening of the "lead" the point is triangular or multi-sided in shape!

Allow a few days to go by during which time you only have to hear the word "pencil" and, like a shot a clear picture of your "old friend" comes to mind. It is at this point you turn yourself into a "receiver." You go through the washing hands ritual, sit down in your comfortable chair, close your eyes and begin to stroke the pencil gently between your fingers.

It is important that you make your mind as blank as possible. If you have done your initial work intensely, after a short time you should begin to "see" images in your brain. Perhaps you might see a huge forest stretching for miles with snow-capped mountains in the background. What you could be viewing is a Canadian forest from where the timber originated out of which your pencil was made! You might "see" a paint factory and know that this was where the paint that gilded your pencil was manufactured. You might "see" large clumps of graphite or the building where the pencils were mass-produced and, for good measure, workers packing the finished product!

The more one works on their sensitivity the better will be the results. Psychometry always held a great fascination for me and I spent countless hours developing an ability in this field. A friend of mine, let's call him Michael. who was also a member of the Cork Psychical Society kindly put me to the test. He was often astonished at what I told him, as he knew the history of the object with which I was working.

To illustrate this I am recounting a number of what, to me, were momentous and astonishing examples. On one occasion Michael, handed me a small white envelope which he had received in the mail. It contained a short letter. He asked me to use psychometry on the signature of the letter writer! I placed the middle finger of my right hand on that spot of the folded letter still in the envelope.

After about ten minutes, it was as if I was in a cinema looking at an action-packed drama. There were three man-of-war battleships of the 16th century, their sails fully extended as they sailed across the Atlantic. They arrived in the Caribbean and sailed into a large horseshoe lagoon-type harbour. Tied up at the quayside was a large number of pirate ships. Without warning, the flotilla opened fire and blew the pirate ships out of the water, none escaped. Michael was silent when I came to the end of the tale.

"What on earth have I been seeing?" I queried.

"Open the envelope, take out the letter and read it", he commanded.

I did so and found that it was a short typewritten letter on headed paper. Michael has been an historian all of his life and the letter in question was in reply to a query he had asked of the sender, a gentleman of affluence. I was puzzled as to how the straightforward mundane letter could have produced such a powerful "vision." Michael then told me that an ancestor of the gentleman in question had a relative who had been with the British Admiralty in the 16th century. He had been commanded by Queen Elizabeth I to organise a flotilla of three ships to sail to the Caribbean, to root out the pirates who were the bane of legitimate merchants. To say that I was astonished was putting it mildly.

Another startling session came about when Michael handed me a small brown envelope, the contents of which I was unaware. After I had centered myself, I found that I was at the Old Head of Kinsale in Co. Cork. I "saw" a large liner coming under attack by two German U-boats. It was the sinking of the Lusitania in 1915! What was amazing about this scene was the fact that there were TWO submarines involved in the attack and this was not generally known. I saw plainly the number "30" painted on the conning tower of one of the subs. As it turned out one of the two submarines bore that number!

On being instructed to open the envelope I found that it contained an ordinary common sea shell and nothing else! Michael told me on a visit to the

Old Head one day he had picked up the shell and it was from THIS shell had its antecedents continued to hold and pass on the vibrations of that terrible event in 1915! That still goes on today and will always continue to do so 'till time immemorial.

There were many of these sessions and what I have related are two of the highlights.

The last part of this trilogy pertains to a tragic accident in which a neighbour, two of her children and her mother were killed instantly in a head-on collision. Where I live there are but sixteen houses on the drive and so everyone knew everyone else. One neighbour stood out for her kindness and goodness and she was always there through thick and thin. Everyone loved her. One terrible morning we learned that our good friend and most of her family were killed in an appalling road accident about 100 miles from Cork. We were shocked to the core. A group assembled in our sitting-room where we shared a small bottle of brandy to help us to overcome the shocking news. In common with all around us we were numb with shock, grief and sorrow. We spoke in hushed tones as we hugged each other and the tears flowed. There was a pall over the whole area.

The years rolled by and one day a good friend of mine who was both a Spiritual Healer and a Medium [who has since passed away] paid us a visit together with a woman friend who was psychic in her own right. We chatted for a while and then she noticed that I had a coloured crystal paperweight about the size of a golf ball on a shelf, part of my drinks cabinet.

I was very fond of it, as it scintillated and radiated out wonderful hues when the sunlight struck it. She asked me if she could take it down to look at it properly and I told her to go ahead. She got up from where she was sitting and as soon as she took the crystal she gave a cry! Startled, we looked at her and saw a look of horror on her face. Before any of us could say a word she blurted out what she was sensing and there and then related to us all in dramatic fashion the full story of what had happened to our dear friend and family years previously! We were flabbergasted. As long as I live I will never forget what happened that day. "How did she know?" you may well ask. The answer is simple but profound. The day the group of shocked residents were congregated in our home, the vibrations generated were of such force and magnitude that the crystal absorbed them all!

The lady who visited us with my good old friend Gordon, was top of her class in the field of Psychometry!

Case proven!

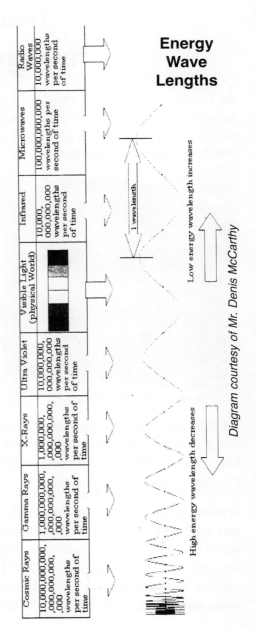

Energy Wave Lengths

Cosmic Rays	Gamma Rays	X-Rays	Ultra Violet	Visible Light (physical World)	Infrared	Microwaves	Radio Waves
10,000,000,000,000,000,000,000 wavelengths per second of time	1,000,000,000,000,000,000,000 wavelengths per second of time	1,000,000,000,000,000,000 wavelengths per second of time	10,000,000,000,000,000 wavelengths per second of time		10,000,000,000,000 wavelengths per second of time	100,000,000,000 wavelengths per second of time	10,000,000 wavelengths per second of time

1 wavelength

Low energy wavelength increases

High energy wavelength decreases

Diagram courtesy of Mr. Denis McCarthy

Chapter 15

"THOUGHTOGRAPHY"

As I write this chapter I can just hear you exclaim, "what the so and so is thoughtography?'" Well, it is a word that was conjured up to describe an ability whereby a person can, by thought alone, transfer a picture from the mind on to unexposed film!

One of the sealed cameras used in these experiments.

The first time that we in the Cork Psychical Society heard of this, was when I read an article in a weekly edition of the London "Psychic News," over thirty years ago. In the course of the article the reporter told of the visit of three Japanese researchers from Tokyo spearheaded by a Mr. Sadao Nakamichi, a 56 year old broadcasting company managing director and vice president of Japan Nengraphy Association. He brought with him albums and films of his test skotographs, photographic images appearing super-normally, with or without a camera! He had been advised to contact "Psychic News" by Prof. Chiyomatsu Tanaka and Yutaka Yoshida, permanent directors of Japan Psychic Science Association.

It goes without saying that our Cork society was very intrigued by what we had read and in particular, by the photographs of the various experiments, some of which are depicted here. What was most intriguing was the photograph of the actual [now defunct] Polaroid camera used in the experiments. It is remarkable to think that I have one of these old models in my possession today, which was used in our own similar experiments!

Part Two

The Japanese were not the only ones engaged in this type of psychic ability. At the time in question most of the attention was directed to the work of "thoughtographer" Ted Serios in America who had produced utterly astonishing results. I can recall reading about him at the time and the article contained a graphic picture of the Eiffel Tower in Paris projected on to film by thought alone by this remarkable man who had never been out of the United States in his life!

Date: 29th May, 1975
Time: 9.00p.m.

Length of concentration period: four minutes

Subject: Ship and boat on sea.

It was in the month of May, 1975 that the members, collectively decided to try out a few experiments. We had two Polaroid cameras, mine which was black and white only, while our atheistic member had a colour model. I mention this for the simple reason that his thought projection was the best of all! As he was associated with shipping and ships in general his subject for projection was a ship and a boat on the sea. His concentration and "exposure" was four minutes. To us, the print was quite extraordinary and while it did not depict the image he was projecting, instead quite a number of spirit lights appeared

The only other success, if one could call it such, was where one would expect to see a black exposure, it turned out to be "light black" in colour, in that the exposure had been affected by the thoughts of the member concerned. The member confessed that she found it hard to concentrate and that her thoughts were wandering "all over the place" during the four minutes!

As Chairman I conducted private experiments - nine in all. For the record they were as follows and all are on file:

1. Lying down on bed, top of head facing east or possibly north east. Camera was placed on small table and concentration applied for ten minutes.

   No results.

2. Lying down on bed, top of head facing east, camera held in outstretched arms and concentration applied for five minutes.

   Result — distinct difference in the black. It seemed as if it had turned into a "light/black" and possibly the makings of an image or two but this could have been a figment of my imagination.

3. Lying on bed, top of head facing east, camera held to the pituitary gland and concentration applied for ten minutes.

   Result – whitish streak appears to be running across the exposure.

4.   Lying down on bed, head facing east, camera held in out-stretched arms and concentration applied for ten minutes and willed the thoughts emerging to appear on film.

Result – remarkable difference in the black in comparison with No. 2 experiment.

5.   Sitting in upright position, back of head to north, camera held in both hands looking down and concentration applied for twenty minutes.

Result – a solid black. [N.B. it seems that the north/south position does not produce the same results as the east/west].

6.   Lying down on bed, top of head facing north, camera held pressed against solar plexus for fifteen minutes.

Result – a solid black.

7. Lying down on bed, top of head facing east, camera was held in outstretched arms and this time concentration was applied to colour picture of a stoutish lady in her late fifties smoking a cigarette.

Result – to my amazement the print was perfectly white and it is possible to discern the arm of the lady! [N.B. in my opinion the picture is over exposed. It should be noted that the picture is one of a lady who is very like my late mother-in-law and the thought struck me if this would have been conducive to better concentration with a pro-rata better result!   I was very fond of my mother-in-law].

8.   Lying down on bed, top of head facing east, camera held in outstretched arms and this time concentration was applied for three minutes to coloured frontispiece of a book "Aku-Aku" by Thor in the Pacific ocean.

Result – quite remarkable. One can see that start of an image forming and if one examines the negative and with a little effort the outline of the carving can be clearly seen.

9. Lay camera on bedside table during the night while sleeping.

Result – was indeed surprised next morning. The film was definitely affected but whether by thought waves from the brain or not I could not ascertain. [N.B. it should be noted that the white portion at the top of the exposure and running diagonally across it came about as a result of tearing the negative. Despite this one can clearly see what could be taken for a face or faces].

My keen interest in this particular type of psychic science brought me to the point where I had the distinction of being the sole Irish representative of the 'Metascience Foundation', founded and financed by Mr. George W. Meek who was President. It was at a news conference in Washington in 1982 he announced that his colleague, William J. O'Neill, had tape-recorded some 20 hours of two-way communication with a dead American scientist.

The communication with Dr. George Jeffries Mueller, a physicist who had died of a heart attack in California 14 years earlier, was obtained via an electronic device which O'Neill and Meek named Spiricom. To encourage further research by others Meek in 1982, released wiring diagrams of the device, a 100 page technical manual and cassettes, that were transmitted world-wide by United Press International.

"Only time will tell if other researchers will replicate our efforts".

In 1983 O'Neill obtained pictures on a TV screen of Dr. Mueller. In 1984 Hans Otto Koenig of West Germany replicated the Metascience research and further developed the instrumentation. In the following years many others throughout the world continued to work on this fascinating research.

It was in October 1988 that researchers in West Germany took the first steps to form an 'International Association of Trans-communication Researchers'. They included physicists, engineers, technicians and parapsychologists in the USA, Germany, Luxembourg and Switzerland.

A "test photo" projected onto a TV set allegedly from other levels of consciousness, Luxembourg, early 1987

A German woman, Hannah Buschbeck, a personal friend of George Meek and founder of the first Electronic Voice Association, allegedly placed this "photo" of herself as a young woman on the TV screen in Luxembourg in 1987, two years after her death.

"Contacts" from beyond the grave

A Corkman is the sole Irish representative on an international body which claims it is now possible to have two-way communication with the dead through electronic instrumentation. MICHAEL KELLY reports on these startling revelations.

Dr. George Jeffries Moeller (left), who died in 1967, "projected" his image (right) on a TV set as he remembered he looked as a young man.

Friedrich Juergenson, the Swedish documentary film producer, who "projected" the photo image of himself after h...

The famous French scientist, Henri Saint-Claire Deville, who lived from 1818 to 1881, "projected" how he remembered he looked as a young man...

As a matter of interest the full story of the development of the Spiricom can be found in a book entitled "The Ghost of 29 Megacycles" written by John G. Fuller who has other books to his credit. The book may be had from New American Library, P.O Box 999 Bergenfield, New Jersey 07621.

On a par with what I have written the following is an interesting case I came across on the local scene. From time to time I would be asked to comment on some aspect of matters psychic as I was well known and thought to be an authority in this field, which, I hasten to add, I am not.

One day I was approached by a businessman, whom I knew well. He had a friend who earned his living as a photographer. He was also one of the first to provide a comprehensive service where he would video weddings from start to finish. He had completed his job and was editing the film and was at the point where one saw the bride and her father come out from the home in west Cork on their way to the church for the ceremony. The pictures were in brilliant colour then, all of a sudden, the film turned black with flashes of white streaking through.

The photographer was completely taken aback especially when a face appeared through what was like the static one can experience when a television is not working properly. For the very short time the face appeared, the person said either of these sentences - "please see me" or "please free me." Immediately after this, full colour was restored and the video worked away normally. It was indeed very strange and I was asked if I would visit the photographer, which I did, together with my second son. I took my camera with me. It was old and one had to work out light and depth of focus, etc. The photographer ran and re-ran the video over and over and, at the crucial moment after the entity spoke, stopped the video. This allowed me to take a couple of pictures of what was on the screen. The features of the spirit [for that is what it had to be] were strained and the garb worn was that of a cleric with headgear that would remind one of Cardinal de Richelieu.

**Spirit Entity which
appeared on wedding video**

What happened to the cut portion of that film I have no idea. I had two small photographs, one was pretty good and the second one much inferior. I wrote to George Meek in my capacity as Irish representative of the foundation. I had an immediate reply from him in which he said it was one of the best spirit pictures he had ever come across. My contribution was passed around the globe to interested parties. For what it is worth the inferior picture is reproduced herewith.

Part Two

Mr. Bill Parfrey

62 Dosel Drive
Grange Heights

Douglas Cork 2

    Ireland

  I R L A N D

CLAUDE THORLIN

Gredbyvägen 4, C

S-632 21 ESKILSTUNA

   S w e d e n

Dear Friend,

As I presume that you are interested in the phenomenon of photo images
of the dead on television picture tube, I send you in this letter a picture of the "Jürgenson-Miracle", which happened here in Eskilstuna in
Sweden, in October 21th 1987 at 1:22 p.m.

It was an fantastic and sensational paranormal phenomenon which happened,
that our old friend, Friedrich Jürgenson, "The Father of the Electronic
Voice Phenomemon", revealed himself for my wife, Ellen, and myself on our
TV-screen – on the same day and at the same time (!) as his burial in the
small village in the south of Sweden, Höör, was started.(Eskilstuna is
approx. 420 miles from Höör).

I documented this phenomenon with my POLAROID-camera, and I send you a COPY
(reproduction) of the original photo.

Yours sincerely

Claude Thorlin

Claude Thorlin

(See UNLIMITED HORIZONS, Spring 1988, page 8 and 9.)

Ellen and Claude Thorlin, Eskilstuna, Sweden

Part Two

The dead are alive!

Communication with another reality

The picture

It was wednesday the 21th october 1987, the same day of the funeral of our friend Friedrich Jürgenson in Höör.

My wife Ellen who is a medium told me on that day that she heard in the morning an inner unindentified male voice who said: "channel four".

At first we were not sure what the voice significated, but then Ellen said that she had a feeling this might be in connection with Jürgensons funeral wich starts at 13:00.

Remembering the paranormal pictures they had made in Luxembourg, I loaded my polaroid-camera with a new film. A few minutes before 13:00 I put on the television and channel four. There is no programme on this channel in Sweden and the television screen showed only buzzing glimmer. I screwed down the irritating sound and placed myself in front of the screen with the polaroid-camera ready to shoot. Ellen sat besides me.

After a while Ellen left the room and went up to the attic to look after the laundry.

I remained sitting before the televisor and had almost lost hope when suddenly something strange happened on the screen: the glimmer passed away and the buzzing finished. It was quite dark on the screen. My first thought was that the televisor had ceased to function. However, suddenly a light point was to be seen on the left side of the screen. At this moment I put my camera ready to make a picture. The light point on the screen expanded quickly and vanished quickly - as if someone opends and closes his hand during 6-7 seconds.

During this moment (I understood that afterwards) I pushed the button of the camera. Suddenly the buzzing and glimmering came back on the screen. I looked at my watch, it showed 13:22.

When the polaroid picture was developed, I noticed Ellen, who had returned from the attic and now bent over my shoulder. "O, My God, this is Friedel!" she almost shouted.

On the photo which I held in my hand a face was now to be seen. It is true, the picture was not distinct but there was no doubt about it - it was our old friend Friedrich Jürgenson.

At the same time when the funeral of his physical body starts in the small chapel in Höör in Southern Sweden, he shows himself on the television screen to his friends in Eskilstuna!

It is very possible that Ellens medial gifts have contributed to this and similar manifestations. As mentioned before, Ellen had just gone up to the attic when the picture was taken. But if one takes into consideration that the attic lies above our living room with the televisor and that Ellen was just above the televisor when I took the picture, this fact shows interesting aspects for speculations.

During the last yers of his life Friedrich Jürgenson worked concentrated in his efforts to reach visual contact with the "other world" by means of modern video technics. Is it therefore not logical that he is the first one in this country to show himself on the screen after he had passed away?

228

Friedrich Jurgenson
(The Father of the E V P)

This is a copy of
The "Eskilstuna-Miracle"
Photographed by
Claude Thorlin,
Eskilstuna, Sweden

october, 21th 1987, 13.²² p.m.

Part Two

Chapter 16

RESCUE WORK

As the title of this chapter implies something has to be said about this serious and sometimes dangerous spiritual work. It can often happen that when a person departs from this world, because of very strong ties with what is being left behind, the spirit of that person becomes earth-bound!

We are spirit; always have been and always will be as we journey from a past infinity to a future infinity! Passing from one dimension to another is rather like a snake shedding its skin! One finds oneself with the same likes and dislikes, with thinking at whatever state of development it was when the soul was on earth.

There may be those who had great wealth, were very successful in business, had many possessions which were of no value at "death" but the memory of what they had achieved in the physical world was so great it acted rather like an anchor and instead of moving on to The Light the soul became earthbound.

This can account for the many ghosts and haunted places we hear about. On the other hand there is the person who is confused about what is to happen at death and where is he or she to go?   Many good living people for one reason or another do not find the answer in the religion into which they were born and perhaps there is a conflict within themselves as they debate the pros and cons of faith versus fact.   Each and every one has been given that most wondrous gift - an ability to think.

The value of a strong faith is that one does not have to think, but can blindly go along their own personal path. They do not have to question themselves as they endeavour to make sense of it all, commensurate with the current state of their spiritual development.   Our journey can be likened to running the spiritual marathon race of 26 miles 385 yards. A contestant at the

14 or 24 mile mark has a very much greater understanding of what the race is all about as distinct from the person who is at the 2 mile mark. No disrespect should be shown to this person for he or she will eventually arrive at the 14 and 24 mile point and indeed finish the race! "Judge not and ye shall not be judged" would appear to be the apt biblical quote.

While I was never involved in rescue work I was fully cognisant with it. I have a very spiritual and close friend who was the leader of a Rescue Circle. Let's call him Richard.

My own father passed away in December 1960 at the relatively young age of 62. Dad and I were close and we often had discussions on what lay ahead of us after we departed this life. I can remember him asking me the question "what happens after I die? Do I go to another planet or what?" I did not know then what I know now so I was unable to be of much help but we had some interesting conversations from time to time.

Sixteen years elapsed. One day I was walking down the street and met a friend who was much involved in spiritual healing. We chatted for a while and the matter of Richard and his rescue group came up in the course of the conversation. Harry said suddenly "Richard was just commenting that you had not visited him for a long time."

I concurred, adding that as Richard lived a fair distance outside of the county I had put off visiting him. I decided to phone him and we arranged for me to travel on the following Saturday and overnight with him and his family As it happened this particular Saturday coincided with a meeting of the Rescue Circle and I was invited to attend the session. As I was not a member of the group I would be in an observer capacity only.

A special room had been dedicated for this type of work and was in fact a little sanctuary where the same six people met on a specific Saturday monthly.

I believe that everything happens when it is meant to happen and this was borne out with a vengeance on this occasion. The room was comfortably warm and the smell of incense and the low playing sacred music produced a very spiritual feeling which felt good. An added touch was the beautiful floral arrangement and lighted candles.

Those taking part in the session sat around a table on which were cards bearing the words "yes" and "no." It was a form of Ouija board. I took my seat outside the circle and the ceremony commenced with a prayer for protection and guidance from the advanced spiritual being who came to help with the work. When Richard asked if the group's controlling spirit was present a pointer moved to the word "yes." From that moment on communication was received on a mental level. Without warning my father came through!

I knew it was my father for when Richard asked his name he replied "Bill Parfrey." He continued, "I do not understand. All is dark!" To Richard's query "can you see any light? Do you have any awareness of God? Can you see your mother? Back came an agitated reply "I do not understand; all is dark."

I was shocked beyond measure, but as it was my father who was communicating I was asked to join the circle. Flowers are very psychic and these were placed on the table in the middle of us - Richard said, "all will be well." I cannot describe my emotions as under Richard's directions we collectively on a mental level projected God's love, light, understanding and comprehension into the beautiful flowers. A power built up which was so intense that it was as if we were being driven back by what I felt as heat, but was in effect massive spiritual energy.

When it reached its zenith, Richard directed it to my father! Immediately he exclaimed excitedly, "I can see light, I can see my mother, I have an awareness of God!" I was simply overcome. I will never forget how one moment that mass of spiritual energy was present and then it was gone! After the meeting I was given a drop of brandy to recover from the shock.

Believe it or not the following Saturday [I was not present] dad came back to thank the group for what they and the controlling spirit brought about the previous week.

There is no such thing as time or space in the spirit world and so far as my father was concerned he was opening the door from one world to the next completely oblivious to the fact that sixteen years had gone by! He could have been there 1,000 years and not realised it. God certainly moves in mysterious ways His wonders to perform.

It cannot be stressed enough as to the importance and how valuable it is mentally to send The Light to those who are passing over or have already gone. They are certainly aware of it and it DEFINITELY helps them. I often wish that everyone would learn how to breath in and expel The Light. Think of the help that could be given at a funeral to the person who has passed over, as well as to their family and friends.

An interesting and personal point is the fact that Richard's father and mine both died at the same age - 62. My dad died in 1960 and Richard's dad died in 1968. Both experienced similar difficulties when they did pass over!

Part Three

A I S C H E   Ä R Z T E K A M M E R

rperschaft öffentlichen Rechts

Mitglied der World Medical Association

w · PARFE(R.Y
21/dd, C cok Street
____ ___ / Ireland

WIEN, I.,
WEIHSBURGGASSE 10-12

POSTANSCHRIFT:
POSTFACH 913
1011 WIEN

Fernschreib-Nr. 7701

Fernruf: 52 69 46

Giroconto: 000-00167

Erste Österr. Spar-Casse
Wien, I. Graben 21

Unser Zeichen 1661/73   Ihr Schreiben vom 23.7.1973 Ihr Zeichen   —   Wien, am   30. Juli , 1973

Betrifft: Anfrage Dr. Karl ROSENTHAL.-

Sehr geehrter Herr !

In Beantwortung Ihrer Anfrage vom 23.ds. erlaubt sich
die Österreichische Ärztekammer Ihnen die gewünschten Angaben
mitzuteilen.

Herr Hofrat Ob.Med.Rat Dr. Karl ROSENTHAL.
ist am 16.6.1953 gestorben, seine letzte Adresse lautete:
2500 Baden bei Wien , Antonsgasse 4.

Die Österreichische Ärztekammer hofft Ihnen damit gedient
zu haben.

Mit dem Ausdruck der vorzüglichen
Hochachtung

Der geschäftsführende Vizepräsident
Präs. Dr. Georg Lechner

N.B. *Dr, Karl Rosenthal was born in Salzburg and practised medicine in Berlin. Was of the Jewish Faith, held by the Nazis and was tortured. Died as a result of the atrocities perpetrated upon him [Information given through power of Spirit]*

236

Chapter 01

THE BIRTH OF A GIFT
Österreichische Ärztekammer
Körperschaft öffentlichen Rechts

W Parfrey,
21/22 Cook Street,
Cork/Ireland.

Vienna,1
Weihburggasse 10-12,
Postal Address
Post Office Box 512,
A-1010 Vienna.

Date 30.July.1973

Subject: Enquiry re Dr. Karl Rosenthal

Dear Sir,

In answer to your enquiry of the 23rd, The Austrian General Medical Council wishes to inform you that:

> Privy Councillor Obstetrician, Dr Karl Rosenthal,
> died on 16.6.1953. His last known address was:
> 2500 Baden near Vienna, Antongasse 4.

The Austrian General Medical Council hopes this is what you require.

Yours faithfully,

The Executive Vice President
Dr Georg Lechner

I have often thought that I was not born at all but issued! In common with everyone else there is meaning and purpose in life and from a very early age I had an ambition to be a medical doctor and surgeon. I had this Walter Mitty concept of being "out there" helping those that were in need. I was dreaming an impossible dream.

In those bygone days unless one was the son of a family with means, there was really no way that one could enter the portals of the university. My school endeavours were in my opinion mediocre due in large part to the fact that I knew my dream could not become a reality, in consequence of which there was no incentive to study. Round about the age of nine I used to browse through a medical book an uncle of mine had in his possession. Where he got it from I do not know for he had not the slightest interest in medicine. The diagrams fascinated me and I would spend hours poring over illustrations of digestive tracts, blood distribution systems and all that went up to make up the marvel of the human body.

I always felt "different" from everyone else and wondered why I should feel this way. I do not wish to infer that I was superior or better in any way - it was, simply that I felt out-of-step with all concerned. I had a feeling that I was on a path all by myself and so it has been all of my life. Perhaps the fact that my grandmother on either side of my family had psychic abilities had something to do with it. Again, my mother was similarly endowed and I, in turn, found that I could "see" things and "hear" things. These abilities have remained with me all of my life.

As has been related already the first four to five years of my life were turbulent to say the least. There was the feeling that I was being called back to where I had come! I have had many illnesses and set-backs in life but I realise now only too well that it was all for a purpose. If one does not experience the trauma and awfulness of pain, anguish and hitting rock bottom, how can a person relate to those who come for help?

I never lost my interest in medicine and read whatever I could understand about it overall. The years rolled by and in common with so many others I asked myself "what is life all about?" "Where do I, Bill Parfrey, fit into the scheme of things?" In time I came to the realisation that it was a lonely search and that everybody, whether they come to know it or not are simply a majority of one but still part of the whole!

In life the test of a person is the fight that that person makes; at least that has been my experience. On losing my job with the company with which I worked for eighteen years in Cahir, County Tipperary I was forced to return to my native city , Cork. I had a wife, three young children, and a ten pound note and had to start all over again.   The going was tough – very tough. The economy in 1962 was not good. Jobs were very scarce and thousands of people were leaving the country weekly to work in England. Fate stopped me from following so many of my countrymen and women when I was fortunate to secure employment, but with very small pay.

Despite the commitments I owed to my family I was instrumental in founding the Cork Psychical Society. I was its chairman for ten years and continued my studies of as many aspects of psychic science as was possible.

One of the subjects was Numerology which I found fascinating. As time went by I began to notice that the number eight was coming into my life a great deal. Eight is the number associated with fate and it can mean that a challenge is in the offing. I took up the challenge and went out of my way to accentuate the power of Saturn's number in every way possible. The number eight started to crop up everywhere. Stuck in traffic, the number of the car in front would be eight. Go for a meal and the table number would be eight and so it went on and on.

Around about this time I began to feel an irresistible urge to learn the German language. I had in the past made a number of half-hearted attempts to master it but to no avail. The year 1970 [an 8: $1+9+7+0 = 17 = 8$] was a disastrous year for me. I had to enter hospital six times; four times for operations. I had a very serious nervous breakdown, was on the suicide trail a couple of times and felt compelled to enter a mental hospital. Those were the darkest days of my life and I did not think that I would recover. With an inner strength I overcame my demons but it took me six years to recover fully.

The difference between mental illness and a physical complaint is that one cannot see what is going on in another person's mind but can observe a physical disability. I always felt that the book "One flew over the cuckoo's nest" was based on my experience.

The year 1972 saw me in Germany on two occasions. I had never been in the country previously but as soon as I stepped off the plane at Hanover I felt as if I belonged there! I could speak but ten words of German. This was a business trip to visit the Hanover trade fair. The second visit was for pleasure when two friends and I went down the Rhine Valley for a wine festival. Returning home through London we were booked to stay in a small hotel. On taking up my reservation the receptionist said to me "room eight, please." This matter of the eight's had now been going on for a couple of years and had reached a peak.

The following day was the 26th October - another eight! (2 + 6 = 8). I knew without the shadow of a doubt that there was a reason for me to be in London on this particular day. I do not like big cities and had been wondering what I was going to do all day as my flight was not until 5.00pm that afternoon. While I was musing, I heard a voice say to me "Go to the Spiritualist headquarters in Belgrave Square!" So off I went.

I was met by an elderly gentleman at reception. "Can I help you?" he enquired. I found myself exclaiming "I'm Bill Parfrey from Cork and am the chairman of the Cork Psychical Society." "Oh yes, Mr. Parfrey, you wrote to us on a number of occasions about psychical matters." Confirming that this was indeed the case

"May I see a medium, please?" I found myself asking

"Of course you can at 4.00pm" came the reply.

"Well," I said, "that's no good as I have to be at Heathrow airport at that time as my flight departs at 5.00pm."

I felt a little foolish and began to try and back out of the situation when the man said "you can see a medium at 1.00pm!" The time was eight minutes to one! I looked at him, surprised and said "but you just told me that I could not see a medium until four in the afternoon." He looked me straight in the eye and said directly "I KNOW that you have to see a medium!"

With that I paid a small fee on receipt of which he said "go down the Conan Doyle corridor into room eight, please." I could not believe it and it was at this point that something outside myself was carrying me along. I entered the room. It was about fifteen by 12 feet in size.

I was there but a few minutes when in bustled Mrs. Doris Collins, one of England's leading mediums.

"Mr. Parfrey?" she enquired to which I replied, "Yes."

"Mr. Parfrey" she continued, "I never see anyone at one o'clock but I was TOLD that I was to see you!"

She did not mean the man at reception but by sources in a different dimension. I was now well and truly out of my depth.

Commencing with a prayer she informed me that I had the gift of healing and that for the preceding fourteen years an Austrian doctor named Dr. Karl Rosenthal had been working through me. She went on to say that this help would increase dramatically during the following four years, as indeed it did. I began to hear German words and phrases in my head. I returned to Cork and straight away people with problems started to come to me from nowhere and each and every one was helped.

At this time I was studying the German language intensively and one evening my teacher - a German lady - suggested that I try to find out something about Dr. Karl Rosenthal. After some months I was informed by the Austrian Medical Council that he had been a professor of Obstetrics and had come from Salzburg. I was given his last known address which was in the Vienna district. I was also informed that he had "died" on the 23rd July, 1953!

As the years went by I became conscious of the fact that I had other helpers in the world of Spirit and through their good offices many people were healed. I had difficulty in coming to terms with what was happening and I often felt as if the whole thing was something I was imagining and perhaps I was heading for another breakdown.

As if to give me confidence and encouragement an extraordinary event occurred. One day on local radio there was an appeal for a healer. I responded and was put in touch with a young woman. She told me that, for the last two months, her grandfather was in a local hospital with gangrene of one of his legs. He was due to have it amputated on the following Wednesday morning.

"I was with my grandfather" she told me "and was thinking what might be done when suddenly into my mind came the suggestion to call upon the services of a healer so I put out the request on local radio and lo and behold you come on the scene."

Off go the two of us to the hospital. Her grandfather was a great old man well into his seventies. I did what I was directed to do and told him that I would call to see him again on the following Monday morning, which I did. The next morning a nurse came to dress his leg which, the night before, was black from the knee down to his toes oozing putrid fluid. To her utter astonishment, on taking off the bandages, the old man had a brand new leg! She screamed and ran for the doctor. He came and shaking his head in disbelief said "I don't understand."

"What will I do now?" asked the patient. "Get up and go home" came the reply. The old man did just that and walked out of the hospital where he had been for so long. He came to see me where I ran a business. At first I did not recognise him. A tall dignified man, he was dressed in a tweed overcoat and soft hat and carried a stick.

"I have come to tell you of a miracle", he began and went on to relate what had happened at the hospital. I was awe-struck and spent that entire day thanking God for what had taken place.

This experience changed my life. It was a huge milestone for me in coming to terms with the enormity of the universal power that is there.

Healing comes about through compassion and love of one's fellow being.

The power to heal is, in my humble opinion, in direct proportion to one's own inner understanding and concept of the power of God. This traumatic experience was instrumental in changing my whole life and ultimately making me decide to give up the business upon which I depended for a living and, in trust, go out and help as many people as I could.

In this regard it is astonishing to think that in the past 35 years [it is now 2006] over 31,000 people have sought help world wide. This does not include the 2,901 others who are on my Distant Healing list! Let me hasten to assure the reader that I, Bill Parfrey, have NO power but am simply a conduit through which the Power flows. I have been very privileged to have had a myriad of experiences which have brought me to my current understanding. In essence the fact is that I know nothing. The profundity of it all is that it is the "nothing" that does the healing!

Chapter 02

SOUL SEARCHING

It is over forty years since I really began to be aware that there was something passing through me. This "something" was intangible and impossible to put into words.

All my life people from all walks of life were drawn to me in many different ways. Even as a child older children than myself would seek me out to tell me of a problem that was a worry to them. In adult terms the difficulties would be looked upon as being trivial but of major importance to those seeking guidance. Invariably after discussion the solution would pop up out of the blue!

A lesson I learned early in life was never to give advice to anyone. Invariably such advice was what the adviser needed themselves! There is a tendency for one's Ego to suggest that it knows it all! Over the intervening years I began to realise that if I happened to visit a sick person in hospital or at home they improved and I would receive a 'phone call or a note later. The message would read "Bill, I don't know what you did but I felt great after you came to see me." It was ironic that I did not know either!

The greatest gift any of us has is an ability to think, so I started thinking.

Was it possible that some form of healing energy was passing through me?

Was it this "something" I had always felt?

I started to read books about others who had developed a healing gift; people like the famous Harry Edwards. He was a printer by trade and became world-famous. As far as I can recall he was known as "the reluctant healer!" My reading led to a whole new understanding and I came to know without doubt that I was being led into the field of spirit communication. I had mentors - Spirit guides - as has everyone else. My awareness of them became stronger to help me in the work I was destined to do. Little did I realise at the time that my guides were like John the Baptist, preparing the way for me to begin my slow torturous search for understanding. My discovery of the awesome and vastness of God and where I, an infinitesimal microscopic speck, but still part of GOD, slotted into part of His plan.

I vividly remember the first time I was introduced to a guide. A medium from the north of Ireland came on a visit for a couple of days. One afternoon he said, suddenly " you have a spirit guide, a Red Indian, his name is White Feather." I was completely taken aback and must confess that I found this very hard to take on board. I was prone to think the whole thing ridiculous. He told me that what he had said was true and would be borne out by the fact that I would come across a white feather the following morning. So I did - loads of them!

The area where I parked my car was home to many birds and there were feathers all over the place. I took it all with the proverbial grain of salt. Arriving at my place of work I was taken by surprise at the sight of a huge white feather, albeit an artificial one used for advertising purposes - but still a white feather! From that moment on I sensed the presence of a kind, wise and good man. I could "see" him. He was sixty-two years of age, was over six feet in height, had long grey hair neatly brushed back to the nape of his neck in which he sported a white feather He had a thin gold band on each of his upper arms.

Stansted Hall, England is the home of Spiritualism. I was prompted to attend a week's course on spiritual development at this renowned college. It was an amazing week and my experiences there opened a floodgate of further understanding. One morning during meditation White Feather spoke to me. I was completely taken aback.

"You speak," he repeated the two words a couple of times.

I was with a group of people enjoying coffee when White Feather said that the lady sitting opposite was sad and depressed because, he said, her seven year old son had lost his life in a millrace. His parents had converted an old mill into a home with the mill-race still attached.

Part Three

"You speak!" commanded White Feather.

Clearing my throat I leaned across the table and addressed the lady in question.

"Excuse me," I said, "but I want to refer to the passing of your seven year old son who lost his life in a millrace."

There was a stunned silence.

"How do you know of the death of my son?" The woman blanched and said in a hushed voice.

I explained and, as I did so, more and more information was being fed to me to relate to the little boy's mother. As pertinent and personal details were given, a most wonderful change came over the countenance of the mother. Her face radiated out happiness as if an enormous weight had been lifted from her shoulders and where dark clouds had gathered, now there was nothing but beautiful sunshine. A healing had taken place.

I "worked" with White Feather for quite a long time and we became firm friends. I might add that healing work was not confined to human beings but also included animals. On two occasions I was asked to help heal horses, one being a very ordinary animal and the other, a race horse valued at over £51,000 [€64,756.64].I know nothing at all about horses except to be able to differentiate between the front and the back. In the first instance the poor horse was suffering from joint evil which is the swelling of the fetlocks. In this particular case I was not aware of White Feather. In retrospect he must have been there for the horse was healed of his complaint within the space of a few hours! On the second occasion the request came from an affluent family in the midlands who reared and trained horses. One of their most valuable stallions became lame and was unable to put his left hind leg on the ground. Vets from all over the country were called in but to no avail. Even an English veterinary surgeon was flown in to examine the horse but to no avail.

Part Three

It was a cold crisp night with frost on the ground when I stepped off the train to be met by the lady who had requested help. There was then a journey of some fifty miles by car. I was met by a reception committee comprised of the owner of the estate, his wife and some friends and two of the staff who were groomsmen. I really felt out of my depth as we went to the magnificent centrally heated stable in which this prized horse was housed. He was a huge animal much taller than myself. He stood there majestically with his left hind leg raised from the ground. as if in pain. I do not know the first thing about horseflesh and when we met face to face all I could say was, "Good evening horse!"

It goes without saying I did not receive a reply. There was an expectant look on the faces of the assembled gathering as I went to the rear end of the horse. I had not the semblance of an idea as to what I should do so threw it all over to the powers-that-be! Placing my right hand high up along the spine to my utter astonishment I heard myself say,

"I think the spine of the horse is out of alignment!"

There were gasps of astonishment from those present. I did not know at the time that the English veterinary surgeon gave as his opinion that the animal's spine was indeed out of alignment! I then found myself being directed to bring my left hand into the groin area and I could feel a power running from my right hand which was still on the spine of the horse to my left hand which was firmly placed in the groin. Then quite an amazing thing happened. The horse turned his head and looking at me actually nodded his head as much as to say that I had found the root cause of the trouble! Within the space of a few minutes the horse slowly but surely lowered his leg and placed his hoof firmly on the ground.

The horse was led back into his comfortable stable while I in turn was led back to the house for a fabulous meal which lasted for hours during which time the sole topic of conversation was about healing and ancillary subjects. Around one o'clock in the morning we went back to the stable to see the patient. The horse came cantering over to us, all four legs working in per-

247

fect harmony. Much later that night as I lay in bed thinking over the extraordinary events I knew without the shadow of a doubt that White Feather had been instrumental in channelling the necessary energies which had brought about the healing of this prized stallion.

On the matter of spirit guides it is my considered opinion that as a person's awareness develops over a long period of time the tiniest semblance of understanding begins to make its presence felt. The awesome structure of the spiritual Hierarchy and of what this entails; the enormity of what is beyond stretching to infinity. All this affords the person developing any kind of spiritual gift to make a link with the Universal Intelligence using, as if teachers in the kindergarten, spirit guides.

We also have help from angels and archangels and all the company of heaven. We must not forget our personal guardian angel It is generally accepted that we each have a minimum of five and a maximum of eight guides, not necessarily at the same time The day can dawn when one's spirit guides leave having served their purpose. In bringing the person who is developing to a certain point their job is done. This happened to me when suddenly I found myself entirely alone.

I seemed to be lost in an incomprehensible void. I knew I was out of my depth but at the same time was certain that what had happened was for a purpose. As time went by I began to sense "The Luminous Ones." After further progression I became conscious of "The Shining Ones" and a new inner knowledge that had been within myself all along was slowly revealed. The ability to be used as a conduit for healing energies increased in direct proportion to my understanding of what was being made clear to me at my new level.

I have learned that in this field of spiritual development the rule is make haste slowly! One cannot go from the kindergarten to the school of cosmic physics in one step. The maxim that when the pupil is ready the master will come is also so true, The path is not an easy one, there being many set-backs and many times when one feels like packing it all in. There is a great deal

Part Three

of anguish to boot and continual soul-searching is the order of the day as
one tries to come to terms with the enormity of it all.

Chapter 03

AWARENESS LEADS TO TRUST

Awareness is defined as having knowledge, consciousness; not ignorant.

In the field of spiritual development this necessary ingredient comes to fruition extremely slowly. It can be so slow that a person is not conscious of the fact that progress is being made at all! Then suddenly when one least expects it, to coin a phrase, they become aware of awareness!

Progress has been made inwardly and there is a sense of personal satisfaction. It is only as time goes by that one comes to realise that the inner satisfaction is stemming from one's ego! The ego can be a real disruptive force if not controlled. The more one notices that they are using the personal pronoun "I" over and over again they have a problem which has to be dealt with in the early stages. The reality of the situation is that no matter how well awareness develops the truth of the matter is one really knows nothing when what is to be absorbed is taken into account . How this awareness develops for each of us is unique for the simple fact is that each of us IS unique!

Those who read this book will discover how the powers-that-be decided to develop MY awareness. To many it may seem strange and hard to believe. It is of no consequence because it was relevant only to myself

Many incidents in my life contributed to my development and I have come to know without the shadow of a doubt that everything happens for a purpose. As an example, one day I was approached by a lady who asked me if I would be prepared to visit a priest who was in the ICU of one of the major hospitals in the city. I have never refused a request in my life and said that I would be more than happy to help in any way I could.

The lady explained to me that she was acting on behalf of a friend who was the sister of the priest in question. He was extremely ill and had suffered two heart attacks together with two brain haemorrhages. He had been unconscious for over two months and his prognosis was not good – a complete understatement.

On the appointed day at seven in the evening I met my contact and off we went to the intensive care unit. We rang the bell and in a very short space of time a nurse opened the door.

"Yes?" she enquired.

"I would like this man to see Fr. O'Brien?" [not his real name]

"Are you his relations" was the next question.

On confirming that we were not the nurse told us that it was impossible for us to enter the ICU. On hearing this my companion, pointing at me, blurted out "he's a faith healer!" - a term I detest.

The nurse took one look at me with disdain and her nostrils twitched as if there was something wrong with the drains!. She said not a word as she togged me out in white and led me into the inner sanctum of the ICU. I have to confess that I was not really prepared for what was before me. I had never seen a person on a life support machine.

Suddenly I was confronted with this heavy-set man, completely naked. He was lying on what to my uneducated mind was a flat board. Wires appeared to be attached to him everywhere and tubes came out of every orifice of his body. A pump beside him literally forced life-giving oxygen into his lungs with such ferocity that the whole board shook regularly as if to the beat of a drum.

I stood beside his unconscious form and had not the slightest idea what to do. The nurse twiddled various dials, checked tubes and all the paraphernalia that goes to make up today's ICU. I was out of my depth big time.

Taking a deep breath I appealed to the Higher Power for guidance. There were only two places where I could touch the patient. One was the middle finger of his left hand and the other his elbow. The nurse left me to my own devices - a pun, but in reality, it was the truth! Suddenly I felt a power running through me which in turn was transmitted to Fr. O'Brien. I was startled when without warning he opened his eyes and looked at me knowingly. He said not a word. After a few minutes he opened his eyes yet again and I could see that he was looking at me intelligently. He closed his eyes once more and I saw clairvoyantly his soul was going through a count-down procedure preparatory to leaving his physical frame. I left the ICU and sought out my companion. I recounted what had transpired and gave as my opinion that Fr. O'Brien was on his way to higher climes. She was amazed that he had opened his eyes. His sister had been visiting him for a number of months and never had this happen.

Ten days went by and one evening around five o'clock I bought a copy of the local daily evening paper. There was a sub-heading on the front paper which read "Death of great priest." The report went on to tell of the work that Fr. O'Brien had done for the blind and the mentally impaired. I read the report as I walked across Patrick's Bridge in Cork city at the height of the city traffic and as I did so Fr. O'Brien spoke to me on a mental level.

"I would like to thank you Bill for coming to see me in the hospital a few weeks ago," he said.

As he spoke I could see him clairvoyantly in the company of other spirit guides who at the time were my constant help. There was a confused look on his face. Our "conversation" continued for quite some time. He said, suddenly, "I'll help with the healing work." With that, for want of a better word, he went off the vibration!

A further two weeks elapsed when out of the blue I received a 'phone call from a musician in Dublin who was a member of the national symphony orchestra. She told me that she was having hearing difficulties and that conventional medicine was unable to help her. She insisted on travelling to Cork to see me. Following introductions I commenced to administer healing and while doing so, to my astonishment, I became aware that Fr. O'Brien was making his presence felt.

"Bill," he said, "I've come about the lady's eyes."

Mentally I replied.

"Father it is not an eye job at all but a hearing problem."

With that he disappeared.

When I had finished my patient told me she found a distinct improvement. Saying how happy she was the good lady shocked me when she said,

"You know, I had a very peculiar experience as you were administering healing."

"Is that so," I said casually.

"Yes," she continued, "I heard a man tell me that there was nothing wrong with my eyes."

"Is there something wrong with your eyes?" I asked quite startled.

"There is I am afraid," came the reply, "My hearing difficulty is linked in some way to my sight problem."

I was astounded and could hardly believe what the lady said. One week later I was asked to call to see an elderly lady with a severe back problem. Her husband suffered from Meniere's disease, a most distressing ailment with deafness and disconcerting noises in the ear, In a taunting manner he asked if I could relieve him of his complaint. I told him that I had no idea. I did my best to allow the power to go through but to no avail. I sensed resistance. His face said it all. The following week I paid a return visit to the lady who was vastly improved. I was quite taken aback when her cynical husband asked me to see what I could do for him yet again. I had barely commenced when who should come on the vibration but Fr. O'Brien!

"I'll fix his Meniere's disease" he said and there and then all traces of the disease vanished never to return again!

Fr. O'Brien turned up once more, one month later.

I happened to be in Dublin and called to see my sister who had lived in the capital for many years. By a most extraordinary coincidence [I know now that there is no such thing] a first cousin of mine who lived in England and who I had not seen for over thirty years paid a surprise visit to my sister at the same time. It goes without saying we had a great deal to talk about and the matter of my healing work up in the conversation. My cousin was born completely deaf in one ear and had partial hearing in the other. She had to wear a powerful hearing aid. When the matter of Fr. O'Brien came up my cousin exclaimed suddenly,

"Do you think that he could help me?"

"We can but try" was my reply.

Fr. O'Brien obliged to such an extent that my cousin's deafness went from both ears! We were amazed. I have to confess that half an hour later the deafness returned to the ear which was deaf since birth. The other one maintained the vast improvement that had come about. From that day to this, many years after the events described, I have neither heard nor sensed anything of Fr. O'Brien.

Truly does God move in mysterious ways His wonders to perform. The enormity of it all is so hard to grasp. Just when we think we have come to grips with some aspect of ourselves, who and what we are, where we slot in starts to give us the illusion that we are peeling an onion. There are countless layers, each of which has to be dealt with and thought about. The more we think we know, in reality, we know less and less! It is as if we are but pawns in an awesome cosmic game of chess.

Checkmate!

Chapter 04

A NON–DREAM EXPERIENCE

I have to stress yet again that the experiences I have had in the development of my personal awareness of how God works is unique to me and no one else. The same holds good for every other individual!

"Why is this so?" one may well ask.

The answer is simple but profound. It is because we are all unique; separate certainly but at the same time part of the whole. We live and have our being in God. It is as if each of us is a minute tiny cell that goes to constitute the body of God on all levels. Yet, the magnitude of it all is that this incomprehensible body of God is itself but another single cell on yet a greater body, ad infinitum! The mind boggles at this concept. It is as one meditates on this profound thought that the personal awareness begins to blossom.

How many of us appreciate the fact that should we have the opportunity of examining our own bodies with the aid of an electronic microscope we would be looking at a world of what appèars to be mountains, gullies, rivers. A whole panorama of 350,000,000 infinitesimal creatures live and have their being. Like us they are born, grow up, reproduce, live their short lives and die. God is in them just as much as He is in us. So far as these creatures are concerned our bodies are their universe! As these infinitesimal creatures are to our bodies so too are we to the body of God. In truth there is no beginning and no end. Whether it is a good thing or not I have never ceased to ponder whether it is a good thing or not.

To my mind, of the two great gifts that we have been given, viz. an ability to think and free will, the former reigns supreme. No matter where a person is, no matter what their circumstances are, rich or poor, sick or well, happy or sad, one can think! We must never forget that thought is a force and we have the freewill to think in a positive manner or a negative way. Energy follows thought so when we think in a positive way, positive energy streams out.

Energy invariably comes back to its source and marries into the five million new cells that are born in the body every second. We feel good. Precisely the opposite happens when we think in a negative way. From where does our thinking stem? Certainly not from our brains for these are physical and are the servant of our minds. Do our thoughts originate in the mind? I do not think so. The mind is dependant on our soul which, in turn is dependant on our spirit of which it is part. At this time of our evolvement, as we cannot go higher, it stands to reason that all our thoughts stem from this source. If we accept that God is a spirit it shows graphically that all our thoughts, both good and bad, are being directed to us from on high.

Our ability to come to terms with this concept is in direct proportion to our current understanding of the purpose of being!

In common with everyone I have wrestled with this cosmic conundrum, often to such an extent I felt my brain heating up as if the circuits were being overloaded. I am sure that they were.

As if in recompense, on rare occasions I have been given the privilege of having my personal understanding shown to me from a different angle. These were instrumental in elevating my inner awareness to a higher plateau with a consequential increase in the healing power. What I term "non-dreams" are the catalysts which come about when I am neither asleep nor awake. It is a trance-like state. I mentioned previously the help I received from my spirit guides, one of whom was a Zen Buddhist.

He was so far advanced spiritually that he had neither shape nor form and, on the few occasions he made his presence felt, invariably appeared as a shower of golden granules. Rather like a beautiful cascading waterfall.

At that time I was conscious of being guided by five personages. Each appeared to be on a separate level of consciousness, one above the other. At the top was the Zen Buddhist who I nick-named "10-10-20" as the golden granules reminded me of the granulated fertiliser used by the farming community. I could not think of any other name, nor was one given to me and 10-10-20 seemed apt. On reflection I think I was inspired to link him in this fashion after all.

It was slightly after 3.30p.m. when I arrived at St. Luke's. Bearing in mind that the Absent Healing session was to commence at 3.00p.m. I felt very reluctant to enter the church at all. The ceremony will be over I thought to myself. Something prompted me to go in. I entered through a side door near to the choir stalls and found seven people sitting there, one of whom I knew personally. I sat down increasing the number present to eight, which to me was significant.

I had barely settled myself when a clergyman opened the door of the vestry/sacristy and came into the church proper and entered the sanctuary. I was delighted with myself. The ceremony was commencing half-an-hour late. After a short period of silent prayer the clergyman asked us to state the names of those seeking help. Only first names were used and each person in turn would list those who had requested healing. For example, one might say "I submit the name of Michael who is suffering from terminal cancer." All present would then concentrate on Michael and one could sense a shaft of power rising heavenwards. It was quite an exhilarating experience. When each had been prayed, for an invitation was extended to the eight of us to approach the altar for the laying on of hands. This we did as a group.

At this time of my life I was searching frantically - and still am - for answers and was convinced that something dramatic was going to happen to me when I experienced the laying on of hands. There was a lady kneeling beside me to the left and when she was about to have hands laid on her head I heard her say, "I have come for Peter."

I expected an instant revelation when my turn came but to my chagrin I felt nothing. I felt let down. I left the church and returned to my place of work. The following Friday afternoon the cleric who had officiated on Wednesday came into my shop to purchase a technical drawing pen. He being a brilliant artist. He visited my shop every so often. On entry I went forward to greet him, noting at the same time that he looked rather pale and haggard.

Referring back to the previous Wednesday I remarked how lucky I was that he did not commence the ceremony until 3.30p.m. He looked at me with a queer expression in his eyes.

"What are you talking about? I started the session at 3.00p.m.!"

"I beg your pardon but you did not. as I was stuck in traffic near the city hall at that precise hour," I replied.

"I did commence at 3.00p.m.," Somewhat irritatedly he exclaimed, "As you are probably aware it is necessary to prepare oneself for the ceremony for the best part of two hours and I was in the church for that time. The clock on the vestry wall showed 3.00p.m. precisely as I entered the church proper."

"There is something very strange here," I, in turn replied, explaining my sequence of events. He looked at me oddly.

"I have felt most peculiar since Wednesday. You will have noticed that I had to sit quietly on one of the chairs in the sanctuary for nearly ten minutes," he replied, quietly, "I found myself out of my body and flying over the countryside in west Cork and was not in the church at all! As a matter of fact I have been granted three weeks furlough to come to terms with what happened."

I knew a good deal about Astral Projection and explained to him that this is what he had experienced. It was two weeks later that I learned from my friend that Peter, who had been terminally ill and for whom the lady requested healing, within a few days regained his full health.

The two experiences that I had on the Monday and Wednesday of the same week where time and space were involved affected me profoundly. Both episodes were for a purpose as indeed is the case for us all. Many years have gone by since then and I am convinced that both episodes were stepping stones to further enlightenment.

May each and every one of us become more and more aware of the power of God that guides our destinies and spurs us along the path chosen by our respective souls.

Chapter 06

GIVING AND RECEIVING

We are familiar with the phrase, 'It is more bless-ed to give than to receive'.

All my life I have been giving of myself in every field of endeavour. I confess that, on the other side of the coin, I find it extremely difficult to receive. This caused me problems and when someone I was able to help wished to thank me in some practical manner, I invariably declined. If they insisted I would tell them to give it to some charity or someone that was worse off than myself. Sometimes the parties concerned would be a little peeved by this but I still held my ground. Oh how I had to learn that it was necessary for me to receive. It was one of the most difficult lessons of my life.

I worked extremely hard and long hours to provide the three basic essentials. These are, some sort of a roof over one's head, some food in the belly and a light! The roof may only be of corrugated iron, the food frugal and the light a candle but it constitutes home, be it ever so humble. I financed the healing work from very limited means. I never refused a request and if some one in a distant part of the country contacted me and asked if I could visit them, off I went. I would accept overnight hospitality, a meal perhaps, but that was all, I would never accept anything towards the overall costs.

One day, many years ago, I met a friend. We were not close but he had been a member of the Cork Psychical Society. I had not seen him for some considerable time and it was quite extraordinary how we met up on this particular occasion. Both of us happened to be walking along a street which neither of us frequented that often. Again neither of us would normally be in that part of town at that particular time. We espied each other at the same moment as we walked in opposite directions.

"Good morning Sean", I said as we passed and he returned my greeting.

We continued on in opposite directions for about ten yards and then stopped suddenly. I turned around and found that Sean had also stopped just as suddenly and we came back to meet each other.

"I don't know what pulled me up short," exclaimed Sean.

"I don't know either", I replied.

We exchanged a few pleasantries and then he enquired as to how things were progressing in the society of which he had been a member but had resigned a few years previously. I brought him up to date as to the activities and then he asked me how my healing work was getting on. I explained how I found myself developing a new sense of awareness. I told him about Dr. Karl Rosenthal who I referred to earlier on in this book.

Hearing this he became quite excited and said I was the answer to prayers.

"What do you mean?" I inquired.

The flood-gates opened as he went on to tell me that his daughter aged twelve had no vision in her left eye and this had just been discovered. He and his family had been praying for her, making Novenas in an effort to invoke a miracle but all to no avail.

"Now", he said, "I meet you on this street and at this particular time and place and you tell me about Dr. Rosenthal; it is beyond coincidence. It must be that you are the answer to our prayers!"

"Sean," I said, "that's a tall order, nevertheless I will visit your daughter."

This I did. As a matter of fact I went to see her on twelve occasions over a period of a year and on my last visit she had her vision restored! Around Christmas time her father came to see me in my office.

"Bill, I really appreciate what you did and my wife and I would like you to accept this little gift from us."

"I don't want anything for it was nothing I did." I retorted.

He was very insistent so reluctantly I accepted the box of chocolates and the bottle of after-shave lotion. I gave the chocolates to the children and being stuck for a small Christmas present for a friend wrapped up the bottle in Christmas wrapping and wrote my best wishes on the accompanying card.

Part Three

Well, immediately after the festive season I seemed to be debarred from helping anyone. It was quite extraordinary. Positively no requests for healing came from anywhere. I found myself in the spiritual doldrums and so it went on for seven months. I began to wonder what it was all about and came to the conclusion that it had something to do with the acceptance of the gifts from Sean. I had a great deal of anguish with which to contend. One day I went for a long drive in a lonely part of the country and there I stayed where I talked with God, personified by the river, the trees, the stones and wild flowers with all the insects hovering round and about.

I looked in awe at the majesty of the branches of the trees moving and, as always, pondered what made them move! I can visualise people saying "surely to goodness he knows that it is the wind that makes the branches sway!" Of course I know that but I ask in return "have you ever seen the wind?"

"Come to think of it, 'no'" is the reply."

I believe that there are adepts and mystics who have actually seen the wind. It must truly be an awesome and terrifying sight As I sat there musing and meditating, I sensed a voice telling me that because I had accepted a gift this was the reason there had been no calls for help during the interim. There and then I swore an oath that as long as I lived I would not take anything for the healing work.

It is important to note that it was my ego that said all this; another lesson I had to learn. I came back to Cork and that very day there was a request on local radio seeking the services of a healer. I answered the call. In earlier chapters of this book you will have read about the astounding miracle that came about where an old man in his late seventies with a gangrenous left leg from knee to toe which was to have been amputated was given a brand new leg through healing. I never looked back from that day.

During the next few years I went to extreme lengths to make sure that I never received anything for the work I was privileged to do. It became rather like an obsession. If someone wrote to me enclosing a stamped addressed envelope I would refund that person the cost of the stamp! No matter where I went in the country I would not take anything towards costs. I was becoming frenetic and it was really putting me off balance.

By this time I had packed up the business and was earning a living as best as I could as a business consultant! It sounded great but I was a jack-of-all-trades-and-master-of-none! Through a chequered career I know something about nearly everything but haven't a degree in the world. As time went by the powers-that-be started to lend a hand. I remember on one occasion travelling from Cork to Belfast to visit a lady who was very ill. The journey is, give or take, one of nearly 300 miles from one end of the country to the other. On the return journey my car travelled 250 miles on three-quarters of a gallon of petrol! I would hear a voice instructing me to go a fruit machine in some amusement arcade. I would put in 50p [63c] in the slot and out would come £10. [€12.70] and the voice would say "that is to pay for the journey to such and such a place."

I remember one year during the month of November I arranged a day's healing session under the auspices of the Dublin Psychical and Spiritual Studies group where I treated upwards of twenty people. On the 17th December I received am unsigned Christmas card with a Dublin postmark and which contained within the sum of £100 [€127] in notes. I knew instinctively that it had come from someone whom I had been privileged to help so I promptly gave the money away! This despite the fact that it would have been mighty useful with Christmas but a few days away. On Christmas Eve at 9.45p.m. an envelope was pushed through the letterbox of my home. I opened it and it contained £200 [€254] in notes! The money was accompanied with a short letter thanking me for something I had done for this person in July and as it had nothing whatsoever to do with healing I could hold on to it! I gave away €127 on the 17th December and received back double the amount within seven days! Talk about casting your bread upon the waters!

The one thing that I have learned in life is to TRUST the Power that made us. The Bible tells us that the very hairs of our head are numbered and if one sparrow falls to the ground God will know about it. To me there is a great difference between belief and trust. I always feel that when we say "I believe" it means we doubt. Belief is not knowledge. For example one might say "I believe the number 20 bus will be here at 6.00p.m.," It might and it might not. Now if we substitute the word "know" for "believe" we are really firing on all cylinders. In the field of healing I do not like the word "hope." Sometimes after a healing session the patient would say " I hope I will be better now." For fun I'd exclaim "did you not see the sign at the door, "abandon hope all ye that enter here?" Of course there would be no such sign; I merely say it to startle the person and catch their attention.

The bottom line is that all healing is on trust. If our trust is from the top drawer we need to ask God but once. To me, the reason why people continue to beseech God for His help is because they doubt! In the field of healing I find it vital to KNOW that the person is going to improve as distinct from BELIEVING that the person is going to be restored to full health. Very often it is the healer who blocks the very power coming from the universal source due to the fact that he or she is human and the trust might slip from time to time.

Healing is a vast subject and the more one learns the more one comes to the realisation that they know nothing.

But by making it simple one finds that it is the "nothing" that does the actual healing!

Chapter 07

EVERY ACTION HAS AN EQUAL AND OPPOSITE REACTION

I have learned something very profound. It is that the Universe expands and contracts in direct proportion to our requirements, provided we trust!

You will recall reading about the oath I swore after my seven month sabbatical. In a most extraordinary way I came to the realisation that I had not made a promise to God, but to myself! To my shame and chagrin I had let pride come into the equation and I wanted to do God's will my way while He wanted me to do it His way!

Every action has an equal and opposite reaction so when one gives one must receive in some form. I had to learn the hard way to come to terms with this fundamental fact.

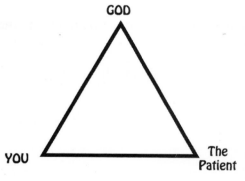

Picture a triangle. The healer and the patient are at the base, one at each angle while the universal power which is GOD is at the apex. The healing power - a positive force - comes from this source and is directed by the mind of the healer, who is in effect the channel through which these majestic and awesome energies flow. All illnesses can be looked upon as a negative force. The healer endeavours to balance this with a positive force thereby helping to overcome the "dis-ease" which one could describe as "not being at ease" As I stated previously, in all my years I have never made a charge of any sort.

Going back to the Bible we read what Jesus said to His disciples: "Go out and in My name heal the sick and preach the gospel." Note that He did not say preach the gospel and heal the sick but rather show them something first of all! He continued "make the lame to walk, the blind to see and the deaf to hear" He told them that as He gave the power they were to "make no charge!" He did however add a rider to the effect that as the labourer was worthy of his hire if something was offered "accept it in My name."

I steadfastly adhered to this instruction and had a donation box in my clinic. If someone wished to make a contribution for the continuation of the work envelopes were provided to afford privacy. It did not matter to me if the donation was great, little or small, or indeed if anything was given. Everything is relative and we only have to think of the poor woman who gave but two "mites" which, in our Lord's eyes, was a greater donation by far than that given by the affluent person who was not hurt financially while the widow had given everything she had!

It is a strange fact that because a healer makes no charge it is assumed that he or she cannot be any good! I have also noted that when a person makes a charge [I am not speaking of professional people] they can become quite well off while those who do not will find that they will just have enough to make ends meet. Another thing I noted over the years is that the story of the ten lepers holds good to this day! I have been privileged to have helped thousands of people over the years and invariably one person in ten might give a call to say they felt better. Many healers cannot resist the temptation of ringing up a patient the following day inquiring as to how they felt after a healing session. Those who have this habit do it for two reasons. In the first instance it is the ego that comes to the fore and, two, lack of trust! It is hard to swallow but it is the truth.

For years I knew intuitively that I was doing things the wrong way. In my heart of hearts I was aware of this but my pride would not allow me to come to terms with what God required of me. I was being torn to pieces mentally and was in great anguish.

Following the giving up of the business where I slaved for eighteen years I had to earn some sort of income. I set myself up as a private business consultant ghosting reports for people, manipulating money, setting up accounting systems and so on. I continued financing my healing work as heretofore. I was barely making ends meet.

This was in 1988. It is a year that I will never forget. In January God decided to force the pace and this He did with a vengeance. Everything started to go wrong. One by one I lost my few clients and, to cap it all, I was let down by a friend whereby I found myself over £5,000 [€6,348.69].in the red. I had to sell my car and take out a loan. Finally I ended up with one small job which netted me £14 [€17.78] and signed on at the unemployment exchange!

When we are at our weakest we are at our strongest.

One day while reading the current edition of "Psychic News" I saw an advertisement regarding a Spiritual and Psychic weekend course being held in Swansea, Wales. I heard a voice within telling me to attend. Though funds were at a low ebb I raised the necessary cash and attended the seminar. What happened there was profound and I returned to Cork knowing that something was happening to me while at the same time not knowing what it was. I thought things were going to change, but no, I was still in the same predicament.

During the months that followed my mind was in a turmoil. At the end of June I saw another advertisement in "Psychic News" a repeat seminar was to be held in Swansea. I knew that I had to attend once more. Something told me that it was necessary for me to have confirmed that which I had experienced on my first visit. Somehow or other I raised enough to travel. On this occasion for the first time in my life I heard the voice of my controlling spirit speaking to me using my own voice box! It was one of the most extraordinary experiences of my life.

I was back in Cork about a week when out of the blue I received an invitation from Professor George Canning to attend his clinic for four days in Dunmanway, Co. Cork. I accepted his invitation. Here I witnessed stupendous examples of God at work. I saw the crippled walk, the blind receiving their sight, pain disappearing and many other wonderful healings. It was like something out of biblical times. The clinics went on without a stop for fourteen hours at a stretch. Each morning at seven I walked the country roads with George for an hour while he propounded concepts and ideas. To my astonishment I found that all he had to say I knew already. What really blew my mind was the fact that the voice I heard in Swansea was the voice of Professor George Canning! He explained to me that his function in the overall universal plan was to confirm that which I already knew!. It was he that made me realise that the oath I had sworn was to myself and not to God. This is where I had gone wrong He made it graphically clear to me that when one gives one must receive as every action has an equal and opposite reaction. He pointed out that donations of any kind are in fact energy which goes back to God to balance that which He had given in the first place.

After our walk each morning I felt what I can only describe as "different." Shortly after 8.00a.m. I would lie on my bed in the hotel and feel my body on fire. One morning as I lay down I felt an enormous pressure developing in my solar plexus to the point where I could not breathe. I felt a power surging through me. It became stronger and stronger. Suddenly without further warning I felt a burst of energy shooting from my forehead and could see all sorts of colours flashing about the ceiling. I heard a voice instructing me to go into the bathroom and look in the mirror until my features disappeared! The voice was so insistent I did just that.

Gripping the wash-hand basin I stared into the mirror. In a short few seconds to my consternation my features disappeared completely. Then miraculously I saw ten Bill Parfreys in the mirror, one behind the other. One was gold, the second silver, the third, purple, the next dark blue followed by a lighter blue, then green, yellow, pink, orange and finally red! I was like a concertina. How long this vision lasted I cannot say. It could have been five seconds or five minutes; I really do not know. Suddenly the ten images merged together and I found myself in my normal physical body. It was as if I had been in a spiritual abyss. When it was all over I felt a tremendous power within myself, especially in my hands. I felt as if I was a different person. All the anguish was gone and I felt balanced. I was still myself but changed completely radiating power; I could feel it oh so strongly.

I related the experience to George when we were next alone and all he said to me was "now go out and do God's work – my job is finished." These experiences had a traumatic effect on me. At that precise moment I decided to dedicate my whole life to healing and nothing else.

Dates are and were very significant to me. I had received the invitation from George on the 8th August of that year - the eighth of the eighth 1988 - 8 - 8 + 1 + 9 + 8 + 8. These figures add up to 42 and when expressed as a unitary figure becomes a six.. The number traditionally associated with Jesus the Healer is 888 which, when added together and expressed as a unitary figure becomes six. The 8th of the 8th 1988 happens but once in the twentieth century! The date on which I commenced to work the way God had wanted me to work all along was the 15th of that month. I have never looked back since. Requests for help poured in from that day onwards.

As I understand it, God's healing power passes through the central nervous system and if the channel for conducting healing energies has any hang-ups these will have to be rectified. Over the following months I experienced some dreadful clear-outs. Uncontrollable sweats which were so bad that the perspiration went right through the mattress on to the floor! These would be accompanied by very strong vibrations of pain that went right through the body as Kundalini – the sleeping serpent – started to rise through my chakras. This continued for a number of days until they left through the base of the spine.

Shortly after this the left side of my face went numb and there was no hearing whatsoever in my left ear. This continued for four weeks until I thought I would not be able to contain it any longer. Suddenly it left me without warning and I collapsed on the floor with relief. Five minutes later the right side of my face went numb and with it the loss of hearing in my right ear. had to endure this for three weeks until suddenly it cleared a couple of days before Christmas. It was the best present I had that festive season.

The final trial came in February, the following year. This was the clearing of the heart chakra. In truth this very nearly killed me and I ended up at death's door, in the ICU of a hospital . I did not think I was going to make it but God thought otherwise and I recovered. There is no such thing as a free lunch and I found there was a very high price to pay for the privilege of being allowed to serve others. It is the pain and anguish, both physical and mental, that a healer suffers that makes him or her stronger. This leads in turn to the build up of that trust I speak about. These are the secret and necessary ingredients.by which Almighty God's power can work.

God moves in mysterious ways His wonders to perform. The material aspect of life becomes less and less important. Very seldom do I watch TV or read the papers. Most of the time I have little or no interest in what is going on in the so-called real world which, when one thinks about it, is an illusion. I sit back and ponder in wonder what has happened in my life and especially since the 15th August, 1988. I am only too well aware of my imperfections and often ask the Higher Power how it is that I am allowed to do this work. Invariably I receive a reply "you did not choose us - we chose you!" Note the use of the royal "we!"

As a result of this I carried on the struggle from day to day wrestling with my failings, anguish and believe it or not, doubt. Over the intervening years it was the accumulation of these factors that has brought about peace of mind, peace of soul and peace of spirit now near my life's end.

Chapter 08

THE SWANSEA LEARNING CURVE

As a tail-piece to my visits to Swansea I am going to relate a couple of experiences I had after attending the first seminar.

Round about 9.30p.m. I was back in the guest house in my room sitting on the edge of the bed.   I was thinking over in minute detail that day's events. For fifteen hours I had been in an atmosphere of very high spiritual vibrations and was, for want of a better expression "coming down" back to the illusion of reality. Lost in thought I saw clairvoyantly a stream of grotesque human beings who had the most appalling disfigurements with misshapen limbs imaginable. They were passing in front of me. I did not know what to think when all of a sudden my controlling spirit spoke to me.

I was informed that all of those that were passing me by were very advanced souls who had purposely taken on their afflictions in order to bring out the latent good that was dormant in others. It was incredible and I thought to myself how highly evolved these souls must be. The experience humbled me to the quick. I felt my heart opening up with compassion. I was so grateful for the lesson that I was being taught. The second night I was again in my bedroom and had yet another vision.

What was happening smacked of Charles Dickens "A Christmas Carol!" On this occasion I saw a bungalow on fire and a 26 year old woman trapped in the inferno. She was screaming for help and my controlling spirit ordered me to assist her. Nothing could be done for her physical body and I remember being guided to pull her spiritual body out of her physical body. I know that this sounds crazy but it is impossible to put into words something that is non-physical.   I caught her by her ankles and pulled and suddenly there was a popping sound and she was free. To my utter consternation I found myself "flying" rather like Peter Pan. Her hand was in mine as we flew through the astral world and I could feel the astral winds blowing through us.

I started to panic. I knew that I had not died but my female companion had done so. Just when I did start to become frightened I heard a voice say "he descended into hell" Immediately my hand was loosened from that of my companion and while she carried on her journey I, in turn felt as if I was as light as a feather. A gentle zephyr carried me down gently and I found myself seated on my bed. All in all it was an exhilarating and wonderful experience.

About a year later a lady rang me up and asked if I would speak with the sister of a girl 26 years of age who lost her life in a bungalow fire in the north of Ireland! There was an eerie feeling as I spoke on the 'phone to the woman. I knew as sure as night follows day that I had been pressed into service in helping the deceased. I did not know whether to tell the lady about it or not but as I had a compulsion to do so, reiterated to her the Swansea experience. She was taken aback in amazement. The sorrow and grief she had been living with just evaporated.

Incredibly a healing over the telephone had come about!'

I want to refer back at this point to the matter of the exchange of energy. There must always be balance. A simple example is when a person visits a friend or relative in hospital. One can feel on top of the world on entering and feel utterly drained on the way out. Leaving aside the matter of the positive ions that pour out from fluorescent lights doing their own draining, the prime cause is the compassion of the visitor! Knowingly or unknowingly the heart chakra opens up and soul energy streams out to the patient. The visitor in turn receives back negative energy in direct proportion to that which was given. Unless one knows how to deal with this problem it sticks in the overall psyche, hence the feeling of being drained.

It is a good idea to learn how the chakra system works. It is through a visualisation process as the mind is always king. When you next visit your friend he or she is bound to say, "you know I felt great after your last visit." Inwardly you confirm to yourself that you are well aware of the fact.

Part Three

No one is an island and while this is true it is also true to say each of us is a loner in our own right as each is unique and no two people are the same. Each of us is a consummate actor or actress. We get up each morning to face the day and have the mask which is our persona well in place. "Good morning Mrs. Dineen how are you today?" If we are absolutely frank and honest with ourselves we really do not care how the good lady is. The reason? Because society expects us to act out the part.

Another typical example would be something like this. "Good morning Jack, I'm so sorry to hear that the dog was killed the other day; you had that dog for a long time" at the same time thinking to yourself how well you can sleep now that the night barking has stopped! In most cases we are not sincere in what we say. For example a pain in one's big toe would appear to be be far more serious than the death of Jack's dog.

Each day none of us is true to ourselves.

The consequence of this is that we build up tension which translates itself as negative energy. And where does this negative energy go? Into the five million new cells born in the body every second lodging in the liver, spleen and other vital organs. When we get home after the day we look in the mirror and say to ourselves, "thank God I can be myself again after walking the stage of life for yet another day!"

I have been privileged to have been a conduit for healing energies for over forty years. The intuitive knowledge that has been given me, and how I interpreted it, provided the catalyst by which countless healings have come about. All this has been, and had to be, coupled with compassion and love for my fellow human beings. We are told that we are fearfully and wonderfully made. How many people ever give a thought to the fact that our bodies are worth approximately 60c made up of roughly 80% water and the remainder carbon and trace elements?

The body is not us but can be looked upon as a diving suit! This protects the real us as we sojourn here on spaceship earth hurtling through the physical universe at seven miles per second! We must come to understand that we are spiritual beings with physical bodies and NOT physical beings with spiritual bodies. We live in the grand illusion of thinking that the physical world is reality, whereas it is the exact opposite. As I pointed out we are fearfully and wonderfully made and are comprised of seven bodies. As a matter of interest the number seven is God's number. God made the world in seven days. We have the seven seas, the seven deadly sins, the seven colours of the rainbow, seven notes on the scale and so it is ad infinitum. St. Peter asked Jesus how many times should he forgive his brother, suggesting "seven times?" The answer he got was "seventy times seven." The power of the number seven is quite extraordinary and is used all the time by me in my healing work. The seven bodies of which we are comprised are, namely:

1. A physical body [diving suit]

2. An etheric body [the matrix upon which our physical body depends and which is connected at 21 distinct points which goes to constitute the Silver Cord].

3. The astral body

4. The lower mental body

5. The intermediate mental body

6. The higher mental body

7. The spiritual body

[Please refer to diagrams on page 324]

We have to look upon our bodies, and that includes the brain, as a computer; an inane piece of equipment that we plug into the wall, and all that it can do is blink. The computer requires a programme and the programme that operates our personal computers is comprised of our mind, soul and spirit. As we think, so we are. Our bodies react to the way we think be it on the mind, soul or spiritual plane. We must never forget that we are in charge of our own computers - no one else. Our bodies comprise of somewhere in the region of sixty billion, billion cells so each of us is like the owner and managing director of a company that has sixty billion, billion employees. 5,000,000 new employees join the company every second while 5,000,000 get their P45's and get kicked out! (A 'P45' is the official dismissal notice)

Cells have intellect, intelligence and understanding. It astounds me when I think that a cell's life is one five millionth of a second during which time it has to grow up, be educated, procreate, wither and die and it does all this in a minuscule part of a second. As our bodies are comprised of these very same cells our existence in turn is also but one five millionth of a second on the plane we find ourselves as we travel from a past infinity to a future infinity. Cells will absorb positive or negative energy as we, the owners of the company run our respective programmes. The real us inside the diving suit is or should be in control and the cells have to react to the way we think. Think in a positive manner and the cells will react in a positive manner. The opposite is the case when we think negatively.

The bottom line is that thought is a force and energy follows thought. As we think, so we are. We live and have our being in a vast sea of energy. Our physical bodies, which in effect are slowed down energy, give us the illusion that we are separate and apart from the whole while the truth is that we are not!

Part Three

Chapter 09

COMPREHENSION – THAT DISTANT GOAL

All my life I have been thinking!   I suppose it is the same with everybody else but all I know is myself. I am now 80 years old and from as far back as I can remember I used to look up at the stars and was staggered by the concept that the stars I was looking at had long since disappeared and that it was only the light of those same stars I was observing! In my innocence I would ask the Universe:

"Who am I?"

"Why am I where I find myself?"

And the biggest question of them all – "Who or what is GOD?"

I am still asking the same questions but I think I have become better aware of the awesome majesty of this physical universe of which I, Bill Parfrey, am an infinitesimal part of a nano particle! The skies fascinated me and I always thought of other worlds and had the strangest feeling that I had come from another galaxy! I know that now to be true and that my origins are from the Triangulum Galaxy which is two and a quarter million light years beyond the galaxy of Andromeda which itself is four and a quarter light years from the Milky Way Galaxy where our solar system finds its home!

I appreciate that no one can know God for we live and have our being in God and to know that - in my book - is enough. However, to comprehend the tiny amount that we can understand is in direct proportion to comprehending the size of our universe!   I have come to the realisation that there are countless parallel universes to our universe occupying the same space but vibrating on a different level! It is accepted that we live and have our being in a three dimensional world - length, width and height, or putting it mathematically X, X2 and X3. But what about X10?; X1,000,000? What about the recorded cases of people disappearing into the 4th dimension? Did they, perhaps, disappear into the 100th dimension? Who knows? God alone knows.

Coming back to the Milky Way Galaxy. It is roughly in the shape of an egg. It is 100 thousand light years in length and about ten to fifteen thousand light years in width! Let us say that the room that you, the reader, are in as you read this is the Milky Way Galaxy. The longest part of your room is the length of the galaxy and the width is how wide the galaxy is. Light travels at a speed of 186,000 miles per second, so to work out the distance from one side of the room to the other we have to multiply 186,000 by 60 x 60 x 24 x 365 x 100,000 and the answer is the number of miles there are between the two ends! A similar exercise provides the number of miles from side to side. The whole galaxy is travelling at the speed of light so while a coin falls from one's hand to the floor we have all travelled seven miles!

Scientists have counted [give or take a few billion] 2,600 billion solar systems in our galaxy around which countless trillions of millions of planets move and have their being! These solar systems could be deemed "Sons of God!" Our solar system is out near the edge of the Milky Way Galaxy and our world is but an infinitesimal speck of dust on one of the smallest ball bearings in a tiny wheel of the overall universe!

How dare we propose to set ourselves up as if we were masters of our domain! In reality, all the countless numbers of other worlds are but tiny little globules dangling on strings which are being controlled by the maker of it all! It is hard to believe that a little over one hundred years ago the telescopes of the day could just about make out the outer periphery of the Milky Way Galaxy and it was thought [I stand to be corrected on this point] that they were observing the end of the universe!

Today, thanks to radio astronomy and the Hubbell telescope it is now estimated that outside our galaxy there are between one hundred and one hundred and twenty-five million more galaxies!!! The mind boggles! Just thinking about it gives one an awareness and one stands agape, speechless endeavouring to take it all in! The greater the awareness of the understanding, the greater is the healing power that passes through the healer.

How can a grain of sand comprehend the desert of which it forms part?

Chapter 10

SERVING OTHERS AND IN TURN, OURSELVES

Those who have an interest in healing usually ask of themselves two questions. Initially they first mull over in their minds why the subject has such a fascination. Secondly what do they understand healing to be. Sometimes it is forgotten that the only person that can answer these two questions is the person her/himself! Anyone reading this book that has reached this stage in the narrative proves that they have an interest. On the matter of understanding what healing is all about there is no hard and fast rule.

In consequence of our uniqueness everyone has their own personal understanding. I do not believe the art of healing can be taught. It is something we discover within ourselves and the quality of any healing is in direct proportion to our own personal understanding of the universal power of which we are all part. Healing can be translated as service. All of us have a need to serve in whatever walk of life we find ourselves to be. Why do we have this need? It is because we need to give of ourselves. Service has to be selfless. It stands to reason therefore that healing has to be selfless. One gives without counting the cost, toil and not seek any rest, and work without seeking any reward. This can be a hard thing to take on board but it is so well worth while when we know inwardly we are doing what our soul decrees.

Our soul in turn is being directed by our spirit which is being guided by the creator. We live countless lives as we progress along our individual spiritual paths from a past infinity to a future infinity. Many may not be able to accept this but it does not matter one way or the other as it happens any way. Contrast our spiritual journey of awareness to a marathon race of 26 miles 385 yards. There are some who are at the two mile mark, some who have "gone through the wall," and dare we say it, some who have reached the 24 mile stage or even reached the last 385 yards! When one reaches this point they will have a much better understanding of what the race is all about than does the person at the two mile mark. This does not mean that one has the right to feel haughty and look with disdain at the person that is so far behind. That person will reach the 26 mile mark and indeed finish the race eventually!

The old maxim that the speed of a convoy is based on the speed of the slowest ship is brought to mind. Service is selfless, ipso facto, healing is selfless. Healing can be a two-edged sword. We serve ourselves in service to our fellow human beings. Life should be both service and balance. The strongest force comes from a balanced individual. Our inner balance is of the utmost importance and we need to know what we are. It can happen that we are looking for more than we are prepared to give.

So far as spiritual growth is concerned an unbalanced sensitivity is a danger. It is a good idea to ask oneself how they know that they are of benefit to others. The answer is both simple and profound - inner knowledge! We know because we know! Once a person can understand this concept it will never leave them. It is beyond emotion and is that still small voice to which we listen and receive all the answers.

A person who has the privilege of being a healer has a duty to help others whether it is physical, mental or spiritual. All my life I have had difficulties in all three of these fields.

The darkest days of my life were when I had to enter a mental hospital as I was informed 'my mind was disturbed!' I was on suicide trails and very nearly succeeded on one occasion. Suicide is pointless for all one destroys is the body. If one is successful there they are in another dimension with the same problems as the problems are not physical in the majority of cases. The difficulties we experience in life are in reality the examinations we have to pass as we go through the university of life. It took me six years to recover but I always thank God for the experience. If a person has a mental problem at least I am able to talk the same language. I term all mental hospitals "colleges." So when in conversation with a person who has been in a mental institution I will inquire as to what "college" they attended. In turn, I would talk about the experiences I had in my college! They would see the dark humour of all this, thus giving support one to the other. There would be a psychological bonus in that we felt superior in some way as if we had gained a metaphorical degree which, in turn gave a fillip to the overall personality.

I do not think it is far from the truth.

The real and only function of a healer is to activate that intangible something that is within us all. Knowledge is already within and we are often not aware of it. We search for it outside ourselves following this guru, that guru, this belief and that belief. All the time failing to realise that what we search for "out there" is now, always was, and always will be within us!

In essence, we are all healers in some form or other albeit at various stages of our progression and we have a serious responsibility to develop that which is within us. We thereby strengthen the link we have with the incomprehensible hierarchical structure which is supporting us in all that we endeavour to do.

We are never alone. One thing common to us all is to be receptive to that still small voice with which we are constantly in touch.. In effect our personal understanding of God.

The energy with which we work is universal and can be directed by our minds in a positive or negative way. It is essential to come to grips with the fact that in essence we are the product of our thoughts. Understanding ourselves can only come from within and it is important to realise that all we do and say has a direct effect on others. It is vital, therefore, that we unfold, in balanced understanding, at the same time. We are energy.

There is an exchange of energy within ourselves which affects our physical, emotional and spiritual selves. We all have a higher mind that knows what we can achieve. We should all strive to access this serene part of ourselves. Inspiration can be defined as a transference of energy from one level to a slower rate of vibration. Another source of inspiration can come from a person who can fire us with enthusiasm simply by being in their presence. A person like this has an ability to be quick-fired and his or her actions radiate purpose and expresses this physically. When we are inspired we are lifted up beyond the so-called reality of the world.

Because we are human we have human frailties and such being the case we are indeed imperfect. This realisation can bring fear in its wake. Where healers are concerned fear is a blockage to communication and this can have a direct bearing on the quality of the healing. We are all but channels through which all energies flow, healers and non healers alike. As we think so we are and it is we ourselves and no one else who creates all the barriers. It falls back once again on trust. Trusting is the secret ingredient no matter what our walk in life is. Whatever one knows and truly trusts can happen will happen. If one just believes it will, rather than trust, in most cases it will not happen. In the field of healing there is no room for doubt. "Trust and KNOW and all will be well!"

Summing up we all have this "something" within ourselves which gives us the desire to help others. It is hard to define or describe. When we think about it in depth it dawns on us that we feel for other people. This translates as love for our fellow human beings. The bottom line is that healing is love and compassion together, which manifest themselves into one thus forming the healing energy itself.

Chapter 11

BELIEF VERSUS TRUST

A few words on the matter of Absent Healing, more often referred to these days as Distance Healing, would seem to be appropriate. We are all aware of the value and power of prayer and in essence distance healing could be looked upon as prayer in action. Thought is a force and prayer is the same.

Personally I have been aware of the power of prayer over many years. Despite being on borrowed time for a very long time I am still here because of two reasons. One that God wants me to be here and secondly the extraordinary good will of so many hundreds of people who pray for me. Every day I receive phone calls, a message of good will, a mass card, people make novenas on my behalf. I have holy water from nearly every holy well in the country and this is backed up with blessed candles and gifts from sacred places. A couple of years ago when the medical people were sure that I was not going to make it a kind lady made a special trip to Lough Derg. She spent two days there on bread and water, walking on stones and without sleep. The goodness and kindness of so many comes over like a force.

People tell me that I look great but what they are seeing is a reflection of all the prayers and goodwill I receive from so many. The spiritual part of me benefits dramatically but the body has to play second fiddle. When we pray for somebody we believe we are talking only with the Power. In reality the format is a triangle (see diagram on page 269). The person being prayed for and the person that is doing the praying are at the base of the triangle and the Power is at the apex. Distance healing works in the very same manner. Where I am concerned I sometimes ask for a photograph of the person for whom a request is being made. With this I can sense the person's aura but this is not really necessary for God knows what those vibrations are in any event.

To me, positive thought, coupled with trust, as distinct from belief, works wonders. When we say "I believe" this can be construed as having doubt. On the other hand when we say that we trust and know that all will be well, if it is part of God's overall plan all WILL be well.

People often ask me how do they learn to trust. I point out that all of us are trusting every day of our lives! For example it is dark at night. One stretches out a hand to the switch and they trust the light will come on, and it does! They go to the bathroom and trust that the toilet will flush and it does. They go into the kitchen to make a cup of tea or coffee, turn on the tap and trust water will flow out and it does. They fill the kettle and trust that the water will boil at 100 degrees It does so.

I will agree that it can take a lifetime to have complete and utter trust. We work at it all our lives. At least that is what I have found to be the case. Nothing is impossible when Almighty God enters the field of play. It can happen that it is not meant that a given person is to be made well. Perhaps it is part of their Karma. On the opposite side of the coin one will find people that even if Jesus himself was to walk into the healing room they would not get better? Why? Because they could not afford to give up what they are suffering from! It is a prop and without it they could not carry on. Strange but true. Seneca, a physician from Roman times, said "it is a step to the cure to be willing to be cured." The man was spot-on then and it is precisely the same today.

One of my very first requests for distance healing came from a man in England who I did not know from Adam. He wrote to tell me that he had a critical back problem and his doctor told him that he would be unable to work again. He went on to say that everything depended upon him holding down his job. I went through the procedure I used at that time so long ago. I wrote to him and enclosed a small healing card which would act as the bond between us. Ten days later I received a joyous reply telling me that he was back at work, his back perfect and his doctor could not understand. I offered up a short prayer of thanks.

With his letter he sent me a copy of "A Healer's Prayer." At the same time he informed me that the prayer had been composed in a pub in England in six minutes and written down on the back of an envelope! Some power greater than myself prompted me to print the prayer on the back of my cards which I send to people. To date nearly 13,000 cards have gone all over the world. I lost count of the number of people who thanked me for the prayer. However it is to the man that made the request for healing that should be thanked. God certainly moves in mysterious ways His wonders to perform

Since that day many years ago I have received 2,903 requests for Distance healing to date. I expect it will continue until my work is finished.. Where contact healing is concerned the number of people I have seen on a personal basis exceeds 31,000.

A Healer's Prayer

Dearest God, to Thee I pray,
Heal my loved ones ill today.
Make them whole and healthy, too,
And swift to recognize it's you
Who works the miracle of healing
In themselves, Thy grace revealing.
May their gratitude find vent
In thanking — not this instrument —
But Thee, from Whom all blessings flow
To us Thy creatures here below.
I am but a channel lowly
For Thy healing, pure and holy.
Cleanse me, keep me true and bright,
Worthy to convey Thy Light
To those who live in constant pain,
And help Thee make them well again.
Let me freely learn to serve
Those in need without reserve.
May I also from them learn
The patience I do not discern
In those who relish robust health,
And do not understand the wealth
Of knowledge learnt, when all else fails
Only Thy Grace and Love prevails.

D.P. Stocker

Chapter 12

WITH THE UNIVERSAL GOD IN CHARGE NOTHING IS IMPOSSIBLE

Sometimes I look at the map of Ireland I have on the wall of my little office. A large area of the south and the midlands is pock-marked with coloured pins indicating the many towns and villages where I held healing clinics over the years. The more isolated ones covered parts of Co. Galway, Aran Islands, Dublin and even Belfast.

Outside the country I did healing work in Wales and England. The amount of travelling was very considerable In addition to the foregoing I ran a daily clinic in the centre of Cork City from 1.00p.m. to near midnight. Here I would see people on an individual basis.

Every three weeks I organised open clinics around the country in hotels, lounge bars and wherever I could find appropriate accommodation. There was a good deal of planning involved what with the booking of a room in some hotel, arranging accommodation for myself and the placing of advertisements in appropriate local papers giving details of venues, times and such like. In numerous towns I would receive support from a local individual who would be kind enough to arrange for small posters to be displayed in various shops and cafes.

A typical monthly trip would embrace driving to Co. Galway on a Sunday night, clock into the hotel where the clinic would be held all day Monday. That night, pack up and drive to another town and work there all hours on Tuesday. The third day would find me in the town of Roscrea which is in the northern part of the county of Tipperary. Again a long stretch of at least twelve hours. The following day I travelled to the town of Thurles. I would leave there late in the evening and make the long journey to Waterford city and hold a day-long clinic on Friday before leaving for Cork and home.

Looking back I stand in awe at the energy and ability that was obviously bestowed upon me to carry on at this pace. A spiritual atmosphere is of enormous help when healing. The logical place one would find this to be would be in a church. Never once was I offered this facility by any denomination!

I always thought that strange. More often than not I would have to hold the clinics in some lounge bar where the spiritual levels virtually did not exist, especially after some bawdy party the night before. It took a tremendous effort to raise the spiritual ante. This was achieved to an extent by burning incense, playing semi-sacred music for a few hours before the clinic began. The sprinkling of some holy water would not go amiss and the use of sage as a cleanser is also very powerful. By the time I would be ready to commence the clinic the vibrations would have improved dramatically.

People came from far and near. The greatest number that ever attended one in one day was a staggering two hundred and thirty-four patients. The clinic was in the ballroom of an hotel in Thurles way back in 1989. People seeking help arrived very early in the morning and were prepared to sit for hour after hour until their turn came around. The difference between an open clinic and a one-to-one session is entirely different. The energy and prayerful goodwill emanating from a large group is very powerful and this collective power can be directed to help a given person more quickly than a one-to-one session. The longer a person sits in such an energy field, unknown to themselves, they are healing away! It is quite extraordinary.

I remember on one occasion in Waterford a man arrived in a wheelchair. He had suffered a severe stroke and was unable to use his right arm or leg. He had arrived early with his wife in tow. His thinking was that being one of the first to be seen he would get away fast. He did not realise that healing does not work like that. I passed him by and treated someone else. I did the same thing a second time and as I passed him by yet again he remonstrated with me for not looking after him first of all. I left him sitting there for five hours! I would come over to him every now and then and say, "not yet!"

Then when I knew inwardly that the time was right I caught his two hands in mine and said rather roughly "get up!" He stood up and catching his arm I said "now - walk!" Linking his arm in mine we walked slowly down the hall. I started to sing that old childhood ditty "the Grand Old Duke of York."

We started to march. With every step he got stronger and stronger and walked faster and faster. After traversing the length of the large room twice I told him to walk up and down by himself. And he did! People were blessing themselves and probably saying a few prayers. The man who arrived in a wheelchair pushed it out of the hotel all by himself!

I have seen utterly and extraordinary healing. Referring to the huge clinic in Thurles, that morning I commenced at 12.15p.m. and believe it or not I never stopped once until 2.45am the following morning. Never once did I have to answer the call of nature or eat anything during the long hours. In open clinics I found that time seemed to speed up. I would be conscious of the first four hours but after that not have an iota I vividly remember that day specifically when a lady told me that it was nearly midnight and that I had been twelve hours on my feet. I said not a thing but carried on until nearly three in the morning. I had been privileged to have helped 134 people.

I was holding a four-day clinic on this particular occasion. Word had gone around the town and countryside so on the following morning the ballroom was packed. There was no way that I could possibly attend to them all so I dealt with the balance from the previous day. It was another marathon session and on one occasion I had no less than seven wheelchair patients all lined up and in between seeing individuals I would treat the seven collectively. As I said, strange things seem to happen in open clinics.

A given patient would come out on to the centre of the floor. Then, there was what I can only describe as 'a cone of silence', descended around the patient and me. No matter how far or close the onlookers were there was no way that they could hear the conversation between the two of us. Wonderful healing was experienced that day also. The help received by all those present was a humbling experience.

Of those present, three stood out. The first which astonished everyone was when a woman about sixty years of age with the aid of two helpers was brought to the centre of the floor. The unfortunate lady was utterly and completely crippled with osteo-arthritis. Her poor arms hands and legs were misshapen and she was in terrible pain. Once or possibly twice in the lifetime of a healer he or she will come across [it would be more correct to say guided to] a person of such spirituality that an instant healing of no matter what disease will take place. This was such a lady. With the thumb and forefinger of my right hand I "gripped" the disease at the top of her head and on the count of seven [God's number] her complaint was whisked out within the space of fifteen seconds. I told the two aides to stand aside and allow the lady to walk off the floor on her own. To the gasps of incredulity she did just that.

An instant healing had taken place. When such an event as this takes place a healer must never dwell upon the awe of what has taken place, but rather concentrate on the next patient who might have a pain in a big toe. The following night this same lady arrived back in the clinic, crippled and unable to move without the help of her two aides. She came on to the floor. I turned to the assembled crowd, many of whom had been there the previous night. I told them that what Almighty God takes away He never gives it back!

I went on to explain the reason why the lady appeared to be in the same condition was due to her saying to herself that her healing was not logical. In physical terms she could be deemed right but in spiritual terms it was a different story I explained that she had allowed a thought form of her complaint to come into her aura. With complete trust, I turned to the patient and clapped my hands smartly four times on either side of her body. As if by magic her complaint left her and she was able to walk freely once again. I had simply been guided to break-up the thought form!

The second prominent healing was that of an attractive woman aged about 32 who had been born with a clenched left hand There was no way it could be opened – perhaps by surgery – I do not know. Her fingers were solid as a rock. Taking her hand in mine I found myself telling her to direct her brain to clench the unopened hand harder and harder. She thought I was mad and I do not blame her. I said rather stridently "do it!" She closed her eyes and visualised herself clenching her 32 year old unopened hand as hard as she could. I found myself pushing the thumb of my right hand in between her fingers which seemed to have become rather like putty. Slowly but surely for the first time in thirty-two years she opened her hand but not fully. The episode was so moving.

Part Three

The last person I saw early in the morning before packing up for a few hours sleep was a middle-aged man with a huge hump on his back, like the Hunchback of Notre Dame. I placed both my hands on his back. I did not feel that I was there at all as the hump started to melt like butter and reduced to about half its size.

I went to bed after that.

Chapter 13

THROUGH THE GLASS DARKLY

My permanent little healing clinic was in the centre of Cork city situated over a wholesale fish merchant's premises. As people mounted the stairs they had to pass through what I termed the fish smell barrier which on a hot summer's day was very pronounced. The entrails drew the flies and the electric fly-killing machines used by the fish monger on such days sounded like a continuous volley of rapid fire from an army under attack. The building was old but it did have that intangible something. I rented two floors and the contrast between the street entrance and that of the clinic was so marked that people could not believe how the atmosphere could change in an instant.

As if by magic one moment the atmosphere was permeated with fishy smells and the next the subtle smell of sage and incense changed the vibrations dramatically. They brought in their wake a wonderful sense of peace and tranquillity. This was accentuated with the aid of the sound of quiet music playing in the backgrou

Down on the ground floor th
subtle places and their ingen
and large. I have always had
left my portion of the buildir
al visitor. The narrow stree
other premises in the same
opposite to what I was do
would result in the sound
would be loud footsteps o

From time to time there
was not large and it had
were on the floor beneat
little clinic. One evening
her Margaret. She was a

she told me that her mother had passed into the world of spirit eleven months previously and she missed her very much.

I could feel the negative energy surrounding her and as I went to clear this her mother "spoke" to me. I could hear her voice in my mind and also "see" her. Without further ado, she said to me "Would you please tell that daughter of mine that I am alive and well. Tell her to stop carrying on as she is as she is holding me back!" She continued, "… and to make sure that Margaret knows that this is her mother speaking to her through you remind her how I taught her to make St. Bridget's crosses when she was eight years old." I relayed the message to Margaret and she nearly jumped off the chair. She was dumbfounded. I sat in front of her and said casually, "God moves in mysterious ways His wonders to perform!" This was like another electric shock. She blanched as she said that those were the very words her mother used to utter whenever any kind of a problem came up in life.

Stress is invariably to be found in the liver and the spleen as well as the solar plexus and this was removed. I was closing up her aura when suddenly I saw clairvoyantly a small terrier with one black ear and one brown ear. I asked Margaret did this have any significance In hushed tones she told me that the animal I described was her mother's pet dog and was alive and well in Margaret's house. The change in that woman was phenomenal. She was radiant. "Come with me", I said and taking her by the hand we descended to the floor beneath. When I rented the building there was a St. Bridget's s on the wall. I ripped it off and gave it to her, "this has been the most dinary night of my life," she said. I told her that she would be telling hildren about this night some time in the future.

example of the way that the power of God works.

what is going to come about at a healing session. If er may decide what is the best thing to do. Over realisation that any of us are but a conduit or ss it all over to a higher authority. It fine- rity and if the directions being given be greater pro rata. From memory I had two similar experiences like that of Margaret. There were many others but difficult to recall straight away.

One of these involved a full-time hospital nurse. She was in her late thirties and was treating her father-in-law who had terminal cancer and had come home to die. The strain of this, coupled with her hospital job, was further compounded by the death of her own father some seven months previously. We sometimes endeavour to burn the candle at both ends but it has never really worked. She was under great strain when she came to me where she was able to pour out all that was within. She shed a few tears also. Crying is good and this stiff upper lip business should never hold sway. Inside us all is just a small girl or a small boy and we are pretending to be big. As in Margaret's case, as I was clearing her aura her father spoke to me. I "saw" him in my mind and he was holding a fishing rod in his hand. In an imploring kind of voice he instructed me to tell his daughter that all was well with him and that her grieving was holding him back and that he was very anxious to go fishing! The girl burst out laughing. Her father was an ardent fisherman and was longing to make a cast into one of the beautiful fishing lakes that abound in the world of spirit.

Sometimes we fail to realise that everything that exists in our physical world is in fact a projection of that which already exists in the spiritual world. A weight lifted from the shoulders of the young woman – she was changed instantly. I really could sense her father's joy on two counts. One, she was relieved of all her stress and two, her father could go fishing!

Yet another such experience related to a young man aged 23 whose father died and he just could not accept or come to terms with the fact that his father had left him. His inability to cope landed him in a mental home for a number of years. A relation brought him to see me, more or less as a last resort. The young man was full to the gills with medication and his whole frame was rock hard. I was seriously worried that he was not with it at all. While sensing what was going on in his overall psyche I heard an instruction in my mind to the effect that I was to relate to the patient a lewd but humourous story. I always do what I am instructed to do and while it seemed completely out of place to relate this coarse joke in a place of healing I did so. I came to the punch line. Suddenly the young man started to shake and it was as if lumps of ice were breaking away from his body.

I could hardly believe it. It was as if he had been encased in a mountain of ice for many years. He exploded with laughter. The tears ran down his face and the huge guffaws were catching and we all laughed until we could laugh no more. It was the belly laugh of all belly laughs. The blockage was in his solar plexus and his heart chakra. Weak with our experience, suddenly I "saw" a man of about 45 years of age. He was wearing gaiters, boots, a soft hat and was carrying a shot gun in the carrying position. There were forests in the background with a range of small mountains in the distance. The man was the father of the patient. He was an out-doors man and had died from a heart attack at the point I described. The young man's life was changed from that moment on.

I have been privileged to have had other similar experiences in my life. Last year a spinster in her late sixties came to see me with her niece. She had suffered three bereavements within one month. Two brothers and a cousin. Without going into full details, after the stress was relieved, she saw her three relatives standing behind me. Her face radiated like the sun. I could not see anything nor could her niece but the lady did. It gave her the ability to carry on. She had one remaining relative who lived in England and the day following the healing she purchased an air ticket to London to be with her relative for the Christmas period..

These kind of experiences have had a profound effect not only on my life but on my thinking. The ability to think is, in my opinion, the greatest gift that Almighty God has bestowed upon us.

Part Three

Chapter 14

OUR COMMON HERITAGE – UNIQUENESS

I keep mentioning the fact that in my humble opinion the greatest gift that we have is an ability to think. I have been thinking all of my life. Looking over some of my many files I came across a few thoughts that occurred to me in August 1977, nearly thirty years ago!

I was lying on a hospital bed on the 8th August that year endeavouring to take an objective look at myself. I came to the conclusion that, inwardly, I knew I was a strange person. On the other hand, outwardly, I appeared to be rational [at least most of the time]. It was and still is a fact that my inner-most thoughts are complicated. I suppose that is the way it is to be. My mother told me that during her lifetime she never ceased thinking and I am just the same. Even when I am doing something mundane or out for an evening, the cinema for instance, a part of me ceaselessly keeps thinking The same must hold good for when I am asleep at night.

There is a reason for everything – there has to be – otherwise the huge jig-saw would not fit together. We strive to put our own few personal pieces together to help and contribute to the whole, but how difficult it all is. Still, we must keep striving. If my assumption that everything happens for a purpose is correct, it stands to reason that there is a reason why I was to become a healer. It must be so. If one looks at the heavens, one sees that all the stars and planets and moons are dependant one upon the other. The gravitational pull keeps everything moving in correct order. If this is true for the heavens as a whole, surely it is also true for those of us that are passengers on space-ship Earth?

But how many people can see and reason along these lines? It is said to be coincidence, pure chance. I do not accept this tenet I know there is freewill, but overall, everything happens for a purpose. It is the incorrect use of our freewill that creates the problems and not the destiny. When people begin to notice the little things and then see the connections in between they are gradually able to build up a picture of their own personal jigsaw. It is fascinating and, to me, is the whole purpose of existence. Over the intervening years I have come to observe everything in finer detail. This has enabled me to create my own particular picture with my personal in-built electronic microscope. I can see things in finer and closer detail than heretofore.

The concept of life, for me at least, seems to be the correct one. I can readily appreciate that there will be many who could not possibly hold my views and they would be right not to do so. The reasons? Each and every one of us is unique and, must therefore find our own answer and so it will ever be. Reading helps, as does discussion. However one must never forget that what one reads, or the views expressed by another no matter how eminent they may be are merely their own viewpoints. It does not follow that they are correct for anyone but the person expressing them!

Still, little nuggets will be found from time to time that fit other peoples' patterns and, in this way, one can - it is in fact the only way - build up his or her own particular concept of their life in the current "now." The only thing that matters is the 'now'. There is no such thing as the past and there is no such thing as the future, All there is is the on-going now! It brings to mind something I read when learning German that remained with me. A broad translation is "Time has three dimensions. The past, the present and the future. The past is gone the future is not here yet and the present does not last. Humankind is physically in the present but by virtue of the ability to think and use imagination it is possible to live in the past and in the future."

This brings up the interesting question as to what is the 'now'? to me the "now" is but a fleeting nano second of our spiritual journey as our soul travels from a past infinity to a future infinity. Our soul chooses our body, our parents, our destiny and even how long we are going to stay in the body. The many and varied difficulties we experience in life can be looked upon as the examinations that we have to pass as we go through the university of life. To me it is all part of an awesome and incomprehensible plan and whether we like it or not we are part of it ever progressing.

Hence my becoming a healer! My ego wanted me to be a medical doctor but that was not part of the overall plan in my case. So, I find myself in the field of complementary and alternative methods of healing. I have learned much over the many years I have been privileged to do this work. Many of the younger medical practitioners from time to time recommend that a patient of theirs come to see me.

On one occasion I had a call from a young woman in the west of Ireland. After the birth of her second child she ended up with a trapped sciatic nerve. She had suffered for weeks on end and her father suggested that she travel to Cork to see me. An appointment was arranged for the following Saturday. With her was an entourag of her father, husband, and her elder son. It was a difficult job to get her up the stairs but finally we reached my little clinic at the top of the house. She was unable to sit so she stood upright holding onto a chair. I worked away. After about twenty minutes I enquired if she had attended her doctor with the complaint. Pointing to her husband she startled me when she said "my husband is a doctor!" Her husband said not a word and after the initial shock I carried on. Ten minutes later the woman was walking from the clinic to the waiting room with very little pain.

"My God", exclaimed the doctor, "how did you do that?".

With a chuckle I replied "magic touch!"

His wife sat down without pain and as she did so he told me that he had been suffering with a bad back for a long time.. He asked if he could be helped. The bottom line is the doctor was touching the floor within fifteen minutes. I held day-long seminars in different parts of the country for those who were interested. Some weeks after treating the doctor's wife and himself it happened that I had arranged to hold a seminar in his area. Forty-two people turned up. Included in the group were two nurses and the doctor himself.

Around seven in the evening the seminar ended and the doctor came up to me. Taking my hand in his extended his right hand.

"Bill Parfrey, you have changed my life!" he said,

I was overwhelmed as I thought of this young vivacious medical man with a string of degrees after his name telling me that I had made a profound change in his life. I felt very humbled. What happened was meant to happen.

On this score a married woman in her thirties came to see me, together with her husband. She was unable to speak. She communicated with me by writing on a pad what she wanted to say. She had been involved in a car accident and her throat received the full brunt in the crash. Her vocal chords appeared to be damaged. I could sense that the cause of her being unable to speak was due to a blockage in the throat chakra in her astral body., Such being the case this was the area in which to administer healing energies.

With the use of a tumbler of water [two atoms of hydrogen and one of oxygen] and guidance from the universal power I said to her suddenly out of the blue "how are you?" Without a moment's hesitation she replied "I am very well thank you!" She was a trained musician and singer and the clinic reverberated with the most glorious voice tripping up and down the full gambit of her range of octaves, tears of joy and happiness intermingled with the resonance of her voice.

What is to be will be. It is as simple as that.

Chapter 15

THE VIRGIN MARY LENDS A HAND – BIG TIME!

It may seem strange for me - a healer - having to confess the difficulties I have had all my life with Jesus. Somehow or other I was unable to handle it. Strangely enough I had no difficulty with the Blessed Virgin Mary. She had been with me all of my life but in the background and it was only in latter years that she made her presence felt big time.

It had been a long day that Monday 18th August, 1998. It was 10.35p.m. as I walked along George's Quay in Cork city going over in my mind the cases I had been privileged to have handled since 1.30p.m. that afternoon. I was tired as I made my way slowly along the road to where I had parked my little car. I was saying a few prayers to myself as I walked along.

On the other side of the river is a church – Holy Trinity Church – which was flood-lit and always looks well. I was just about opposite to the church when literally, from out of the sky something fell at my feet. I could not see it in the dark but bent down to examine it. I found it comprised of a small key-ring which had a leather covering and had but one key - the type used to raise up a car aerial from the bonnet. Attached to the ring was a Miraculous medal!

I was completely taken aback. Where had it come from? I looked for a rational explanation but there was none. All the buildings around me were in darkness. There was no light, nor was a window open. The buildings were for office use only. Even if there had been a window open, who could or would have thrown a key-ring such as I have described out of the window? Again, how could it have come down right in front of me as I was at the edge of the pavement? I was astounded.

Where it happened is a shop that sells all sorts of second-hand goods from the proverbial needle to an anchor. The shop front is always full of valuable junk and, believe it or not, on Monday night, right in the middle of the window display was a two-foot high statue of the Blessed Virgin Mary!

I knew that this experience was a message for me to keep on the hard road. [This was definitely an apport - see reference in Part 02 of this book].That week was a tough one spiritually. As I continued to walk to my car I received a message to the effect that I was not to say a prayer of any sort until 3.00p.m. the following Friday! Not an easy thing to do. I related the experience to a very close friend in whom I confide. He offered to do the praying for me and also those due to come to see me that week .

Every Wednesday for quite some time I had been calling to see a very sincere man who had suffered a stroke. He and his wife have a mentally impaired son. When I called that morning, Matthew [not his real name] said to me "do you notice anything different in the room this morning?" I looked around and there, to my utter astonishment on the sideboard under the window stood the statue of the Blessed Virgin Mary that had been in the junk shop window! I was simply lost for words. Nan, his wife, a very religious and spiritual woman had seen the statue in the shop window.

That night she heard a voice telling her to buy the statue for a junk shop was not a fit place for the statue to be. She went to the shop the next day and purchased it.   Nan carried the statue which was together with all her other purchases. She told me that she had asked the Virgin Mary to be a lightweight and she obliged - like a feather! Nan carried the statue and all her purchases quite a long way to catch a bus and so the statue came into their home.

Then the bombshell came!

"The statue is for you, Bill, and no one else!" they said in unison.

"Promise that you will never give her away!" they said together.

I was awe-struck! A very special wheel had turned a full circle! The tailpiece to this extraordinary story is itself extraordinary. I phoned my friend to tell him of the amazing events that had taken place since the medal fell from the sky. At six that evening we had a snack together and we parted company. He told me that when he got back to his small flat he found a Miraculous Medal on the floor! Truly God moves in mysterious ways His wonders to perform. I found myself changed also.

Part Three

The further astonishing thing is that Friday night at 7.00 p.m. a lady came to see me, accompanied by her husband. She had last been with me the previous November.

"Bill, do you remember the last time I was here and you told me that I would become pregnant?"The pleasant woman, aged about forty said to me.

"No," I replied, adding "I never remember anything that I may say to a person for it is not me saying it!"

"Well," she went on, "despite what doctors had told me, I am pregnant and have but seven weeks to go!"

I congratulated her and then enquired what could we do to help on this occasion. She told me that the placenta was not in the correct position and if it did not move to its rightful position, she would have to enter hospital for about six weeks and have a section. With her husband present, I sensed an imbalance of energy between her throat and sacral chakras and was guided to balance this. Then I found that the sacral chakra at her back was not in sync with the one in the front. I was guided to move away from her and work on her etheric and astral bodies, directing healing energies through my hands and my brow chakra, thereby forming a triangle of force. Nothing happened for four minutes then suddenly her whole womb gave a jerk, stopped and then moved again.

"Oh my God," she cried to her husband, "my whole insides are moving." – then, in a hushed tone, she added, "do you smell what I smell?"

"I smell nothing," he replied.

It was then my turn. "Is it the smell of roses?" I asked casually."

"It is," she said, "the whole room is full of the scent of roses!"

I knew this but did not personally smell the roses! While I had been administering healing, I was thinking all of the time of the Blessed Virgin Mary in the shape of the statue that had been presented to me and had said, in a prayerful way, "well, if anyone knows about pregnancies, you the Blessed Virgin Mary do!" The woman went away with her husband and I knew that

Part Three

all would be well.

Some months went by and the proud mother brought the baby to see me. He was a grand little chap. All was well.

Chapter 16

THE FR. ROOKEY EXPERIENCE

It was 11.45p.m. on a Sunday night when the 'phone rang. I was just finishing my third nightcap before going to bed. It is a little unusual for the phone to ring so late on a Sunday night. The lateness of the hour suggested a sense of urgency and I immediately thought that a member of the family in Dublin had something urgent to say. I lifted the telephone and the caller happened to be a business man. I knew him personally though we would not meet very often.

His voice was charged with emotion as he went on to tell me that his sister was very seriously ill with Bacterial Meningitis in a Cork hospital. She was in a coma and not responding to treatment and dependant on a life support machine. He asked me if I would go and see her there and then. Arrangements had been made for her to be taken off the life support machine at 3.00p.m. the following day.

I knew that I was over the limit as I drove my car to the hospital which was about five miles distant from where I lived. It was well after midnight when I arrived. All was quiet as I made my way along corridors to the ICU. In an adjoining room members of the family were gathered together. They spoke in hushed tones through their tears. Unity is strength at a tragic time like this. When I think back on that night I cannot believe that I more or less breezed in and just said, "Don't cry, Zena [not her real name] will be ok" or words to that effect.

On the physical plane my nightcaps probably were the cause of the utterance. On the other hand it probably was the Higher Power that was really steering the conversation. Within a few minutes I was with the patient. She was a young married woman aged thirty-four and had two children. She was in a private part of the ICU and I looked at her still body being kept alive by a machine. The nurse made some adjustments to the equipment and though not far away I was alone with the patient. In situations like this the only thing one can do is to pass the whole problem over to the universal

God. This I did and I was guided to direct healing energies to the patient's liver.

I have found over the years never to question what is being given intuitively and no matter what is being suggested, go and do it. I found myself being directed to Zena's head which I held in the palms of my hands. I lifted my head and saw a small plain mother-of-pearl cross on her chest. As I have said elsewhere in this narrative, for a very long time I had problems with crosses and crucifixes. I was aware that the crucifix represented the crucified Christ while the plain cross represented the Risen Lord. I found I could deal much better with the latter.

FATHER PETER ROOKEY
MAN OF MIRACLES

The plain cross held my gaze and as I looked upon it I found my mind wandering and lost in reverie. I had read a book not only once but twice. It was the life story of an American priest named Fr. Rookey. As far as I can recall when he was eight years old and celebrating American Independence day a large firework exploded in his face blinding him completely. Medically there was no possibility of him regaining his sight. His family had tremendous faith and year after year they prayed the Rosary for a miracle.

Their prayers were answered. The young Rookey was given back his sight. In grateful thanks he decided to become a priest and dedicated his whole life to the ministry of healing. He travelled the world with an old worn cassock and a battered cross. He had visited Waterford on one occasion but it was impossible for me to travel to see him. The halt, the lame and the blind were healed through him. He would explain to those seeking help that he had nothing to give them but the power of the cross. They fell back in the spirit, healed. These thoughts were going through my mind as I stood holding Zena's head my eyes transfixed on that small mother-of-pearl plain cross.

I found myself speaking to Fr. Rookey. I had not a clue as to what part of the world he was in just at that moment but I did speak to that 77 year old priest who helped people sixteen hours a day, ate little and owned nothing!

I found myself telling him that I wish I had even a fraction of his trust in the cross. It was then I asked him for help. I found myself standing at the side of Zena and I placed the palm of my right hand on the cross. It was like a block of ice. I found my hand beginning to burn. It was staggering. For the life of me I cannot recall how long my hand was on that cross but I knew that something very special had taken place.

I was guided to grip Zena's two ankles, one in either hand. Counting backwards from seven [the holy number] I reached number one. With complete trust I "pulled" the problem from her body! I passed the family gathering in the ante room, gave a wave and told them all would be well. It was only when I arrived home a couple of hours later that the enormity of my hospital antics dawned on me. The whole thing was like a dream. It was as if I had acted out some part in a play in another dimension.

Monday dawned and as usual I was at my little clinic shortly after 1.00p.m. At 2.30p.m. precisely Zena's brother 'phoned me. He thanked me for visiting his sister in the hospital but advised that there had been no change in her condition. She was still in a coma and the life support machine was being switched off in thirty minutes. I suddenly exclaimed, "it is not three yet!" I am sure he must have thought I was crazy. At three in the afternoon the life support was switched off. Immediately Zena sat bolt upright and said in a loud voice, "could anyone get me a bottle of 7-up please?"

Everyone was dumbfounded. Two weeks after this wonderful healing she was out playing tennis. All the family came to my little clinic one night about a week later to thank me. I told them the whole story as I have just reiterated. I told them that the thanks must go to Almighty God through the complete and utter trust of Fr. Rookey in the power of the cross. I often wished that I had been able to write and relate the healing saga to him personally. If he is still alive he must be a man in his eighties. I think that he lived in California somewhere. This tremendous experience had a profound effect upon me and gave me much to think about. It was another part of my learning curve and a huge one at that.

Part Three

Chapter 17

STEPPING STONES TO INFINITY

In common with many others, from time to time I write to myself. In essence the conscious part of a person finds out what is going on in the deep recesses of the subconscious mind. To me the knowledge gained from the subconscious is something well worth striving for. It brings enlightenment in its wake. It is rather like collecting all the sediment at the bottom of our individual pond. Bringing it to the surface we learn what makes us tick. The muddled thoughts eventually come to fruition when we take away the sediment and leave the nuggets of knowledge.

Seven-eighths of our overall psyche lives in this realm which has a vibrant existence in time and space. From what I have experienced and because we are all made from the same spiritual material it stands to reason at some stage of our existence our awareness develops along these lines.

Stepping-stones to Infinity!

Our minds are realms of spiritual reality and just as "real" as the physical world appears to be. We all must pass through this door in order to progress to eternity and beyond.

Beyond eternity? How can one comprehend this? With the aid of the gift of thought and the practice of meditation sometimes I get a little closer to understanding a semblance of this problem of two existences. The value of meditation cannot be emphasised enough. It is a discipline to be followed and is never mastered. By persevering, meditation can lead to one's own personal haven of refuge – so peaceful and serene that those who make it are in awe at the peace that is found within.

We are in a timeless and spaceless part of ourselves. Here we start to comprehend the path we must tread. Life and lives, aeons of time and space are here – in fact, another dimension! When we pray, we talk to God. When we meditate God speaks to us. The strange thing is that if one remembers what God said, it was not God!

If we are fortunate enough to hear God speak to us in meditation while we do not remember what was said, what He did say is reflected to others from our own soul! Seers sometimes catch a glimpse of this existence with finely attuned eyes with which to see. They see beyond the normal seeing and hear beyond the normal hearing. We develop awareness along these lines. Our schooling in the field of psychic abilities leads here as we travel in eternity. We try to grasp with a finite mind some of the marvels of infinity and that which goes to make up one of our worlds without end. Slowly the gap between our consciousness and subconscious opens. It is a beginning.

If one finds this hard to comprehend how can one expect to comprehend the next step in the future of humanity? As I have consistently stated we are of spirit. When the sheath is shed the spiritual makes its appearance While still within the bodily sheath the spiritual expresses itself through love, compassion for others and consistently giving of oneself. Gifts of leadership, clear thinking, guidance and indeed healing for the common good demonstrate the spirit at work. The price for the prize is high but so well worth while.

Suffering to me – often referred to as the cross one must bear – in my case at any rate - was meant to be part of my overall plan. I found that it is only as one progresses in time does this become clear. It is difficult to write about such an abstract subject. One may be excused for thinking that I am not sane or rational but I have to explain things as best I can. My thoughts have always been deep as I endeavour to understand the purpose of my being.

I recall some years ago when I left my thinking-cap on far too long as I struggled with a certain line of thought. It was as if my brain had gone on fire. The brain is the servant of the mind and it was becoming obvious that my thinking had gone far outside the parameters permitted. I had to go to bed. Suddenly I heard a voice say to me, "how can a grain of sand comprehend the desert of which it forms part? Get back in to your grain of sand!"

I did just that and all was quiet on the mind and brain fronts. A quite extraordinary experience and another one for the book.

I recalled to mind the story of the man who was walking by the sea and a fish popped his head above the water. The man said to the fish "it must be wonderful to be a fish and swim in the vastness of the ocean." To which the fish, a questioning look on its face replied "what is the ocean?"

What is life but the opportunity to know about oneself - the real self. Nothing else is of importance. We will do great things and help others by the experiences we will encounter.

Apropos the foregoing the following is a prayer that I use daily. It is entitled "The Prayer of Cardinal Newman" [also used by Mother Teresa of Calcutta].

"Dear Lord, help me to spread Thy fragrance everywhere I go. Flood my soul with Thy spirit and life. Penetrate and possess my whole being so utterly that all my life may only be a radiance of Thine. Shine through me, and be so in me that every soul I come in contact with may feel Thy presence in my soul. Let them look up and see no longer me but only Thee O Lord! Stay with me, and then I shall begin to shine as Thou shinest; so to shine as to be a light to others. The light O Lord will be all from Thee; none of it will be mine; it will be Thou, shining on others through me. Let me thus praise Thee in the way Thou dost love best, not by words, but by my example, by the catching force, the sympathetic influence of what I do, the evident fullness of the love my heart bears to Thee. Amen."

Part Three

Chapter 18

PSYCHISM – A HELP AND A HINDRANCE

Understanding and developing the latent abilities within ourselves is a daunting task. The answer to this lies in the fact that there is no ending to that understanding! As I have so often stated each and every one is unique and the only true common denominator between us is this uniqueness. Such being the case none of us can teach another how to understand that "something", that inner feeling which is our common heritage. It is we that teach ourselves.

Awakening our inner psychic ability is a good place from where to start the journey of exploration. A good trigger to start one off might be found in such subjects as clairvoyance, clairaudience, clairsentience, astral projection, numerology, astrology, crystal gazing, psychometry, divination of all kinds, precognitive dreams, the use and misuse of Ouija boards, ad infinitum. These are, by analogy, the leaves which in turn are attached to the twigs which are attached to the branches which lead ultimately into what I term the psychic tree [See left]

When translated the tree is in effect oneself! It stands to reason, therefore, by studying, as much as one wishes, any or all of the "leaves" will prove to be or enormous benefit in heightening one's sensitivity. It is a truism to state that psychics are the tools of spirit. It stands to reason therefore that the more one strives to develop one's ability in this field the greater the opportunity is to become an instrument of the Universal Mind and help others in whatever direction one is guided. In helping others we help ourselves into the bargain.

It must never be forgotten that psychics are merely a means to an end. There is great glamour and excitement and a feeling of power as one's abilities develop and one runs the risk of the ego taking over. Psychics per se can also be a deterrent to spiritual progression. It may appear to be a contradiction in terms to exhort one to develop their abilities and at the same time state that these same abilities are a handicap.

This apparent contradiction becomes clearer when one commences to come to grips with the fact that there are countless levels of awareness. Psychic awareness finds its home in the very low register of this cosmic keyboard. Too much attention paid to these lower vibrations acts as a distinct barrier. Imagine the biblical Jacob's ladder. For argument sake let us say that it is comprised of one thousand rungs reaching to infinity. On this scale we can place the whole gambit of psychics on or about the seventieth rung of our personal ladder we are endeavouring to climb. From this analogy one can see the point I am trying to make.

Too much attention will halt the personal climb! It is so important to keep an open mind at all times. If one comes across something which is difficult to accept and does not appear to fit into one's own personal jigsaw just reject it. Lay it aside until such time that particular piece fits snugly into some obscure part of the picture. Tunnel vision is bad news but tunnel thinking a million times worse. It is worth remembering that what one seeks "out there" is now, always was and always will be within oneself. No matter where one goes in search of knowledge, to the east or to the west, to the north or to the south that which one searches for travels with them for it is within all the time!

Chapter 19

THE LONG HAUL

When endeavouring to come to terms with healing on all levels, viz. spiri
guides, gate-keepers, controls and help from the masters one has to ask two
specific questions.

The first is why they have an interest in the subject and secondly what do
they understand it to be?

There are no hard and fast answers to the questions raised. Each person has
the answers within themselves. Thinking over the matter one comes to the
realisation that the quality of any healing is in direct proportion to one's
own personal awareness of what the universal power recognised as God is.

Having said all this there is one common denominator and that is service.
Healing can be translated as service. We all have a need to serve and deep
down we are aware of the need to help our fellow human being. The answer
to why we have this need is simple but profound. We need to give of ourselves. Service has to be selfless. It stands to reason therefore that healing
has to be in the same category. One gives without counting the cost; toil and
not seek rest; work without seeking any reward except in the knowledge
that we are doing what our soul decrees. We serve ourselves in service.

Where spiritual growth is concerned an unbalanced sensitivity is a danger.
One can often wonder how they are being of benefit to others? The answer
is by inner knowing. Once this is taken on board it will never leave a person. It is beyond emotion. It is that still small voice so one goes within to
find the answers! Whether we realise it or not every one of us is on a path
from what may be termed a "past infinity" to a "future infinity" but is only
conscious of the on-going now! We can look upon this path as a marathon
race of 26 miles 385 yards. Some of us are at the two mile mark, some have
gone through the "wall" and are at the 24 mile mark. Dare we say it, there

are those who are at the last 385 yards. One can rest assured that those who have reached the twenty-four mile mark have a much greater appreciation of what the race is all about in contrast to those at the two mile mark. There should be no disrespect shown to those who are at the lower end of the scale. They too will reach the 24 mile mark and indeed finish the race! What I am endeavouring to show by this example is the degrees of awareness.

The awesome truth is that each and every one knows what they need to know already. This knowledge has been lying dormant and I know that these few lines will be sufficient to trigger-off a personal search. Each and every one of us irrespective of the stage of our current progression has a serious responsibility to develop that which is within. In return one strengthens the link one has with that incomprehensible hierarchical structure which is our individual support in all we attempt to do. We are never alone. One thing common to us all is the ability to be receptive to the voice within. One should never forget and always remember we are constantly in touch with a power which, in effect, is our own personal understanding of God.

Energy is universal and it is vitally important that with development comes balanced progression both physical and spiritual. It is important to realise that our mind is king! One is essentially one's thought. This concept is profound and requires a great deal of hard thinking. We are comprised of spirit, soul, mind and body. We must understand that the brain is the servant of mind, mind the servant of the soul and the soul the servant of the spirit.

Spirit is, in turn being guided and directed by beings far, far in advance of us mere mortals. These beings form part of the hierarchy which to us is intangible but nevertheless of which we are part. Visualise a triangle. The overall power is at the apex, the person requiring help and the conduit constitute the two angles at the base. Until such time that this is clearly understood one falls back on spirit guides. The mind allows the directed healing energies to flow. It is so vitally important to dissolve and be completely free of the ego which can prove to be a great barrier.

The word "spiritual" means being of spirit; the awareness of the inner self the part that is God. Spiritual growth has to do with the essential self Spiritual also means being true to oneself. It is so important that one comes to recognise oneself as one is, and always and ever allow God an expression in one's life.

> 1 **Higher Mind**
> 2 **Subconscious Mind**
> 3 **Conscious Mind**

We are all energy! There is an exchange of this force within us which affects the physical, emotional and spiritual self. Each of us has a higher mind that knows what we can achieve. We must strive with all our might to access this serene part of ourselves. Because we are primarily energy we are in a position to manipulate it. Inspiration can be defined as a transference of energy from one level to a slower vibration. Group minds can also inspire.

All species of plant life and all animals have a group soul. We can trap the group mind i.e. the collective mind of maple or oak trees or any other living thing. Life is well worth sharing and we have much to learn from the group lives of nature. There are many forms of life that exist on other planets and these also affect us.

There are three identifiable areas of mind; higher mind, subconscious mind and conscious mind. Spirit guides and other entities commensurate with our current understanding work on the higher mind level. The subconscious part of the mind is full of all kinds of rubbish, viz. phobias, fears, fantasies, inhibitions, complexes, inherited traits; the list is endless. The conscious mind is that part of us of which we are aware in our waking moments in the so-called real world. One must allow the mind to blend beyond the areas of mundane psychic experience already mentioned. While, in all probability, much will be impressed upon the mind from these areas one must pay no heed to what might come. There is a tremendous temptation to do so. Just be and trust entirely on the inspiration one receives from powers far greater than ourselves.

It is a good idea to look upon oneself as just a pipe or channel and let that which is within radiate out. People sense this radiation and benefit accordingly. Inspiration is constantly and silently being directed to us. Each person has a controlling spirit which will always work with the mind so there is always need for attunement.

The equation is Attunement + Experience = An Ability To Heal. The daily practice of meditation is of great value. Perhaps one should say that it is an essential. Because we are human we fluctuate and such we must come to terms with the fact that inspirational links will also fluctuate. The transfer of healing energy is a spiritual expression and we must always keep in mind that all life is connected.

It may not be readily appreciated that colour has a direct bearing in our lives. We must learn to use colour and at the same time be conscious of the colour we are wearing. Every colour produces a vibration. For example one might say "he was red with rage; green with envy, in a blue mood, yellow with fear." One can even learn to distinguish colour by touch.

There are seven primary chakras. The word is an old Sanskrit word which loosely translated means a wheel or vortices of energy. In addition to the seven primary chakras we have twenty-one minor chakras connecting the etheric body to the physical frame. Then there are forty-nine sub-minor chakras all of which have a direct effect on the physical body is worth about 60 cents; 80% is made up of blood and water. The remaining 20% is constituted of carbon and trace elements. It is true therefore to say that we are spiritual beings with physical bodies and not spiritual beings with physical bodies. The mind boggles when one thinks deeply on the wonders of creation.

Because we are human we have human frailties. Such being the case we are indeed imperfect and with this realisation can come fear. Fear is a blockage to communication and this can affect the flow of healing energies. As we think so we are and it is ourselves who limit the quality of any given healing. With the power of God and complete trust everything is possible. How was it that Jesus was able to walk upon the waters? Because He trusted that he could do so. What enabled Him to calm the storms? Because he trusted He could do so. And it is just the same with ourselves. Whatever one trusts and knows can happen will happen but without faith very little can come about!

To me, belief is not knowledge. If I say "I believe" I am really saying that I doubt. If I change the word "believe" to "trust" a whole new force comes into play. In the field of healing there is no room for doubt. One must trust and know that all will be well. This is not something acquired overnight, rather is it an understanding that develops ever so slowly as one goes along life's path. Many times one can feel like packing it all in. My own development just when I thought I was making progress the power would cut the legs from under me. I have lost count of the number of times over the years when this happened. Then I would metaphorically pick myself up and continue. As time went by I began to notice that I was gaining in awareness and spiritual strength because of what I thought were failures.

Summing up there is this something within ourselves which makes us want to help others. One finds it difficult to describe but on reflection it dawns on one that there is feeling for others. The bottom line is that we love our fellow human being.

Healing is in fact the highest form of love in action.

Part Three

Chapter 20

WE ARE BUT ENERGY

When one speaks about their body invariably there is a tendency to think of it in physical terms only. When we do so we are in effect talking about nothing. If one includes every part of the human frame that can be viewed under an electronic microscope nothing remains for the scientist to hold on to. Every atom of which we are comprised is more than 99.99% empty space and the solid particles whizzing around are themselves just compact bundles of energy vibrations. The structure of an atom can be contrasted with the size of a small orange in a massive cathedral.

As one sifts through this solid-looking convincing body one has only to go so far before ending up with a handful of nothing! Yet this nothing is not really a void but a womb. As Dr. Deepak Chopra points out in his book "Unconditional Life" and I quote:

> *'with incredible fertility our inner space gives birth to love and hate, joy and sorrow, misery and happiness, pleasure and pain, right and wrong, purpose, meaning, hope, courage, despair, God, heaven and hell, grace, sin, salvation, damnation, enlightenment, wisdom, compassion, evil, envy, malice, generosity, camaraderie and everything in fact that makes life worth living.'*

Our physical body is really slowed-down energy. Outside of this we have our etheric body which has all the organs that the physical body has but vibrates so fast that one is not aware of it. It is connected to the physical frame at twenty-one distinct points which go to constitute what is termed "the silver cord" just as the umbilical cord joined us to our mothers.

The etheric body is the matrix upon which the physical body hangs. Beyond the etheric we have an astral body which vibrates faster than the etheric. Beyond this we have our lower, intermediate and higher mental bodies and finally comes our spiritual body. In between each of the seven bodies are a further seven and in between these seven are a further seven ad infinitum. One must look upon these bodies as fields of energy. The seven primary chakras therefore are not confined to the etheric body only but all the other bodies. Etheric chakras materialise as endocrine glands and control an area of the body, usually a number or organs.

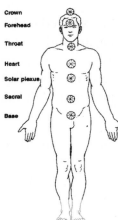

Crown
Forehead
Throat
Heart
Solar plexus
Sacral
Base

Disease in one organ usually relates to problems in a relevant major chakra. Chakras can be likened to ice-cream cones, one on the top of the head, one at the forehead, the throat, heart, solar plexus, sacral area and at the base of the spine. These vortices spin and are associated with various colours. Look upon the chakra at the top of the head as being God's inlet non-returnable valve for the power that is passing through and the one at the base as being God's outlet non-returnable valve. All the time there is a positive force passing through our chakra system on the right hand side of our spine from the cosmos to the centre of the earth along a channel called pingala.

On reaching the centre of the earth this energy takes on a negative aspect and returns to the cosmos on the left hand side of the spine through a channel called ida. The central column thus formed is called the Sushumna and when it leaves the top of our heads it is called the Sutratma. Though we live and have our being in God, this channel ultimately makes us aware of the Spirit of God passing through us. It should be noted that this force wraps itself around the sashumna thus forming the caduceus. There are corresponding ice-cream cones behind us and the energy that comes to us through the throat, heart, solar plexus and sacral chakras comes in from the rear. In the case of the pituitary gland the energy enters from the front. The top three chakras viz. crown, brow/ajna and throat go to constitute a triad with the apex pointing upwards. This is the spiritual us. The chakras at the solar plexus, sacral and base of the spine go to constitute a triad with the apex pointing downwards – this is the material us. In this particular context the soul resides at the heart centre.

Our function in life is to balance these two aspects of ourselves, the spiritual material, and endeavour mentally to make each triad equal in size and density. Then draw the spiritual triad down to the heart and the material one up to the heart. If successful we end up with the Star of David - the Jewish emblem for balance!

With this picture in mind let us take the case of a hypothetical business mogul who has been hugely successful, money-wise. In this day and age one has to be ruthless and prepared, metaphorically speaking, to go even to the point where they would kick their mother's teeth down her throat. A person in this category would end up with a material triad which is strong, thick and coarse while the corresponding spiritual triad would be obtuse and well out of alignment.

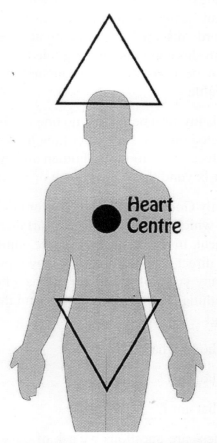

Heart Centre

Conversely one can come up against some hot-gospeller or religious fanatic who is so heavenly he is of no earthly use! In such cases the party concerned has a thick, coarse spiritual triad equivalent to the mogul's material triad while his material triad is obtuse and out of alignment! They are off balance.

The crown chakra represents the highest point of one's spiritual self and the base the lowest point of the material self. We are both and sometimes inclined to forget this important fact. Concentrating too much on the spiritual side of ourselves and neglecting the material can cause us problems, upsetting our equilibrium. The same thing applies if we place too much emphasis on the material side of ourselves thereby neglecting our spiritual. Again we become unbalanced!

What I am really referring to is the constant battle we all have as the soul endeavours to balance itself with the personality. Balance is the key! People visit healers with some disease - mental or physical. The meaning of the word "disease" is not being at ease! A healer's function is to act as a conduit directing energy as guided to replace the disease with easement. This can be translated as balancing the energy fields thereby restoring good health.

It is my firm belief that no one can be taught to heal but I am open to be corrected on this. No matter how high one may go - even to the Masters themselves - they too were human and even though they were at an exalted level far beyond the average man or woman, their knowledge is finite!

Only God knows everything for God IS everything and it is from this source of which we are an integral part do we have the privilege of being a healing agent. In my own very humble opinion the quality of one's ability to heal is in direct proportion to one's own personal understanding of God. Over the many years of my life acting as a healer I have learned one thing - I know nothing! In my case I have found that it is the "nothing" that does the healing!

Who or what is God?

Who am I?

What am I?

These are questions we ask of ourselves. Many seek God outside of themselves following this guru, that guru, this church, that church. All of this is an outward manifestation of the search that is going on within. I have found that what one seeks "out there" is now, always was and always will be within oneself! The greater one's personal awareness the greater will be the ability to be used as a channel for healing. KNOW that this is true and do not BELIEVE it is true. As I have said previously there is a huge difference between knowing and believing.

When one takes one's first tentative steps in developing the healing gift the only thing one is sure of is the ego. When one finds oneself with a patient, it is instinctive to ask oneself what do I do now? One endeavours to remember all they read in books on techniques and advice from all quarters, the concentration is on the "I." If a person feels help coming from a spirit guide link up with him or her. Spirit guides are but extensions of the awesome hierarchical structure of which we are part. Many people go through their lives working with spirit guides alone and with great success. Never allow doubt to control.

It takes years upon years of meditation, soul-searching, anguish, frustration, anger with self, anger with God, loneliness, depression. Included is a feeling that one is going mad as one tries to cope with what is being fed in to the mind.

Gradually it dawns on a person that they have nothing to do but trust and know and all will be well. It is imperative that one learns to control their own chakra system, manipulating each as the occasion demands. Visualisation brings reality and it is a good idea to picture the seven chakras as, say, roses, water lilies or burning gas jets. As the majority of people know little or anything about their chakra systems there is a tendency for them to go about with "leaky auras" thereby picking up all sorts and conditions of vibrations.

The more sensitive such a person is, the more they are prone to allowing all sorts of unwanted energies into their overall psyche. One will often hear a person exclaim "I have no energy." If that were the case they would be physically dead. In effect what they are saying is that they have picked up so much dross they unwittingly allowed others to draw off their energy. Their positive energy was exchanged for negative without realising it.

Each and every one of us is affected all of the time by those with whom we come into contact, by the daily stress of living, by what we see on TV or hear on the radio or read in the papers.

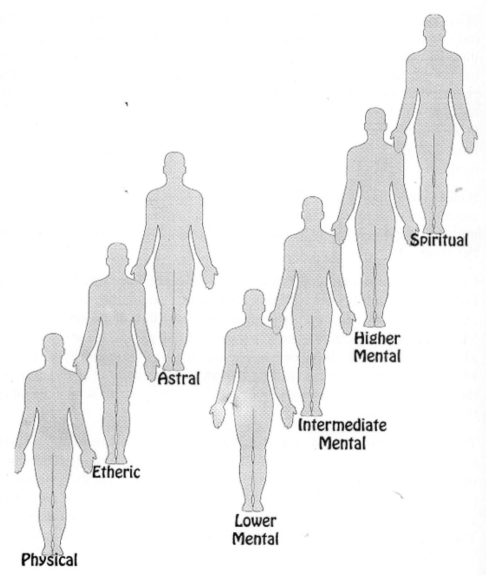

Spiritual

Higher
Mental

Astral

Intermediate
Mental

Etheric

Lower
Mental

Physical

When we give we receive. In the context of giving of oneself in healing we receive back the negative energy from those we endeavour to help. It is so important therefore to learn how to rid oneself of this. One could become like the Dead Sea – everything goes in but nothing comes out. The result?

One becomes worn out physically and mentally exhausted. Controlling the chakras is the key to avoiding this problem.

In conclusion I quote from Elizabeth Clare Prophet's book "Intermediate Studies of the Human Aura" in which the seven chakras are termed "The Seven Centres of God Awareness."

'The seven centres in your being are for the release of God's energy. God's awareness of Himself as power is anchored in our throat in the authority of the Word. God's awareness of Himself as vision is anchored in our third eye. God's awareness of Himself as wisdom is anchored in our crown. God's awareness of Himself as peace is in the solar plexus. God's awareness of Himself as freedom is in the seat of the soul. And God's awareness of Himself as purity is in the base of the spine.'

Chapter 21

KIRLIAN PHOTOGRAPHY

At this point I feel it is necessary to say a few words on the subject of Kirlian Photography.

In the early 1940s, Seymon Kirlian, an amateur inventor and electrician of Krasnodar, Russia, discovered by accident that if an object on a photographic plate is subjected to a high-voltage electric field, an image is created on the plate. The image looks like a coloured halo or coronal discharge. It is said to be a physical manifestation of the spiritual aura or "life force" which allegedly surrounds each living thing. It is a special method of "photographing" objects acting as a gateway to the paranormal world of auras. Actually, what is recorded is due to quite natural phenomena such as pressure, electrical grounding, humidity and temperature. Changes in moisture [which may effect changes in emotions], barometric pressure, and voltage, among other things, will produce different "auras."

The principle of Kirlian photography, as well as all electrography, is the corona discharge phenomenon, that takes place when an electrically grounded object discharges sparks between itself and an electrode generating the electrical field. When these sparks are captured on film they give the appearance of coronas of light. These discharges can be affected by temperature, moisture, pressure, or other environmental factors.

Several Kirlian techniques have been developed, but the basic ones generally employ a Tesia coil connected to a metal plate. The process is similar to the one which occurs in nature, when electrical conditions in the atmosphere produce luminescences, auras, such as St. Elmo's fire.

Overleaf are examples of four items as portayed by Kirlian Photography.

Parsley: *One sprig of Parsley. Note strength and regularity of radiation. This is the normal condition of plants in general, unless interfered with.*

Golden Cross: *The radiation of the object shows the psychological balance of the person, and the relationship to the significance of the cross*

Whole Food Bread: *Freshly cut slice of rye bread. Intensity of radiation shows goodness of the food. Energy dissipates faster when loaf is cut.*

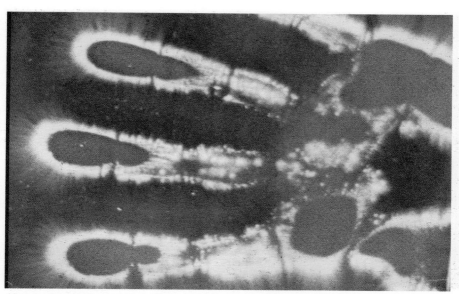

Hand of a Healer: *During Distant Healing this specific blue appears particularly during healing processes. Great regularity of corona signifies harmonious response*

Chapter 22

THE LONG AND DIFFICULT PROGRESSION

The reader will by now be well conscious of the fact that psychics are the tools of spirit. By making use of these tools we can begin to expand our awareness. We all have extra sensory abilities. It is our inheritance. It is linked with our subconscious mind and is part and parcel of us. Living in the so-called real world of gross materialisation dulls this very important part of ourselves.

It is only at certain times, perhaps when we have been subjected to some traumatic experience or in some great danger, that it comes into play. The more finely attuned person will be found to have more frequent psychic experiences. These can range from knowing who is on the 'phone as soon as it rings to knowing who will be at the front door before even opening it.

Then there are those who have experienced hearing, feeling seeing a loved one after they had passed to the world of spirit. No one has gone through life without at least one experience of extra sensory perception [ESP]. The more material the atmosphere we find ourselves in the less will be the awareness of our inherited psychic abilities.

Conversely, the further we get away from the material world and closer to that of nature the greater they will become. Developing one's awareness consistently will ultimately bring about the realisation that we have far more senses than the normally accepted ones of seeing, hearing, feeling, tasting and smelling. In his book "Unconditional Life" Dr. Deepak Chopra states:

' ... the whole notion that we have exactly five senses is completely arbitrary to begin with. Under the sense of touch for example we include our response to heat, texture, pressure, the placement of our limbs, the weight of our bodies and pain - all things we 'feel.' When the nervous system is intact, we may be said to have as many as seventeen senses according to

researchers on perception. We do not give names to most of these and some
are still disputable. Everyone seems to be able to detect pheromones for
example, the distinctive chemicals the body gives off when a person is
afraid or sexually aroused. The pineal gland in everyone's brain changes its
hormonal output by sensing the yearly cycle of the sun. But only selected
individuals count among their senses ESP or the ability to see auras and
light around other people."

In the same book Dr. Chopra recounts the story of a British anthropologist
who undertook a field trip to India. One evening he crept through the jungle and caught sight of a strange scene. An old holy man was dancing ecstat-
ically in the forest. He ran up and embraced the trees; he laughed when the
leaves stirred and bathed his face in the moonlight with an expression of
delirious joy. The anthropologist watched this display in fascination until he
couldn't contain himself. "Pardon me," he said, stepping from the bushes,
but what makes you dance out here alone in the jungle?" The holy man
looked bewildered and replied "pardon me, but what makes you think I'm
alone?" Both questions are mutually unanswerable because they depend on
unique world views. The holy man sees himself surrounded in the forest by
nature spirits while the anthropologist sees wood and chlorophyll. The two
realities overlap and yet do not come alive for each other.'

It is from awareness we progress to comprehension. Comprehension, in turn
leads to understanding and understanding translates itself into knowing. It
is a long and difficult progression and the secret is to make haste slowly!

As each of us is unique it goes without question that our ultimate knowledge
will also be unique. No two people can possibly interpret their inner knowledge the same way. Having regard to this fact it seems right never to accept
anything one reads or has propounded until such time one finds it is com-
patible to their current thinking. If it doesn't, reject it no matter how eminent the source may be. Lay it aside in stock so to speak. At the appropriate
time when one sees where it fits that's the time then to mould it to one's own
unique design.

Chapter 22

YOUR REALITY – WHAT IS IT?

I often wish I could see myself as others see me! Sometimes, like now, I do not feel real -whatever reality means. At this moment as I write I do not know if I am in the physical world or in some other dimension. I feel these two dimensions and struggle to analyse which is which! I think that I feel more content in this other world and wish that it would become stronger so that the physical world would fade away for good. What ties me to the physical world? I feel as if the answer is –

1. Some power seems to keep me here - as in a trap and from which there is no escape.

2. A special bond is the main anchor to the physical dimension and should that bond, itself, transfer to this other dimension, my bond would loosen and I, too, would move to this non-physical dimension.

3. The special bond, in turn, keeps me doing the work that I committed myself to do but only as long as I feel myself in this physical dimension! At this moment the physical dimension is like some wavy existence that does not appear to have real substance but is vibrating all of the time. It appears to make all so-called solid objects seem of little consequence. Where am I? Should I be here or elsewhere? I feel as if I am waiting for something to happen! Something to clarify the position. There seems to be two distinct areas, viz.:

1. The so-called physical.

2. A non-place which exists by virtue of its being and divides the so-called physical from the other world. I am in the non-place at this moment – it is semi-dark and appears to be square in shape – No-man's Land. Whether other people are here or not I do not know. It is neither frightening nor uplift-

ing - it seems to quiver and this is where I am. I have a feeling that I have been here a few times previously - I don't know what or where it is. When I put on my front I seem to return to the quivering so-called real world which all seems so strange - it is difficult to concentrate on what I see and when speaking to those that come to me with their problems it is an effort to do anything for the scene lacks reality - whatever that is. Maybe this non-world is my reality. The non-world is neither good nor bad - it just is! It is like a place where I exist but, at the same time, do not exist! This non-world can expand and contract but will always return to its original size - that of a semi-dark cube or box. I don't know what it is - maybe it is a cube of utter sadness and loneliness - maybe it is either in myself or, perhaps it is myself! Does the cube move on in time or is it a case that I will ultimately move out of it to happier climes and places where the sun will shine; where there will be bright clouds scudding across the clear blue skies; where birds will sing and beautiful flowers grow; where clear crystal clear streams of water will flow and where mountains and hills and utter peace will be really real and not like the travesty of illusion which goes to constitute reality in the so-called physical world.

Why am I in this non-world?" For what purpose? I never asked to be here! Who or what placed me here? Has a non-world got an opposite? I haven't got a clue. All I know is that a non -world does exist - at least so far as I am concerned. It is like The Twilight Zone! It has all sorts of dimensions. Not just the traditional and acceptable three dimensions of the so-called physical world. In the non-world there are any number of dimensions from X to the first power to X to the 1,000,000th power - and away beyond!

All belief and all knowledge seems to be confined to three dimensions only in the so-called physical world but the enormity is that belief and knowledge also extend into these vast regions of other dimensions! Such being the case, those whose thinking is governed by the three-dimensional thinking are limited to an extraordinary degree - and this applies to everything - religion, science, mathematics et al!

Take religion for example. Those with three-dimensional aspects of mind will only be able to understand God, Jesus, the Virgin Mary, the Holy Ghost, the many other saviour gods the millions upon millions of hierarchies that exist now, previously and in the future - within the most narrow of thinking bands!

This can only lead to tunnel vision and worse, tunnel thinking! This is a complete and utter dead end! It leads to number nothing, nowhere street! Perhaps it leads to the non-world where I exist at "present" where nothing matters one way or the other - God, Jesus, Mary, the Holy Ghost, Masters, Saints, Angels, Archangels, Buddha's, Gurus, Rosaries, Prayers, Fasting, this, that and the other thing, Holy Wells, climbing mountains on bare feet, rituals, novenas, baptism, confirmation [of what?] and all the host of other man-made rules and regulations which, when one boils it all down, is reduced to nothing!

It is but yet another illusion! Who or what DOES have the truth? The only thing that does have the truth, the whole truth and nothing but the truth is –

CREATION ITSELF!

Chapter 24

METHODS OF DIVINATION

Acultomancy (by needles)
Aeromancy (by atmospheric conditions)
Ailuromancy (by cats)
Alectryomancy (by rooster)
Aleuromancy (by flour, including fortune cookies):
(Note: Divination by fortune cookies is also a form of **Stichomancy**, see below)
Alomancy (by salt)
Alphitomancy (by barley)
Ambulomancy (by taking a walk)
Anemoscopy (by wind)
Anthomancy (by flowers)
Anthracomancy (by burning coals)
Anthropomancy (by human sacrifice)
Apantomancy (by seeing animals)
Arithmancy (by numerology)
Ashagalomancy (by the casting of small bones)
Aspidomancy (by entering a trance)
Astragalomancy (by dice; see also Cleromancy)
Astrology (by celestial bodies)
Astromancy (by celestial bodies, aka **Astrology**; antiquated term)
Astro-Numerology (through an integration of Astrology and Numerology)
Astro-Tarot (through an integration of Astrology and Tarot)
Augury (by the formation of birds)
Austromancy (by wind and clouds)
Axiomancy (by axes)
Belomancy (by arrows)
Bibliomancy (by books, especially the Bible; see also **Stichomancy**)
Biorhythms divination
Bletonism (by currents of water)
Botanomancy (by burning plants or leaves)
Brontomancy (by thunder)
Capnomancy (by smoke)
Carromancy (by the melting of wax)
Cartomancy (by cards, e.g., playing cards, tarot cards, and non-tarot oracle cards; see also **Taromancy)**
Catoptromancy (by mirrors)
Causimomancy (by burning)
Cephalomancy (by skulls)
Ceraunoscopy (by thunder and lightning)
Ceromancy, or ceroscopy (by placing melted wax into cold water)
Chaomancy (by aerial visions)
Cheiromancy, or palmistry (by palms) where the grooves of the hand are interpreted as signs.
Chirognomy (by hands)
Cledonomancy (by chance events or overheard words)
Cleromancy (by casting lots or by bones; including divination by use of dice or dominoes; For divination by use of dice, see also **Astragalomancy**)
Clidomancy, or cleidomancy (by keys)
Coffee Grounds Divination, Coffee **Tasseography**: see **Tasseography**
Cometomancy (by comet tails)
Coscinomancy (by hanging sieves)
Critomancy (by barley cakes)

Cromniomancy (by onion sprouts)
Crystallomancy/Scrying (by crystals or other reflecting objects)
Cybermancy (via computer oracles)
Cyclomancy (by wheels)
Daphnomancy (by burning laurel wreaths)
Demonomancy (by demons)
Dice divination (see also **Astragalomancy** and **Cleromancy**)
Dominoes divination (see also **Cleromancy**)
Dbutsu uranai (by one's animal horoscope)
Empyromancy (by burning)
Extispicy (from the exta of sacrificed animals)
Favomancy (by beans; a form of cleromancy)
Floriography (the language of flowers)
Geomancy (by earth), includes **Feng Shui** divination
Geloscopy (by laughter)
Graphology (by handwriting)
Gyromancy (by dizziness)
Hepatoscopy, or **haruspication** or **hepatomancy** (by liver)
Hippomancy (by horses)
Hydromancy (by water)
Hypnomancy (by hypnosis)
I Ching divination (ancient Chinese divination using I Ching): (However, as performed by some diviners with heavy reliance on an accompanying I Ching manual, this is, in effect, also a form of **Bibliomancy/Stichomancy**)
Ichnomancy (by footprints)
Icthyomancy (by fish)
Idolomancy (by idols)
Knissomancy (by burning incense)
Lampadomancy (by flame)
Lecanomancy (by a basin of water)

Libanomancy (by smoke from incense)
Libromancy (by book(s); see also: **Bibliomancy, Stichomancy**)
Literomancy (by a letter in a given written language)
Lithomancy (by precious stones)
Logarithmancy (by logarithms)
Macharomancy (by knives or swords)
Mahjong divination (by Mahjong tiles)
Margaritomancy (by bouncing pearls)
Metagnomy (by visions)
Meteormancy (by meteors)
Metoposcopy (by the lines of the forehead)
Moleosophy (by blemishes)
Myomancy (by rodent behaviour)
Myrmomancy (by ant behaviour)
Narcomancy (by sleep)
Necromancy (by speaking to the dead)
Nephomancy (by clouds)
Nggàm (by spiders or crabs)
Numerology (by numbers)
Oculomancy (by eyes)
Oinomancy (by wine)
Omphalomancy (by umbilical cords)
Oneiromancy (by dreams)
Onomancy or **Nomancy** (by letters in a name)
Onychomancy (by fingernails)
Oomantia, or **Ooscopy** or **Ovomancy** (by eggs)
Ophiomancy (by snakes)
Oracle-books divination (e.g., Chinese: I Ching (Book of Changes), Ling Ch'i Ching (Spiritual Chess Classic), I Lin (Forest of Change), T'ai Hsüan Ching (Canon of the Supreme Mystery); African: Ifá; Western: Sabian Symbols): See also **Stichomancy/Bibliomancy**

Orniscopy, or **Orinthomancy** (by birds of flight)
Ossomancy (by bones)
Ouija board divination
Palmistry (by palm inspection)
Pedomancy (by footprints)
Pegomancy (by spring water)
Phrenology (by the shape of one's head)
Phyllorhodomancy (by rose petals)
Plastromancy (by cracks formed by heat on a turtle's plastron)
Pyromancy, or **pyroscopy** (by fire)
Rhabdomancy (by rod or stick)
Rhapsodomancy (by poetry)
Roadomancy (by stars)
Runecasting / Runic divination (by Runes)
Scatomancy (by droppings, usually animal)

Scapulimancy (by bovine or caprid scapulae, i.e. shoulder bones)
Sciomancy (by spirits)
Sideromancy (by burning of straw)
Slinneanachd (by animals' shoulderblades)
Spodomancy (by ash)
Stichomancy (by books and/or lines; see also: Bibliomancy, Libromancy)
Stolisomancy (by clothing)
Taromancy (by specially designed cards: Tarot; see also **Cartomancy**)
Tasseography (or **Tasseomancy**) (by tea leaves or by coffee grounds)
Tephramancy (by bark ashes)
Tiromancy (by cheese)
Xylomancy (by burning wood)
Zoomancy (by animals)

Part Four

WONDER HEALING TAKING PLACE AT CORK HOTEL – CORK WOMAN CASTS ASIDE HER WALKING AID

CORKONIAN REPORTERS ON THE SPOT

The Corkonian News
26th May,1989

They come from the four corners of this country, not really knowing what to expect or what will confront them, but they come in anticipation of Bill Parfrey, very often achieving what medical science has failed to rectify. Parfrey is a grey haired man in is 60's, who claims 25 years of involvement with healing and his remarkable claims are spellbinding to the ears. From severe arthritis to terminal cancer; people in many instances without hope arrive at the Airport Hotel, which is situated on the steep hill leading to Cork Airport, to explore for themselves, the merits of Bill Parfrey. This writer, suffering from acute muscular shoulder pains, unremitting in severity for over 2 years went along to Bill Parfrey's healing sessions, to ascertain the level of scepticism, or indeed confidence, of those visiting the clinic.

Extracting the causes of suffering from her body and casting them to the floor by wayward hand movements, which seemed illogical and difficult to comprehend, Bill Parfrey walked to the end of the room, a distance of about 10 feet, to Jean, he might as well have been a mile away. Simply, since her operations, she had not walked unaided and didn't believe too much in her future ability to walk without assistance. By the conclusion of her therapy, she became composed and very confident like never before to throw away her walking aid.

Parfrey's secret is 4 consecutive days of visits to his hotel clinic, and day I was about to wrap itself up for this East Cork based woman, but not before I took part in another Bill Parfrey healing session. 'I am a Bio Energy Healer', said Bill Parfrey, 'People come to me from all over and I get great pleasure in helping people overcome the tragedies of life'.

He doesn't believe in religion and doesn't profess identity with any one sector of religion. But he is quick to point out, that he does believe in God. I listened with great attention to his Godly outlines and as a total non-believer, found it most difficult to convince myself of his sincerity in this division of life. His Bible quotations and citations of deeds, certainly commend interest and I listened with the intention of picking holes.

He placed his hands on my shoulders, and after listening to my outline of various sectors of shoulder pain, he assured me, that after this session, I would enter a new dawn of life without pain. Reassuring I thought, but If it doesn't work, I haven't lost anything.

On this day of days, I was

also the subject of severe headache, and neck pain, a prominent feature of my life for 2 years. Without medical qualifications, I wondered could this gentleman really be serious about his claims.

Continuing his therapy, Bill Parfrey applied his hands all over, but never touching the body, except to release the aches from head and neck. From a distance, he mentally extracted the origins of my discomforts by more strange hand movements, and again,I thought who's going to believe that I am subjecting myself to such mayhem. From sitting to standing and swinging my arm, I was instructed to follow his movements and I do so with precise detail.

Before I knew what was happening. I had been subjected to almost 25 minutes of Bill Parfrey's method of Bio Energy Healing and somehow, it seemed more like 25 seconds. Could my days of night and day pains be coming to a slow halt, I wondered?

Had I the belief in Bill Parfrey to make a second visit, realising that altogether I was commissioned to make four consecutive visits. I knew I hadn't the belief in myself, but as long as the spiritual healer wanted me to come, I'd go along with my plan. It was I that committed myself to Bill Parfrey. It was my own free choice to do so.

NO HOPE OF FURTHER MEDICAL AID'

I was looking forward to my second visit with much composure, but somehow I was rapidly deteriorating in motivation.Gone was the adrenelin as I climbed the Airport Hotel steps, but once in the healing room, I felt a quiet degree of renewed confidence. The passion of the previous evening was a difficult act to follow, but most pleasing was the sheer joy on the face of my fellow patient from East Cork.

She was, to my utter astonishment walking without her aid, and her sincerity was everywhere in the room. We sat and talked openly about Bill Parfrey, but mostly I was very concerned that medical people had surrendered her to the outside world, with no hope of further medical aid to redress the great imbalance In her life.

Less thin 24 hours previously, this lightly framed lady was unable to walk unattended, and now once more, the subject of Bill Parfrey's roaming hands and scintillating mind, she was walking at a brisk pace, doing an about turn as confident as the soldiers of parade in Collins Barracks.

Mind blowing revelations unfolding in Room 19 of the Airport Hotel, on a beautiful Summer afternoon, I wondered what made an ordinary looking gentleman command such respect.

'MAJOR VARIETY OF AILMENTS'

A middle aged lady from Ballincollig was now also in our midst and she rose to Parfrey's command without hesitation. Suffering from acute neuralysis of the ankle, the was experiencing great discomfort, and came to the Corkman's clinic to explore the mystics of bio energy healing.

With total calmness and much assurances (which I found at times to be dulling my own sincerity in Bill Parfrey), he went through the rituals once again, with all the motions.now so repetitive. Beseated and attentive, Bill's patients listened to my probing questions, and I have no doubt, that his disclosure of not being a member of a particular religious denomination, almost caused a mind explosion for one participant. All present expressed sincere relief from pain and day 2 complete, we awaited part 3 wIth much anxiety. For my own part, I had experienced great partial relief, but still retained the mental scars of the previous two years of discomfort.

It was plain to be seen that many who entered Bill Parfrey's clinic were expecting to be confronted by some vigil from the heavenly planet. They simply wanted to find & human being different to themselves. He doesn't advise or encourage people to slap recognised medical treatment in the few. Indeed, Bill's own life is for a number of years in the capable hands of his own doctor. 'Unfortunately', says Bill, 'whilst healers can lay claims to great deeds in heating power, they cannot administer to themselves or to one another.

Studying Bill Parfrey over 4 days, and approximately 15 hours, provided access to the formulation of many theories and my conclusive analogy bluntly implied, that it the Corkman was a practical joker, without foundation or belief in his bio energy powers, then he was surely putting himself through great and extended daily anguish. I couldn't we the proof of his healing powers, not yet at any rate, but 1 did seethe strain on his countenance time and again.

Day 3 was a traumatic and moving scenario and among those present, was a lady suffering from Parkinsons Disease. She was brought to the Hotel Clinic in a wayward state, totally unable to activate any motionable activity. I made a a special note of her notable improvement on day 3 of the therapy, and assured myself, that I would make a very special insertion in my, diary for her final visit on day 4.

Before my eyes, came a former Cork businessmen, from the motor industry, and also a person I had acquainted with previously at his former garage. His plight was a mixum of ailments from hearing to hip and knee joints severely swollen. In the course of a personal discussion informed me, that he was living out of a tablet bucket.

'I've known Bill a long time', he said. 'I get marvellous relief from his therapy, and only for him, I don't know what I'd do. My life and health is upscuttled, but today, I know I'll feel better when Bill is finished with me'. True and sincere confidence filled the room as he spoke and one could only sit in dismay. By the conclusion of Parfrey's therapy, knee joints that had been locked tight, preventing reasonable mobility, had surrendered to the bio energy healer, and now the willing patient was strolling to and fro the healing room.

Hearing was a major defect for the former motor industry man, and again Bill's skills were put to the test. Music was set to low, medium and high volumes, to test the hearing strength, before therapy commenced. It was clear the healer was indeed looking for a miracle or perhaps an automatic hearing aid. Confidently, he strode purposefully at the awesome confrontation, and within moments decibels of sound were now coming through to the hearing victim that were not there previously. The expression on the patient's face said it all, as he walked beck to his seat to watch other sufferers of various ailments put their trust in Bill Parfrey. The treatment is group orientated, whereby witnessing Bill in action, other sufferers will feel the tempo.

'INCOMPREHENSIBLE TO THE HUMAN MIND'

Day 3 for me was a day of low key. But it was also very revealing. Jean, the East Cork based lady had an uncomfortable previous night, but her mobility without the walking aid had to be seen to be believed. She was blooming in confidence and an example to all.

Sarah presented Bill with a problem of another kind. At two and a half years old, she contacted Polio, end the end product was one leg shorter than the other by one and a half inches.

Her medical consultants were keen to fit a leg brace, but Sarah wasn't too keen. At least not when she heard about Bill Parfrey. Her shoulders were drooping, one below the other, Her confidence was good, without being exceptional.

She arrived on day 1 to commence 4 days of Parfrey bio energy treatment, and by day 3, she was proclaiming great success. As indeed was her excited watching mother.

The 35-year old succumbed to Bill Parfrey's instructions and listened to his every whim with minute precision. By total submission to the healer, she was beginning to look very composed and self-confident,

The 40 year old Southide lady suffering from Parkinsons Disease was quite a different proposition to Bill Parfrey. On day 3, she returned with great willingness, but surely, this was expecting a lot of the healer. I thought. He greeted her on arrival in a manner and style that would not be surpassed at Heaven's gates, immediately bringing her into his confidence.

He spent considerable time pledging his unusual talent to this lightly framed lady, and again, she was only too eager to benefit. Foremost, it was an impossible task, but now latterly, the improvement was very significant

Several more sat in the healing room on day 3. One lady had journeyed from Cashel, and also a West Cork farmer was in our midst. We all had the same mission. By the dawning of day 4, my own condition was returning to it's peak of suffering, and I said forlornly, that I had lost nothing and observed a great deal of satisfaction mirrored on people's countenances.

Bill Parfrey speaks lavishly of George Canning, the man who introduced bio energy heating to Ireland, and also a man of immense healing power. The same Canning took Parfrey under his wing for a special 4 day intensive course and although the Corkman had many years of healing claims under his belt, he left Dunmanway's Parkway Hotel mesmerised at the healing credentials of Canning. ' I saw everything', said Bill, 'from severe cancer cases to spinal injuries, and almost all of the results were incomprehensible to the human mind

LEG FOR AMPUTATION SAVED AT LAST MOMENT'

Bill Parfrey talks glowingly of day 4, as 'icing on the cake' day, because in real terms, you are on your own after day 4, and he further assuringly implies, that there is a 24 day 'powerpack' after the conclusion of the 4 day therapy. This gives his patients real hope, but when asked to explain the reasoning of the time factors, he nods his head, and says 'that in my arithmetic after 25 years of healing. It's not, and can't be a day 1 miracle, but if it is, that's a real bonus to any sufferer who comes to my clinic.

Bill Parfrey cited one very excited heating claim of a former year. 'Local Radio', said Bill, 'broadcast a message on the air looking for a faith healer (which I'm not). I rang them up and found that a West Cork family were desperately looking for a healer to perform on a young member of the family, who was at Cork's Orthopaedic Hospital, preparing for an amputation of the leg. I went along and did my usual routine and observed the immediate progress.

When the nurse came along later to tend her patient, and dress his wounds, she noticed, said Bill, that the green matter had ceased pouring and shortly afterwards, the yellow emission completely cleared up. I was both thrilled and enlightened, and of course delirious with joy for the young man. Shortly afterwards, he was discharged, and that, said Bill, gave me immense human belief in my own ability as a healer.

When I put to him, that finance must come into the reckoning, he smiled and said, 'Look, if I could, I'd go into the room naked. I don't wear a watch or carry money and if I thought this singular moment that money was the motivating factor, then I couldn't do this therapy'.

Bill was being extremely modest, because he runs his clinic with the overheads attached to many businesses. He pays a weekly rent to the hotel for the use of the room, and points out how important it is to have the exclusive use of any healing room, he may operate in. 'The vibrations I create must not be disturbed and that to me is all important', said Bill.

During my 4 days, and nights at the hotel, I couldn't help but notice the trickle of business accumulating to the Hotel. Many infirmed persons need transportation to the clinic, and usually the host driver, frequent the hostelry to while away the passing time. Every story has a spinoff, and people, perhaps are arriving at the Cork hotel, who would not normally stop-off, but such are the benefits of bio energy healing.

The cost of therapy by Bill Parfrey is not specified and though pressed to make a detailed outline, he simply said that he incurs substantial outlay, and doesn't partici-

pate in other work. 'Donations', he said, 'are the norm, and I am pleased to receive any donation'. Of course, it must be stated that if the Cork healer can perform healing acts, no price is too high, and compared to 4 visits from a family doctor, surely a minimum of £20 donation would be only a token gesture to satisfied clients at the clinic.

I put it to Bill Parfrey, that he we, taking on an awesome task, when dealing with human suffering, and what gave him the conviction to tackle such a responsible line of work?

'I have endured ridicule, apathy, you name it', said Bill, 'but I know what I'm doing is right. This healing power was latent and not explored to its full potential by me, for far too many years. Now I'm at peace with myself. I am able to relax, meditate and I have discovered the key to the door, that makes me a more humble person. I'm also of course, extremely aware and confident of my own ability to help my fellow man, when his health is in distress.

'FINAL GOODBYES -
DAY 4'

Recalling his earliest involvement with psychic powers, Bill Parfrey said he was one of the founder members of (but now defunct) Cork Psychic Society. 'That society', said Bill, 'afforded people to come together as a unit and exchange their viewpoints on such matters as crystal gazing, and spirit communication. It was a very enclosed society, and to gain entry was not easy'.

Spirit voices, have on many occasions communicated to him, said Bill, and the family history is credited with many pre-clan members who had peculiar abilities in psychic powers. It was in Cahir as a young man of 18 that Bill encountered his first fling with spirits. ' In the stealth of a long Summer's evening around 1945, with nothing to do, I lazed around the room with only the tick of the clock to amuse me. Suddenly, the ticking stopped and the voice of his deceased grandmother said, 'We're all very happy here. 'Then', Bill continued, 'The ticking recommenced. That was my first major encounter with the spirits'. The Parfrey magic continued into day 4 at the Airport Hotel Healing Clinic and the excited infirmed returned for the 'icing on the cake' day, full of beans and unperturbed at their surrounds. As we made our way to Room 19 for the final scenario, I began to feel deflated, but not somehow downhearted.

I left my pain aching body to the Bio (life) energy healer, and conceded in thought, that for me, it wasn't to be a success, because again on this day, I was not going to jump over the moon. He sensed my anxiety, and in no time. I was pouring out all the sentiments of defeat. He wasn't listening, at least I thought not, but he carried on relentlessly relieving the stress in an afternoon session. By conclusion, I confess to greater comfort and less excruciation; from the body, and now 5 days later, 1 am monitoring (without discomfort), a progression, that hopefully will yield a positive dimension

Sarah's leg, if not of equal length to it's compatriot, was brimful in it's movement, and all present at the clinic. witnessed a sincere improvement.

Jean was revamped, and one could almost say, ·believing that she too, could now become a bio energy healer. Helen, suffering from Parkinsons Disease, asked Bill Parfrey on arrival of night 4, how he was feeling. That truly summed up the wonderful atmosphere on this night of nights and taking into consideration, that Helen on night 1 was as meek as a young chicken, this really did put the 'icing on the cake' for all present. Before the final bows were taken, a 13-year old Douglas schoolgirl, who had missed 6 months of schooling through a mysterious ailment made her appearance.

Hospitalised, and the subject of an exploratory operation at the Wilton Regional, this young and beautiful young lady finally turned to Bill Parfrey to find a remedy. Soon after Bill's therapy, Caroline returned to school once more feeling a new pin, but in her anxiety to account for lost school time, she was perhaps, pushing herself over the top a little too much. Uncle Bill was back in business and one could only sense the implicit trust placed in him by Caroline. I have no doubt that with her confidence and his belief in himself, Caroline is unlikely to miss many more school days.

Treatment at the clinic ranges right across the board from throat, eyes, ears, cancer, ulcers, gall bladder, end a litany of medical complaints, that would fill a bible. All come with one mission, to meet Bill Parfrey, and hopefully relief.

Clinics are held Mondays to Thursdays afternoons 2.30 to 5 p.m., and nightly 7.30 p.m. until late. It is only necessary to attend one clinic a day.

Part Four

PAPER FRONT PAGES
CORKING GOOD STORY

AN Eire newspaper told of "wonder healing claims" earlier this month after its editor spent four days with spirit healer Bill Parfrey.

Deny Doody's lengthy article made the lead story in "Corkonian News" – and told how a woman was able to walk without any aid following treatment.

Suffering for two years with "acute muscular shoulder pains," and associated ailments, Mr Doody – who described himself as "totally unreligious" and without a "belief in the life thereafter" - visited the healer at the Airport Hotel, Cork.

"I put my pride in my pocket," the editor explained,"-and submitted my excruciating pains to the unknown healer."

Entering the hotel's Kinsale Room, where the healer regularly conducts his clinics, Mr Doody continued:

"I was greeted by serenading tape music and a strong, well-built man.

"He placed his hands on my shoulders, and after listening to my outline of various sectors of shoulder pain, assured me that after this session, I would enter a new dawn of life without pain.

On his first visit, "I was also the subject of a severe headache and neck pain, a prominent feature of my life for two years.

"Bill,' he continued, "applied his hands all over, but never touching the body, except to release the aches from my head and neck."

Mr Doody added: "Before I knew what was happening, I had been subjected to almost 25 minutes of Bill's method of Bio-Energy healing

Somehow, it seemed more like 25 seconds.

"I had experienced great partial relief but still retained the mental scars of the previous two years of discomfort."

By the fourth day, Mr Doody "left my pain-aching body to the healer and conceded that, for me, it wasn't to be a success."

Following his last visit, the reporter found he had "greater comfort and less excruciations from the body.

"Five days later, I am monitoring, without discomfort, a progression that will hopefully yield a positive dimension."

Jean O'Sullivan, 60, who underwent a major hip and pelvis operation some months ago, was unable to walk without aid on her first visit to Bill.

"From the comfort of my seat," Mr Doody wrote, "it was obvious Jean was the subject of much ongoing pain and unable to walk without practical aids."

Permanently residing in a convalescent home after doctors said nothing more could be done for her, the patient attended the following day.

"The passion of the previous evening was a difficult act to follow," Mr Doody said, "but most pleasing was the sheer joy on the face of my fellow patient from East Cork.

"She was, to my utter astonishment, walking without her aid. Her sincerity was everywhere in the room.

"Less than 24 hours previously," he noted, "this slightly framed lady was unable to walk unattended.

"Now she was walking at a brisk pace, doing an about turn as confidently as the soldiers on parade in Collins Barracks."

A former businessman in the car industry was another seeking the healer's help.

With ailments ranging from hearing loss to swollen joints, the reporter confirmed that the patient "informed me be was living out of a tablet bucket"

By the end of the healing "knee joints that had been locked tight, preventing reasonable mobility, had 'surrendered'to the healer.

"The willing patient was strolling to and from the healing room."

Bills' skills were really "put to the test" when confronting the patient's hearing difficulties. Attempting to discover the severity of the problem music was played at varying pitches.

Within moments of the healing, the journalist confirmed that "decibels of sound were now coming through to the hearing victim that were not there previously.

"The expression the patient's face said it all."

A sufferer who contracted polio as a toddler aged two-and-a-half was next to receive healing.

Although her leg was left shorter than the other by one-and-a-half inches, the patient refused doctors' demands to fit a leg brace, preferring to visit the healer instead.

She arrived for four days treatment, Mr Doody explained, "and by day three was proclaiming great success, as indeed was her excited watching mother."

Speaking afterwards, Bill - who hails from a family of psychics - commented:

"People come to me from all over. I get great pleasure in helping them overcome the tragedies of life.

"I have endured ridicule, apathy, you name it. But know what I'm doing is right for me.

"This healing power was latent and not explored to its full potential for far too many years. Now I am at peace with myself."

In concluding, Mr Doody added: "Good can be the only theme to adopt. ... and any persons suffering from any disability must surely benefit from his therapy".

MAUREEN FOX on Monday

Healing hands

"JUST a line to say how pleased I was to read how Bio-Energy techniques were employed to help your daughter in England and the girl who had knee trouble," writes Bill Parfrey. "Having been a healer for well over thirty years, I deal with similar problems on a daily basis and find that one visit suffices to put a problem right in the majority of cases.

"I hold healing clinics in Cork on an on-going basis," he says, "as well as in different parts of the country. I have studied the whole gamut of healing techniques for many years and have come to realise that no matter what procedure is adopted, all healing stems from a universal source which we term 'God.'

"The deeper the understanding and awareness of the healer (who has no power himself per se but is merely an instrument through which the energy flows) decrees the quality of the healing. Some may call the ability to heal "a science" but the question must be asked 'who made the science?' The answer can only be - God."

Thank you Bill for your letter - I would be interested to have other views on this complex subject.

**The Cork Examiner
18th October,1993**

350

Cork Examiner, Monday, April 13, 1992

Communicating with the World of Spirit

LAST, week I published a request from a reader who was anxious to make contact with a genuine psychic and this has resulted in a Cork healer coming forward with some information.

Bill Parfrey has been involved in the field of psychics embracing all aspects of what he describes as a ,"fascinating subject" for more years than he cares to remember!

"So far as mediumship is concerned," he says, "let me state categorically at the outset that no medium can state that he or she will make contact with a specific person who has passed from this world. Communication always stems from the world of spirit."

Bill says that many people are unaware that there is a vast difference between being a psychic and being a medium.

"The majority of so-called mediums are, simply, good psychics but they are no more in touch with the world of spirit than the man in the moon," he says. "What in fact they are doing (in psychic terms) is fishing in the aura and feeding back to the sitter that which they sense with their psychic ability."

According to Bill everything that has happened to us in the past is there within the various auric fields for we are made up of many bodies, seven in all. Our physical body is, simply, the "diving suit" which protects the "real" us as we sojourn, here in the dense gross material world; Bill . adds that it should not be forgotten that we are spiritual beings with physical bodies and not physical beings with spiritual bodies!

He then goes on to explain that "true spirit communication comes through a complicated structure and involves a medium's controlling spirit which spirit (an ordinary manor woman who resides on a different plane of consciousness) whose function is to liaise with the medium's "gatekeeper" who, in turn relates to the medium's spirit guides from where the real contact comes.

"The number of true mediums are few and far between," he says. "Off the top of my head those that really stand out are Stephen O'Brien, a Welsh medium (under whom I had the privilege to train as a medium), Alfred Best and a handful of others. These are mediums out of the top drawer who will bring evidence, not only of names and surnames, but phone numbers, addresses, etc.

"Again," he continues, "one can experience those with clairaudience abilities as instance the late Doris Stokes who could 'hear' voices but could not 'see' those that were communicating.

"Again," he explains, "there are trance mediums people who have the ability to allow the features of those that are departed over a long period of, say, 40 years to superimpose their likeness, intontion of voice etc through the trance medium who in the final analysis, has no idea of what has happened while she or he has been used by the spirit of God to prove survival after death as distinct from having to believe (which in reality means I doubt) that such a thing is possible."

Finally, Bill says that he has been privileged to have seen and come to know – having investigated fully – what is real spiritual communication and what is psychic reading the aura which has nothing to do with true spiritual communication.

"Over 40 years my own psychic and spiritual abilities have been steered into the field of healing with awesome results," he says.

The topic of mediums and psychics is a vast subject and if that reader who contacted me would like to know more on the subject, Bill Parfrey can be contacted at 021-364365.

NO SUCH THING AS DEATH SAYS BILL

The Cork Examiner
11th April,1984

BY MAUREEN FOX

IT was seven years ago that I first met, Bill Parfrey, when I called to write an article on his involvement in spiritualism and healing.

I also remember the deluge of letters that followed too! Readers who had had 'strange' experiences, but were afraid to tell anyone in case, they thought them mad, wrote in for more information.

Now, seven years later I spoke to Bill about his continuing work in the spiritual world, asked how it was evolving and congratulated him on his new and prestigious appointment

Bill Parfrey has been invited bv the Executive Director, Mr George W. Meek to be the Irish representative on the Inter-national Advisory Panel of the Life Beyond Death Research Foundation Inc., in the States.

His co-members come from all parts of the world including New Zealand, Austria, England, India, Japan, South Africa and of course the States.

Since the beginning of time, man has built shrines, temples and churches. The presiding priests, rabbi and ministers have grappled with the ages-old question: what comes after death of the physical body? Personal extinction..., eternal punishment..., heavenly reward?

The only answers widely available have been those of the various religions of the world, with very little agreement and almost nothing specific. Always the seeker was told to accept the answers on faith.

A NEW INVENTION

However, in just the past 25 years, more light has been shed on these mysteries than in all recorded history. The explosion of information in many, branches of science has helped to open the door. The research by the parapsychologists, psychiatrists and medical doctors of near death and out of the body experience has opened, the door. Now the base has been built for a full-scale effort to strip away the veil between our present three-dimensional world and the inter-penetrating worlds of spirit.

In April of 1982, engineer and inventor George Meek announ-ced that he and his colleagues of Metascience foundation had attained initial success with an electromagnetic-etheric instrument they called Spiricom.

With this system, they were able to record hours of two-way conversation with 'dead' persons. That breakthrough seems to offer at last possibilities for electronic proof that the mind, memory banks and personality survive death of the body.

The implications of that achievement are obviously enormous - when, and if Spiricom or similar, devices are perfected, George Meek cautioned at his press conference that such instruments are roughly at the stage of the Wright brothers first airplane, which flew for only twelve seconds and covered a distance of 160 feet.

The Life Beyond Death Research Foundation Inc., of which Bill Parfrey is now a panel member, was founded in December 1982 and it exists to support and encourage research aimed at providing conclusive answers to the questions of what happens after the death of the physical body.

It now has a functional world-wide network of like- minded scientists, educators and researchers who will gather information about new developments and share it with all members.

Bill just doesn't merely believe in an after-life: "I know there is," he says, and then illustrates instances where members of his family have come back, through a medium, and given messages that could not be written off as "chance". Why, then, I asked, are the messages' from the other side always so inconequential and oft times trite.

"First of all the answers are just proof that someone does exist", he explained, "but we are also talking about vibrations. We on this earth have a different frequency to that of 'the other side' and we must endeavour to tune in – this is why I am so excited about the Spiricom, it could be the answer."

According to Bill we are spiritual beings with physical bodies. "All of us as we progress are at various stages of spiritual development," he explains.

The first conference of the Life Beyond Death Research Foundation will take place in Atlanta in the Autumn, and Bill is looking forward to being there – and returning to this country with a lot more information.

During the years, while studying all forms of spiritualism, Bill has been drawn to healing and has had some remarkable successes He will travel anywhere to help someone in need, as will a friend of his, Con McSweeney, Cork 500706, who is a practising Catholic. Bill can be contacted at Cork 291926.

"We are having some visitors to Cork who will be of particular interest to many of your readers", said Bill. "Mr and Mrs Sowter, well-known across the water, will be in Cork on Saturday, May 12, to give demonstrations of clairvoyance and will remain here until the following Friday... They will also be prepared to give private sittings."

Bill can sum up his philosophy very simply: "There is no such thing as, death, so far as I am concerned, it is only a continuation of the spirit."

And, for 'those whose reaction to the foregoing is that it is "all nonsense", then perhaps these words of Herbert Spencer (1820-1903) will at least make you pause and ponder.

"There is a principle which is a bar against all information, and which is proof against all arguments, and which cannot fail to keep a man in everlasting ignorance – that principle is contempt prior to investigation".

A journey into the unknown

The Cork Examiner
5 October 1977

I wonder how many readers automatically read the stars in the Evening Echo? Of course they don't believe it but nevertheless it makes compulsive reading.

If someone has a reputation for reading palms (or the teacup) a queue quickly forms because this is a subject that has fascinated people from time immemorial.

Bill Parfrey is presently giving a series of lectures at the School of Commerce for An Tuairim on all aspects of spiritualism – clairvoyance, psychometry, mediumship, etc., and needless to say, he is speaking to packed houses.

Bill has been President of the Cork Psychical Society for the past seven years which is increasing in numbers every year, although as Bill said, "we never seek publicity".

We are interested in all aspects of psychic phenomèna," explained Bill, "with the exception of witchcraft and black magic – it is dangerous to even go into the subject, either white or black."

Bill's particular interest is clairvoyance and psychometry and he explained that clairvoyance meant the ability to see for want of a better word – or pick up imprssions from people.

I see black and white images fleeting across a person's hand", said Bill, "It's either some – with remarkable pereption, I was extremely surprised.

Images have become very much part of Bill's life. He recalled the time many years ago when he was sitting in his car outside a graveyard. Bill took up the story. Somehow I knew she was 21 years old. I stared at her for a long time, then the image disappeared.

Some moments later I was looking at another grave and an old man appeared, again I seemed to know his age, 77. My curiosity got the better of me and I walked over to the graves – one of a young woman who died when she was 21, the other of an old man aged 77."

This ability to see people long since dead is almost a way of life for Bill — his grandmother was extremely psychic and he has obviously inherited this gift.

Psychometry too is something in which he is extremely interested. He holds an object belonging to someone either living or dead and images float to the surface frm the subconscious.

There are many would write this gift off as a mere hit-or-miss affair, the gardai have good reason to be more receptive; for Laurance Hudson, through psychometry has helped them to locate bodies and he is accurate to withion a few hundred yards. According to Bill Parfrey everyone has psychic powers, it's just that we don't exercise this sense and therefore it is dormant.

"Basically, man is spirit," said Bill, "but he is living in a morass of materialism and stress which dulls the spiritual sense in man. He underlined his argument by saying that Iceland is one of the most psychic countries in the world — due to the fact that it is isolated and Icelanders can enjoy a degree of solitude and peace unknown to us."

"Strange enough, the more primitive the society, the more psychic. Bill said that it was due to lack of stress and strain of modern day living. Speaking of spiritualism, Bill felt strongly about the fact one never sees on television or films, it being depicted as anything but fraudulant. "While I accept that there are many frauds in this area, it is totally wrong to brand everyone as a charlatan.

Take Albert Best,' he went on, "He is fast gaining a worldwide reputation as a medium. I have seen him at work and, not only does he contact the spirit world, he gives names and addresses to back up this claim."

Albert Best is now living in Scotland — victim of thew

strife-town North of Ireland. Now, does one equate spiritualism with an orthodox religion, are they at variance?, I asked.

"Spiritualism is not a religion," said Bill, "It is a movement, quite frankly, it is the same as orthodoxy without the trimmings."

Bill, now becoming immersed in a subject near to his heart went on to say that basic Christianity was, after all, founded on the belief that Jesus appeared in spirit form to his disciples.

"When you see insertions in the paper, 'Thanksgiving to the Sacred Heart, St. Jude', and so on this is published as a result of successful intercession by a saint – in other words contacts with 'the spirit world."

This month Bill and, some other members of the Cork Society have enrolled at the Findlay College, Standsted Hall, Essex for a residential course entitled Psychic Development" lectures and demonstrations will be given by Eileen Ison and Doris Stokes.

He wants to learn a lot more about a subject in which he is deeply interested "I would,

like to emphasise the fact that I am just an ordinary person," he explained. 'I am speaking to you from a purely personal point of view, relating my own, experiences. I am in no way an expert.

But he is going to study his subject systematically through approved channels.

"Do you believe in fortune telling?' I asked.

He laughed, "Not in the fairground 50p for a palm symdrome, although some do have the gift, but I do believe that our furure is mapped out for us – just take a look at the prophecies in the Bible. — what's that but another word for fortune telling?"

Bill explained that our lives really resemble a three-act play — act 1, we don't know about, act 2, when we were born, act 3, when one passes into the spirit world.

"Yet we have the audacity to draw conclusions as to the overall purpose of existence when we don't know the answers. It is a question of trust; at the moment we are victims of 'tunnel thinking' but one day it will be all revealed to us."

ANN MOONEYwent to a West Cork hotel and saw physical healer George Canning in action

MORE 'MIRACLES' THAN MEDJUGORJE

PEOPLE are flocking in their thousands to the Parkway Hotel in Dunmanway, Co. Cork, where Professor George Canning is providing special miracles. Some come with hope in their hearts. Many other have no hope at all.

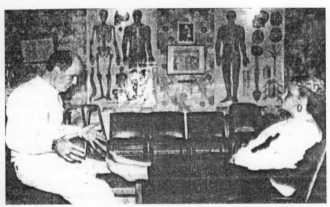

Bill Parfrey is only one of many who feels that a serious quest for knowledge into the world of spirit will reveal, at least, some of the answers.Professor George Canning says he is neither a faith nor spiritual healer. He is a physical healer and the only therapist in Western Europe who has been trained in bio-energy healing by the world-famous Yugoslav Zdenko Domancic. What is happening in the West Cork hotel is astounding to even the most hardened of sceptics. People have

had their sight and hearing restored; back problems fixed, and all types, of ailments sorted out. Even those who have a death sentence from cancer are being reprieved. People who arrived in wheel-chairs have walked out unaided.

But George Canning does not claim to be the new Messiah, nor does he take credit for his great powers. He says his powers come from God and that he is the conductor of those powers. 'The power to heal is all around us and the healer can

teach good people how to accept and use that power. Matter is made up of positive and negative forces and when these forces become unbalanced, illness results. I transmit energy to the area which needs healing and the ailment is cured," said Professor Canning.

No hypnosis

He rarely touches his patients, except when there is a need to improve circulation, but he does not hypnotise them either.

For his treatment, he mades a series of passes with his hands all around the patient's body with fingers fluttering and at times acting as if he is pulling something out, or throwing something away.

To the onlookers it all seems crazy, yet such is the need for some form of cure that they are willing to stay until their turn.

The movements occur while Professor Canning is working on the person's aura. This acts as a protective screen around our bodies. Where there is a hollow in the area, there is a deficiency of positive energy and such an area is generally where treatment is necessary.

The clinics held in the Parkway are completely open. Anyone can drop in from noon to after midnight. The 'healer believes there should be nothing bidden about what he does and people queue for hours In the healing room and outside in the corridor waiting.

DONATIONS

No payment is sought, but people may leave a donation. George is willing to accept any challenges. "Where medicine stops, I start. I take on medicine's failures and I am willing to be tested any time, any where.'

He also admits that there are failures but claims; a success rate of 80% to 90%.

"I am bringing an Eastern form of healing to the West," he states.

Professor Canning has the ability too to tell people what is wrong with them. An example is the case of the woman who brought her mother along suffering from chronic arthritis. After treating the old lady, George stopped the daughter and asked her how long she had suffered with her bad back. "How do you know I've a had back?" she asked. "I just do," Prof. Canning replied.

When he offered to treat her, she refused saying she did not believe in such "hocus-pocus," but when George asked her what she had to lose, she reluctantly agreed. She said she had a spinal condition that was so bad she could not bend from the waist down. She could not even tie her shoelaces.

As he started the treatment, the woman began to bend over, and then backward, and was able to continue doing so afterwards.

POWERFUL

"Bio-energy is the most powerful form of healing. it is so strong that I can even heal in people's absence, once I have a photograph of the sick person.

"1 have moments here too when I have been called every name under the sun - a cheat, a fake etc., but I have my results and for people with little or no hope I am often times the only alternative they have.

"Doctors send me their patients, particularly those for whom medicine has noth-ing left to offer-When I am finished I always send those patients back to their doctors. I believe that my healing and medicine can work hand in hand, but because there are no drugs or big money involved, medicine fears me," said George.

He has taught a number of people to use bio-energy healing, including Bill Parfrey of Grange in Douglas.

"I can teach a mother how to take care of her own child, so much so that she would never have to go to a doctor again. There are more miracles in this room, if you want to call them that, than there have been in Medjugorje.

"I believe chemical illness is killing the western world and the time has come to call a halt to it. We did not listen to the Hanrahans of Tipperary 10 years ago and it is only now that they are proven right. We are being poisoned chemically with the air we breathe and the food we eat, and Ireland should lead the way in a halt to this," said George.

DRUG SOCIETY

"Every modern ill is treated with drugs, even psychological illnesses. We are living in a drug-related society where pill-popping for every ailment is accepted. And while medicine is doing a good job generally, it is not prepared to accept its failures, one of which is treating the symptoms rather than the cause," he added.

The professor claims that all illnesses can be cured by bio energy, even AIDS. Among his testimonials is one from a man claiming to be cured of this dreaded modern disease. People are travelling from all over the country to visit George in his clinic. Among the first people he treated when be first arrived' was Sonny Maybury, the proprietor of the hotel, who was so impressed that he offered him a room and accommodation so that he could establish the West Cork town as his Irish headquarters.

This writer must admit to being the most sceptical of people, but, having seen George Canning in action, I can honestly tell anyone who asks that I was certainly impressed, so much so that if ever I discovered something seriously wrong with myself, I would head to the clinic in Dunmanway.

It is extremely difficult to put into words the things that are happening there, and also difficult to sum up the man himself, who has an obvious inner strength and a presence that makes you realise that yes! indeed there is something quite different here.

When he is treating people, there is an atmosphere that is hard to define. But people sit waiting for hours in that room full of hope and describing a feeling of inner peace.

Bella, Mary and Bill tell their stories.

"I WAS dead. All that was left for me was for my body to die," so said Bella, acknowledged as the miracle of Dunmanway.

Her recovery from being almost a vegetable confined to a wheelchair has astounded the entire town.

She was a long-time patient in a hospital and when her two daughters brought her home she was insisting that she be put into a home to die.

"When I came out of the hospital I could not walk, I shook all over and I could not bear to talk to people or go outside the door. I could not look after myself, I could not even wash a cup. I had no interest In life, even in watching the television," said Bella.

When I called to her home with George Canning during the week, the door was answered by Bella, who certainly did not look like a lady who had resigned herself to dying. Her remarkable recovery she completely attributes to George.

Bella spoke of the day that she went down to his clinic in the Parkway Hotel, supported by her two daughters who held on to her arms tightly in case she might fall.

"Professor Canning treated me, and on the way out of the hotel, I told my daughters that I felt quite different and I thought I might be able to walk unsupported, which I did, much to the amazement of all, including myself.

"Since that day my health has continued to improve thanks to the professor who comes up to my home once a week to treat me.

"I got tablets from the doctors, but I got my faith and my life back from the professor. My medication has been drastically cut and I am a new woman. This Christmas was the best one ever — I had the gift of being able to live back again," said Bella.

George said that when he first met Bella, he knew immediately that she had suffered a terrible trauma in her life and her illness resulted from that. The professor claims to have the ability to see what is wrong with many people.

"I realised too that the people around her, like her daughters, loved her greatly, but did not know what to do, or how to go about taking care of her.

"I could feel she was dying and I knew she had gone through absolute hell. She had no proper circulation in her body and she was on drugs that she knew nothing about, or what they were supposed to do for her.

"When I treated her I got an immediate result. It happens that way with some people. The third week I took her by the arm and brought her out of her home to meet her neighbours, something she had not done in 10 years," said George. Mary, also a local lady, has suffered from dreadful ulcerated legs for many years, but when she sat out in the sun one summer a few years ago, she intensified the problem. She has been treated in hospital, but the condition had worsened to such an extent that they could do nothing more for her. She had skin grafts, but these too failed to even lessen the condition of her swollen, puss-filled legs.

When she heard about this strange man, Professor Canning, who was reputed to be doing wonderful things down in the Parkway Hotel, she felt she haad nothing tolose. So, with the help of her walking aid, she called down to him.

"I will never forget what happened to me. After three therapies - the second and third done in my home — because my legs were so bad the professor called to treat me. I got three stabs of pain in my legs. My circulation was returning and the blood was starting to flow through them again.

Floods of puss flowed out of them and covered the floor and amazingly they started to heal up. I can now leave them without dressings and before the treatment I had to keep them covered all the time. They were so bad the doctor would not go near them," said Mary.

Bill Tatten is a solid, sensible farmer from near Carrigtwo-hill, but George Canning has made such a tremendous impact on him that he spends a great deal of time in the Parkway Hotel, training to be a bio-energy healer.

In 1974, during a bad storm, his motor bike ran into a fallen tree and he suffered head injuries. As the years went on, his condition deteriorated, the most noticable thing being a complete loss of energy, as well as a ringing in his head.

"I had all types of X-ray, cat-scans, etc., but the doctors could find nothing wrong with me. I heard about George through neighbours who had taken their child, who was suffering from severe eczema, and who was cured, and I decided to come to the clinic last September.

"I arrived prepared to wait to be seen complete with a book and sandwiches.

George Canning

The first thing that astonished me was the fact that the clinic was an open one, but I sat down, and was absolutely amazed at what I saw. I was there for hours, but it never crossed my mind to open the book or eat the food.

"When I stood in front of George I told him about the loss of, energy and the ringing in my ears. He asked me if I knew my spine was twisted and I told him that the doctors had found nothing wrong with that area. He treated me and that weekend I found I had endless energy. I walked up mountains, cycled and ran to try and burn it out, and since then I have never looked back."

"I have seen absolutely amazing things happening here," said Bill.

I WOULD have thought he was comical - waving his arms and hands, hopping suddenly backwards and forwards, as if from electric shocks and nuzzling up close on his stool to his patients - If he hadn't such an intense concentrated look in his eyes.

That was when I first set eyes a week ago, on Cork Healer, Bill Parfrey in action - in a lounge bar function room, with soft background music playing and a large "SILENCE PLEASE" cardboard sign. Bill travels countrywide and is some performer to watch.

But the tools of his trade are very portable – his hands and the energy he has derived from being a part of the psychic world for the past 30 years.

He is not, however, to be confused with a Faith Healer; "A faith healer is someone who says I believe or I don't believe against someone like me, who draws on my knowledge of God.

"God can be perceived as a man with a long beard, or a pulsating star, a vibration, a light, even a sound - and it is this awesome power that uses the nervous system of the healer to transmit energies to the patient to heal."

Energy

Bill believes therefore that the whole universe is made up of energy and when there is an imbalance between the positive and negative energy levels, then disease sets in. But wait a minute - we're not just talking on a physical level here. When you or I talk about our bodies – we mean, well, our flesh and blood, don't we?

But not Bill …

For starters, his notion of the physical is this: "The body is made up of 80% water and 20% carbon and trace elements."

We also have an astral body and an etheric body, he explains.

And to illustrate this, he asked me to lift

my arms straight up towards the ceiling, and point my index fingers in the same direction six inches apart and look through that gap upwards.

After a few seconds lo and behold – I began to see a second finger on each hand, aside from my own physical fingers, like two bright shadows.

The cynics, or maybe even scientists, will undoubtedly have some explanation for this phenomenon.

But Bill's explanation is that these 'fingers' are the etheric body which together with the astral body are vibrating energy fields.

They penetrate the physical body, in the same way that radio and television waves do.

Your soul, personality, emotions, memory banks and mental or causal body are all contained in the astral body.

Then when the physical and etheric bodies die. The 'real you, is still alive in your astral body.

And within minutes to a few days, after your physical body gives up, your astral body finds itself on an astral plane to which your life an the earth plane has entitled you.

Philosophy

Without going into any further detail much, this healer's philosophy is based on the notion that we all come back to earth (so to speak), again and again, passing through various planes, until we achieve the highest state of consciousness possible.

It is by dipping into the aura of these bodies that the healer does his work.

And so as to prove to me the existence of my astral body, Bill stood four feet in front of me and asked me to stand up straight. By waving his hands in a 'come forth' sort of manner I found my physical body drawn forward towards him, although my feet were still rooted to the same spot.

His reaction? Just to flash one of his brilliant smiles in matter-of-fact recognition.

An unusual experience for me, maybe, but a pale shadow of what this man has experienced over the years in the psychic world.

Stories

The stories of his supernatural encounters are too numerous to mention here.

His grandmothers on both sides were 'very psychic' and his mother also had 'extra sensitivity.'

Tales are told and retold around Cork of his powers as a medium, in previous years.

And he himself admits: "I have seen, listened to and had conversations with those in the world of the spirit."

But as he has developed, he has opted he said, to "use my powers for healing, instead of mediumship."

And he estimates that 80% of the people he sees go away cured.

Bill can be contacted in Douglas at 021-364365.

He's just the Bill of Health

I WOULD have thought he was comical - waving his arms and hands, hopping suddenly backwards and forwards, as if from electric shocks and nuzzling up close on his stool to his patients - If he hadn't such an intense concentrated look in his eyes.

That was when I first set eyes a week ago, on Cork Healer, Bill Parfrey in action - in a lounge bar function room, with soft background music playing

TAPPING alternatives with MARGARET JENNINGS

and a large "SILENCE PLEASE" cardboard sign.

Bill travels countrywide and is some performer to watch.

But the tools of his trade are very portable – his hands and the energy he has derived from being a part of the psychic world for the past 30 years.

He is not, however, to be confused with a Faith Healer; "A faith healer is someone who says I believe or I don't believe against someone like me, who draws on my knowledge of God.

"God can be perceived as a man with a long beard, or a pulsating star, a vibration, a light, even a sound - and it is this awesome power that uses the nervous system of the healer to transmit energies to the patient to heal."

Energy

Bill believes therefore that the whole universe is made up of energy and when there is an imbalance between the positive and negative energy levels, then disease sets in. But wait a minute - we're not just talking on a physical level here. When you or I talk about our bodies – we mean, well, our flesh and blood, don't we?

But not Bill ...

For starters, his notion of the physical

is this: "The body is made up of 80% water and 20% carbon and trace elements."

We also have an astral body and an etheric body, he explains.

And to illustrate this, he asked me to lift my arms straight up towards the ceiling, and point my index fingers in the same direction six inches apart and look through that gap upwards.

After a few seconds lo and behold – I began to see a second finger on each hand, aside from my own physical fingers, like two bright shadows.

The cynics, or maybe even scientists, will undoubtedly have some explanation for this phenomenon.

But Bill's explanation is that these 'fingers' are the etheric body which together with the astral body are vibrating energy fields.

They penetrate the physical body, in the same way that radio and television waves

do.

Your soul, personality, emotions, memory banks and mental or causal body are all contained in the astral body.

Then when the physical and etheric bodies die. The 'real you, is still alive in your astral body.

And within minutes to a few days, after your physical body gives up, your astral body finds itself on an astral plane to which your life an the earth plane has entitled you.

Philosophy

Without going into any further detail much, · this healer's philosophy is based on the notion that we all come back to earth (so to speak), again and again, passing through various planes, until we achieve the highest state of consciousness possible.

It is by dipping into the aura of these bodies that the healer does his work.

And so as to prove to me the existence of my astral body, Bill stood four feet in front of me and asked me to stand up straight. By waving his hands in a 'come forth' sort of manner I found my physical body drawn forward towards him, although my feet were still rooted to the same spot. His reaction? Just to flash one of his brilliant smiles in matter-of-fact recognition.

An unusual experience for me, maybe, but a pale shadow of what this man has experienced over the years in the psychic world.

Stories

The stories of his supernatural encounters are too numerous to mention here. His grandmothers on both sides were 'very psychic' and his mother also had 'extra sensitivity.' Tales are told and retold around Cork of his powers as a medium, in previous years.

And he himself admits: "I have seen, listened to and had conversations with those in the world of the spirit."

But as he has developed, he has opted he said, to "use my powers for healing, instead of mediumship."

And he estimates that 80% of the people he sees go away cured. Bill can be contacted in Douglas at 021-364365.

Cork Healer in attendance in Fermoy

Bill Parfrey, the well known Cork Healer whose reputation is known nationally and internationally will be holding a series of Health Clinics in Alexanders' Lounge, Fermoy commencing in January 1992.

Having been involved in his field for nigh on thirty years, his knowledge is vast.

"However," as he says, "there is always something greater to attain - some new insight - some new awareness - a greater comprehension - which, when brought into play, can be used to help even further the many people who come for help."

Bill pays tribute to Professor George Canning who helped him so much in developing his abilities as a healer. He has been privileged to have studied the whole gambit of the holistic approach to illness on all levels from a master of the art and a healer of great magnitude.

Where Psychism is concerned, Bill Parfrey's name is synonymous. Founder and Chairman of the original Cork Psychical Society for many years, he is today linked with serious investigating groups attached to universities and similar establishments world-wide. He represents Ireland on the international panel of the Metascience Foundation Inc of America.

Noted healer coming to West Wicklow

A CORK healer who can heal afflictions and relieve pain in both humans and animals is to begin a series of four-day clinics in West Wicklow next month.

Bill Parfrey, whose reputation is known both in Ireland and abroad, has been invited to attend West Wicklow clinics and offer the benefits of his healing powers to people seeking relief from their afflictions.

His clinics are being organised by Victoria Butler, a Northern Ireland woman who has recently settled in the Glen of Imaal area, and Bill and Margaret Flynn from Castleruddery.

The clinics will take place in the Flynns' Glen Lounge in Castleruddery on four consecutive days each month, starting from October 21st to 24th. Bill, who has an extensive following in various parts of the country, is believed to be the first faith healer to hold regular clinics in the area.

According to Victoria Butler, Bill Parfrey is very dedicated to those who seek his help and has achieved some remarkable results, even with cases which medical doctors were unable to help.

Like most healers, Bill does not charge for his skills which he sees as a gift from God. However, people do sometimes make donations where they have been cured or given relief.

Bill's method of healing is bio-energy therapy, which involves using an 'aura' around the body to detect and heal problems without the laying on of hands.

Healer returns

BILL Parfrey, the Cork **healer**, whose reputation **is** known both here and **abroad**, will be recommencing his Cork clinics on Monday, January 7 next.

Hving been involved in his field for almost 30 years, his knowledge is vast. "However", as he says, "there is always something greater to attain, some new insight, some new awareness, a greater comprehension, which, when brought into play, can be used to help even further the many people who come to me for help."

Bill, who can be contacted at 364365, pays tribute to Professor George Canning who has helped him so much in developing his abilities as a healer. He has been privileged to have studied the whole gambit of the holistic approach to illness on all levels from a Master of the Art and a healer of tremendous magnitude.

Where psychism is concerned, Bill Parfrey's name has been synonymous. Founder and chairman of the original Cork Psychical Society for many years, he is today linked with serious investigating groups attached to universities and similar establishments worldwide. He represents represents Ireland on the international panel of the Metascience Foundation Inc. of America.

"Psychics are the tools of the Spirit" says Bill "and a deep and profound knowledge of this vast subject can be a prerequisite in affording one the privilege of helping one's fellow man - or woman".

Part Five

DATE: 27th February, 2005

Venue: Rosscarbery, Co. Cork, Ireland.

Speaker: Fr. Pat Murray on Meditation.

Group: 50 people.

I decided to attend a Meditation Day with the parent of a child I take care of.

The minute Fr. Pat walked into the room I felt as if I knew him. [although I had never even heard of him before] and as he began to speak I then knew I knew him because Fr. Pat and Bill Parfrey became integrated in my mind. Fr. Pat was standing in front of me but it was Bill who was in my thoughts and sometimes they blended to become Bill. That in itself I found strange but in no way disturbing.

The morning progressed and Fr. Pat was speaking about SILENCE and PRESENCE after which we had a short meditation to feel the Silence and the Presence. After this he wrote a question on the board and it said "Did we ask to be born?" As I firmly feel that we choose to be born I could feel myself wanting to challenge this question but I was resisting as there were a number of people from Innishannon where I live, in the group.

Then, before I realized it had happened I found myself speaking and asked the question back that if he felt we didn't ask to be born then surely we choose it? It was then something extraordinary happened. [I don't even know if he answered my question]. Our eyes locked; that's the only way I can explain it. I couldn't blink or take my eyes away from his and time stood totally still. It was then he became Bill [Parfrey] speaking almost through Fr. Pat. All I could see was Bill and yet my eyes hadn't moved from Fr. Pat's eyes but it was Bill who was there. Everybody in the room seemed to have receded or removed from the room as I wasn't aware of any of them. He said to me "you are a beautiful person" to which I replied "thank you." He replied by saying that "thank you" was said too quickly so I will say again "you are a beautiful person." I waited a few seconds and said again "thank you - and was that better?" at which we both laughed. Then he said to me "you have suffered greatly" and I replied that I have known suffering in my life and I have been to the "College of Life" [a line Bill told me when I revealed to him that I had been in a mental institution] and I remembered smiling as I said that because I knew that he'd know what I was talking about. He then asked me if I ever felt like ending it all and if I had wanted to cover up and pretend I didn't - it just was not possible. I could speak nothing but truth to this person so I truthfully replied "many times." And he continued "out of this suffering has come a huge beauty and a sense of presence." He then continued to say that if he had met me fifty years ago his life could have been much different to which I replied and laughed "it couldn't as I wasn't even born and I am only 21 years old next birthday [and if you believe that you will believe any thing. Ha, ha!"]" Then our eyes drifted and the moment which in one way seemed like a split and another eternity - was gone. Fr. Pat continued on with his morning and I spent the time recovering. At lunchtime the girl I had gone with and I decided to go for a walk and it was then she revealed to me there had been a total silence in the room and that time seemed to stand still. She also said that there seemed to be nobody else in the room only Fr. Pat and that she had never experienced anything like it before.

As the girl I travelled with and I were returning after our walk Fr. Pat drove up, stopped, put down the window and addressed me by asking me "was this my travelling companion?" to which I replied "yes." He replied by saying "you are both wise in different ways but in communion together."

When the day was over I went up to Fr. Pat and said to him it had been a pleasure to meet him - to which he replied "and its been my gift."

Signed: Rene McCarthy [Manning]

Co. Cork.
'Phone: 021-4776784

WRITTEN TO BILL PARFREY ON 6TH MARCH, 2005 [MOTHER'S DAY]

Part Five

I first heard of Bill in 1988 when we lived in Clonakilty, Co. Cork. He had healed a friend of ours who had a serious motorbike accident . He was going to have his leg amputated above his knee. He was nineteen years of age. Bill went to see him in hospital and after giving some healing, our friend walked out of the hospital - on two very healthy legs!

We decided then to pay Bill a visit for pains and aches we had in our arms, shoulders and back. Bill fixed us up in no time, it was simply incredible! When my parents came to visit from France they benefited greatly of Bill's healing, and did so for many years.

Bill healed me for so many aches, pain,, problems I had over the years, it is staggering when you think of it. Not only did he heal you physically, but spiritually as well. You always had a feeling of well-being and peace within when you left that stayed with you for weeks. It was simply wonderful

Pascale and Xavier Lutz

Cork 2

Tel: 021-4366066

Cork.

31St May, 2006

Dear Bill.

Just a quick note to say thank you so much for your Healing Touch on that awful wisdom tooth.

I have not had a problem since and never had to have it extracted despite the dentist saying that it would always give me trouble.

Many thanks Bill.

Sincerely,

Aileen

[Mrs.] Aileen Crowley

Part Five

My two cents worth.

Bill has never professionally treated me. He has in fact spoken, advised and gave pointers as a friend and human being.

I cannot speak to Bill's professional healing process. I can only speak to his presence and gift of wisdom. I met Bill professionally, by being one of his employees, and a fairer and more practical down-to-earth employer was and still is so very scarce. To say Bill was the boss would possibly be an insult to this man. He was more of a practical humanist, who helped me, and, I believe, many others to a higher level when looking at one's life, and one's faith in life.

You see Bill knew how to listen, how to guide and straighten a thought frame. You could say this took wisdom, I would say this took belief in a higher influence interceding through Bill. Wisdom was a channel Bill was blessed with and through this wisdom he could put the faith picture in view for any who would receive.

It has been 30 years, I have made some big mistakes and I have made some great decisions. I don't live my life as a fairy tale but I do occasionally think 'what would Bill do or think about in this situation'.

Yes, I have moved on from where I was 30 years ago. Now married, now on another continent, now the advisor to my two daughters. I speak of Bill to them, and it is my hope and belief that some of what I advise them on is spiritually supported by the network brought to me by our paths crossing 30 years ago.

Richard

Letter received from Richard O'Halloran in California, U.S.A. 4th February, 2005

Cork 3.

24th February, 2005

Dear Bill,

I hope this letter finds you well. I got my results today for my D/C at the Bons on January 7th. You were right Bill, everything was fine. Thank you so much for all your help. I find the words "Trust and know and all will be well " very calming for me.

I got your e-mail about your book. I will be looking forward reading this very much, Bill.

I would like to say since I have been seeing you and getting your healing for about the last ten or eleven years now, Bill, I have been getting better and better in myself, being led to the right people, the right medicine. When I have a problem and write to you the minute I send it in the post I feel so positive of your results in healing the situation or the person. For instance, my son was a drug addict and I asked your healing. He was taking drugs and getting worse all the time. Then when I wrote to you for your Absent Healing miracles happened. He is off drugs now for a year so far. He has a great love of animals.. He has two dogs and treats them like his children. That's a miracle Bill to me. It was only when I asked you for that Absent Healing he got help..

I can only tell you that the comfort I get from knowing that you are there is very reassuring for me for I know I will always be helped and healed by you because you have so much trust in God for me.

I will try and get to see you soon, Bill.

Thank you so much . All the best.

Sincerely your friend always.

Margaret

Wexford
May 26th, 2005

My dear good friend Bill,

Love and dearest gratitude for taking care of me last month. Wasn't I a miserable wreck back them? Nervous. frightened, bogged down by uncertainty, pain and stress. I'm sure you know, Bill, the healing you created in my whole body . Not just the old knee, which I thought was "the" problem. But you, as usual, healed my spirit, my whole body.

I could not 'phone or write to express my gratitude, my dearest friend - I was too overwhelmed - and as each day passed, I was amazed at how energetic I became particularly how focused I was. Some days I worked in the garden from early morning, clearing stuff I could only look at for months. I would fall into bed early and sleep. If I had 'phoned I would only have bawled with relief and gratitude.

I feel re-created; YOU were probably drained.

I am so glad, so privileged, to know you - thanks to Oliver I pray for you Bill, every day,

With love from Frances [Flanagan]

From: "Maria Kohlmann"
Date: Tue, 8 Feb 2005
To: "Bill Parfrey"

Hi Uncle Billy

What a mammoth task you have taken on!! I had heard on the grapevine about your proposed book and wish you well with it. I have thought over

the people in my life that you may have helped and can only remember clearly that you were helping Karl with absent healing and of course Peter. He gets very clear skin every so often and then it can flare up again but nowhere near as bad as it had been. He puts this down to your intervention.

On the psychic front I have a clear memory of being in your company and being visited by my grandfather. He asked me to look at a picture/photograph of himself anf my mum and dad near water. Well, needless to say, I did not have the time or inclination to go up in the attic and go over hundreds of photos. One day soon after I arrived to Mum and Dad (I worked there at the time) and on the mantle piece was a photograph which mum had chosen out of a huge pile. She had been looking through them the night before. Dare I say it but it was the photo as described to me by my grandfather during his visit using you as the messenger.!! I was needless to say a little unnerved but very convinced that I had indeed received a message from beyond.

Good luck with the book and I know I will be looking forward to getting my hands on a copy!!

Love and best wishes always

Maria K

Hello Dearest Spiritual Father and Elder of Cork and Munster and Our Sacred Island. Happy Fathers day Bill, I feel like this is maybe an appropriate title for you even though I Know you dont like titles.

(On your last e-mail I thought you were joking when you said let me know if you dont recieve it - So I thought If I dont recieve this how could I Possibly know - to let you know whether I recieved it or not, so I thought that was Hilarious !!! But Now on re-reading it I think I didnt realise that you may have been referring to the previous e-mails !!! So Sorry for the misunderstanding !! e-mails are funny that way sometimes arent they ?? easy to get the wrong idea.)

I feel like in some way you are one of our dearest cherished elders Bill, A carrier of the earth wisdom and the ancient sacred knowledge and all the experience of the years that no one can get out of books, or having a million letters after their names, meaning not a whole lot usually.

I have talked to some people about this and you and so many people love you so dearly and hold you dear to their hearts, Its amazing. I think if we were still living in Tribal communities you would be a wise elder - honoured and Held in a very sacred place in the tribe, probably with loads of feathers and squirrel-fur hanging out of your magnificent hat ! Of course you would have a magnificent Hat !!

I was very touched by the lost bear story on the Gerry Ryan Show, It was beautiful and endearing and a very very enlighteneing and consciousness expanding tale for children to hear, Im sure it has touched many little hearts and many big hearts too around the nation.

I think your Immense and awesome contribution to Cork, and the nation throughout your years Bill has been extraordinary and none of us will ever forget it. Your words and wisdom and all those you have touched with Love, and the Love of God, will be locked in the hearts and minds of many, for generations to come.

Thank you Our wise Elder father for Being and sending so many of us off on our unique journeys into the mystery..............

God bless you Bill... We love you so much

Ger (and Most of Cork and half the country probably.)

Dear Mr. Parfrey

I was given your book by my mother.

Within minutes of reading it, I felt compelled to write to you. I thoroughly enjoyed it and found that your life was very interesting and inspirational.

I myself have always believed in a stream of consciousness running through everyone. I came to understand that only those who seek this consciousness and understand that it exists can really see the power of it. I first realized that it existed when I started to write songs on my guitar.

For a while, I thought that these songs were my own creation. After a few years of songwriting, I came to understand that every word and every line of melody were being fed through me by another consciousness. This is when I realized I had a spirit guide. I am only aware of one. I do not know its name or who it is but I am aware that its there.

I dont know why I am writing this to you but something inside me told me do it. And now I am after realizing that the word 'I' was used too much in this letter...

To round things up, I would like to thank you for inspiring my spirit to further my knowledge of itself. I would appreciate if you could reply, at your own convenience, as I would love to converse with you further about the matter.

Thank You
Darren Johnston

Part Five

Clapham,
London

I've known Bill for nearly fifteen years , and in that time he has been a great help to me in both a healing and spiritual capacity, especially in times of crisis and bereavement, and know that this has been a similar story to thousands of others, whose lives he has enriched immeasurably.

John Philpott

Bill,

I wish you every possible success with the TV show. You will be extraordinary as always and will help thousands by the appearence alone. I can't wait to see it when it is done.

More to the point, your words on trust and knowledge keep in my head and soul and are helping me always. Thank you for sharing them with me, I feel our night was very special for me for some reason and all I have to do to feel good is know that I know you. Isn't that wild also...

Neil's show was very very nervewracking! 16 mikes and a big PA system in a small hall doesn't mix well but I feel and did feel that God was on my side and I didn't worry a bit and it turned out better than expected. I told all it was a big team effort — which it was. I get the credit but my son was more than vital on it as was Ken and everyone helped as best they could. The stars got their photos taken and I took ours! — so its all good.

As an aside, I was reading about you and White Feather and I think he is still around and telling me about you. When I saw the feather, as when I met you I swear I had not read about that part in the book.

Its a magic book you have written and given to me and nothing is an accident! (its in the jeep as I write). What amazes me is that you didn't have a higher public profile with your healing. You should have with the scale of its success but I have told a good few about you and no one heard of you other than Carmel here.

So Bill the Lord didn't want to overwhelm you totally and kept you low in profile, like you say God works in wonderous ways.

Well, its always good to talk and always stay healthy and happy,

Your old friend,

John C